Obscene Gestures

Obscene Gestures

Counter-Narratives of Sex and Race
in the Twentieth Century

PATRICK S. LAWRENCE

Fordham University Press
NEW YORK   2022

Copyright © 2022 Fordham University Press

All rights reserved. No part of this publication may be reproduced, stored in a retrieval system, or transmitted in any form or by any means—electronic, mechanical, photocopy, recording, or any other—except for brief quotations in printed reviews, without the prior permission of the publisher.

Fordham University Press has no responsibility for the persistence or accuracy of URLs for external or third-party Internet websites referred to in this publication and does not guarantee that any content on such websites is, or will remain, accurate or appropriate.

Fordham University Press also publishes its books in a variety of electronic formats. Some content that appears in print may not be available in electronic books.

Visit us online at www.fordhampress.com.

Library of Congress Cataloging-in-Publication Data available online at https://catalog.loc.gov.

Printed in the United States of America

24 23 22   5 4 3 2 1

First edition

To my mom and dad, who taught me to love art
and justice and to think deeply and seriously

Contents

Introduction. Outlaws vs. Outcasts:
Defining Narratives of Obscenity   1

1 Classic Counter-Narratives: Deep Psychology vs.
Deep Pathology in Two Early Twentieth-Century Novels   29

2 Geniuses Abroad, Deviants at Home: Racial
Counter-Narratives of the Global and Domestic   65

3 Porn Wars and Pornotroping: Counter-Narratives
of Obscenity amid Transitions in Feminist Activism   102

4 AIDS Politics Is Local: Narratives of Plague and Place
in the Culture Wars   136

Epilogue   171

Acknowledgments   177
Notes   179
Works Cited   201
Index   215

Obscene Gestures

Introduction
Outlaws vs. Outcasts:
Defining Narratives of Obscenity

Before his death in 1966, comedian Lenny Bruce is said to have warned, "Take away the right to say 'fuck' and you take away the right to say 'Fuck the government.'"[1] Behind the rhetoric meant to needle the prosecutors who arrested Bruce on obscenity charges multiple times and routinely staked out his shows lies the blunt contention that challenging prudish notions is a form of challenging oppressive governments and guarding one's right to intellectual autonomy. That is to say, breaking the rules of propriety is fundamental to the right of self-determination. But Bruce's wording is not entirely beside the point either because words such as "fuck" and others for which Bruce was prosecuted (especially "cocksucker") can have sexual connotations. Bruce contends in his acts that the words lack sexual intent: They are not prurient. Those who prosecuted him contend the opposite: that they cannot be divorced from their sexual connotations and thus potentially are obscene. The fact that this ambiguity about sexual content became a central facet in the story of Bruce's career demonstrates that the terrain on which the political and intellectual questions of free speech and government authority are contested in the United States during the twentieth century was often—if not uniformly—the terrain of sex.

What this quotation gets at, too, is the way that sex is a proxy for combatants on all sides of contestations over freedom and power. Hal Wilner, the producer of the definitive collection of Bruce's recordings, confesses, "I am a believer that his use of 'dirty words' was just a vehicle the authorities used—it was the religious material that got 'them' to want to stop him."[2] What Wilner surmises plausibly explains what seems like a contradiction. To those who follow in the same tradition as Bruce (such as George Carlin, with his "7 Words You Can't Say on Television" routine, and Jello Biafra with his spoken word albums and speaking tour), dirty words are so transparently innocuous that their suppression can only be a pretext for weightier issues. Wilner supposed, in this vein, that it was Bruce's skewering of the hypocrisy of religious sectarians that got him into hot water, though ironically once he was arrested, this element of his routines faded in favor of bits about his obscenity trials. For Bruce and others, it seems that the intent was, indeed, not to lawfully limit First Amendment abuses in defense of public morality, but to simply silence dissidents. As Marvin Worth recalls in regards to Bruce's having died "broken physically, emotionally, and financially," the tolls of fighting censorship were enormous and felt like a targeted assault on free-thinking critics of the status quo (qtd. in Bruce, n.p.). This probably sounds familiar to Biafra, the lead singer of Dead Kennedys, whose record label was bankrupted defending him from politically motivated obscenity charges in 1986 of which he was never convicted. Whether they see the suppression of sexual speech as motivated by desire to suppress religious or social dissent or to quash racial justice or gender equality movements, figures such as Bruce, Carlin, and Biafra see sex as no more than a hollow proxy for contestations over power and belonging—and they are at least partly right in doing so, for this is, indeed, part of the story.

To be sure, Bruce is right: repressing sexual expression does effectively repress dissent. But in his other sets, such as "To Is a Preposition; Come Is a Verb" or "Is It the Word or the Act," where he attempts to reduce sexual expression to something as banal as buying cantaloupes—he might miss the mark. The dense history of twentieth-century obscenity prosecutions—including Bruce's own—signals the vigorous investment of power in this particular site, right or wrong. Sexuality has historically been many things. In the late twentieth-century counterculture, it served as an avatar of pleasure, which was itself understood to be an unjustly stifled means of self-expression. It has also been a locus of identity and subjectivity through much of the Feminist and LGBTQ+ movements. It has served as a tool for the oppression of black people in slavery, and the echoes of that oppression resonate through the late century in the gendered and sexualized culture wars, rhetoric animating welfare reform and Reaganomics. Sexual speech is policed (and used as a means of resistance) because sex is a significant node at the heart of major contestations over national identity. It has played this role because, as a field of identification, it can stand in for exclusion and belonging in terms of race, gender, sexuality, class, ability, and age. Further, as a field of action, it can stand in for cultural pathologies and stereotypes, for notions of deviance, license, decadence, or purity. Sex is simply too rich a site of meaning to be only an arbitrary, hollow site of power's exercise.

Consider, for example, the fates of comedians such as Belle Barth, who capitalized on the fashion for salacious comedy nightclub routines in the 1950s and 1960s just as Bruce did. Though Barth was also famously arrested for obscenity, was memorialized in a popular play, and made a living performing until shortly before her death in 1971, she is not well-known as Bruce is today, nor is she cited as a formative influence by today's most prominent comedians.[3] In 1996, the *New York Times* panned the play *Sophie, Totie, and Belle*, about the lives of Barth and two of her contemporaries, because "No one needs to be told that these three outrageous, resilient comedians paved the way for the sexually unrestrained and otherwise blunt manner of contemporary women in comedy."[4] Today, though, it may indeed be the case that people need to be told this because the women are considerably lesser known than their male counterparts. For example, *Rolling Stone*'s 2017 list of the fifty best comedians of all time ranks Bruce at number three, claiming that "he almost singlehandedly transformed stand-up into an outlaw occupation."[5] The list fails to even mention Barth, though. Or Totie Fields, or Sophie Tucker, or Pearl Williams. Debra Aarons and Marc Mierowsky lament, in fact, that "while Bruce is widely acknowledged as the father of extreme, edgy stand-up (he is remembered, immortalized, and now beatified for his crucifixion), Belle Barth and Pearl Williams are forgotten."[6]

Given the similarities in their sets, styles, and experiences, then, what contributes to the marked difference in their legacies, with Bruce lionized and Barth and others all but forgotten? In what follows, I argue that it is the unequal privileges of the obscene, which accrue favorably to already majoritarian groups, especially men and whites. The encomiums to Bruce's contributions represent classic ways of describing male taboo breakers, casting them as transformative figures whose willingness to trespass norms of decency opens the door for new ways of being. Performers and creators who are women or come from other marginalized communities, however, are forced to contend with more convoluted paths and more considerable challenges defined by societal stereotypes of deviance. Their transgressions are often regarded as confirmation of these stereotypes or must be consciously constructed to refute them, thus centering repressive systems even when they resist them.

This is all to say that free speech defenders such as Bruce, Carlin, and Biafra no doubt resist excessive state power in important ways when they identify restrictions on sexual speech as a covert means of maintaining control in other spheres; they are certainly right, but the story they tell is incomplete. The image of jackboot-wearing thugs at the command of overly zealous prudes, religious moralists, and pearl-clutchers is not without its elements of historical accuracy, but it is also not at all the full picture. While it is true that moralist forces have often attempted to abuse the courts to silence raunchy dissenters and provocateurs, obscenity discourse in the United States is much more complex than that simple binary. In what follows, I will attempt to elaborate some of the relevant complexities, particularly as the repression of sexual expression was used to police the borders of racial and sexual identity.

Genius vs. Pathology: Counter-Narratives of Obscenity

Among the intersecting racial, gendered, and sexual politics that define the literary history around obscenity, I contend that certain throughlines can be seen. In particular, a single common narrative of possibility emerges with two diverging strains that I call the "narrative of obscene genius" and the "narrative of obscene pathology." The opening movements of these counter-narratives are the same. When authors publish literary works that use explicit sexuality to challenge cultural norms, it routinely leads to public uproar. The uproar generates interest and drives sales, while the resulting critiques and defenses of the text generate a body of scholarship that cements the book as a cultural phenomenon. The author and publisher often become rich (or richer) and famous (or notorious) as a result of the controversy, while the text is fast-tracked to possible canonization. This element of the narrative is common enough to provide a recurring script for the reception of taboo literature. However, beyond these commonalities two paths emerge with identifiable themes and echoes, but which are not totalizing.

The narrative of obscene genius can be imagined as open primarily to dominant voice authors: white, male, heterosexual. When they break taboo, their transgression is interpreted as a mark of a transformative or generational talent. They are excused for breaking the rules because they are assumed (or asserted) to being doing so in order to cast off the shackles of received opinions and offering new ways of being. As they do, critics consciously situate the writer or performer in the canon while emphasizing the author's role in transforming it. Consider, for example, how Aarons and Mierowsky describe Bruce: "Lenny Bruce took himself seriously as a prophet and teacher. . . . [H]e transformed stand-up comedy, shaping it as aggressively pointed social critique. And it is in this respect that he can be considered to belong to the tradition of the great moralists" (170). The operative notes here are the emphasis on transformation of the art form as a specific result of the use of obscenity. These strands will echo the treatment of works like Henry Miller's *Tropic of Cancer* (1934) and Thomas Pynchon's *Gravity's Rainbow*, which I examine in Chapters 1 and 2, respectively. In essence, this possibility is a mark of the authors' privilege, often white privilege. It is by virtue of their group belonging that even flagrant rule-breaking does not cause others to question their place in the national community. In fact, it is by operation of the principle of obscene genius that we see it was their belonging that determined the interpretation of their actions, not their actions that earn them belonging. They belong, and so breaking the rules is constructed *post-hoc* as innovative, original, and courageous.

In contrast, even when their works are acclaimed, women, writers of color, and LGBTQ+ folk are not seen as transforming the canon but as exceptions to it or even outside of it, performing ethnographic work or folk art. Even Aarons and Mierowsky, who do laudable work examining and celebrating the work of Barth and Williams, do so largely by representing them as something other than comedians. They write, for example, that "strictly speaking, it might be argued that Barth and Williams were not stand-up comedians in the same tradition, but rather entertainers who performed particular identities, creating a seductive and warm club-like atmosphere different and less dangerous than using only a microphone on a bare stage" like Bruce (Aarons and Mierowsky 174). Though they are celebrating these women, it is striking that the authors openly wonder whether they ought to be classed as comedians at all, while Bruce's stylistic deviations make him innovative. The specific language here, calling the sets "warm" and "less dangerous," also reflects the expectations that the work of women is, or should be, constrained to domestic matters, an assumption that tended to limit the public influence of women cultural creators, as we will see in my analysis of Toni Morrison's *The Bluest Eye* in Chapter 2. Grace Overbeke notes that this tendency is very much in keeping with the assumption that women were not capable of full participation in politics, a contention that negatively influenced their acts.[7] Thus, while these women sometimes get the genius treatment retroactively,[8] in their day, they were consistently confronted with the binary choice between upholding or challenging domestic stereotypes about women, and this confrontation was the cost of admittance to their field and access to their audience.[9] Moreover, it damaged their legacies by preventing reviewers from recognizing their influence in the moment and diminishing the perception of their work's social importance.[10]

In *History of Sexuality*, Michel Foucault describes what he calls "the speaker's benefit,"[11] which is the tendency to hold in awe those who are willing to violate the taboo on speaking about sex. Foucault writes that "If sex is repressed, that is, condemned to prohibition, nonexistence, and silence, then the mere fact that one is speaking about it has the appearance of a deliberate transgression. A person who holds forth in such language places himself to a certain extent outside the reach of power; he upsets established law; he somehow anticipates the coming freedom" (6). With this description of the aura of revolution and prophetic power attributed to those willing to break the codes of repression, Foucault channels some of the more glowing reviews of Miller, Philip Roth, Pynchon, William S. Burroughs, or any number of other literary figures of the mid-century who gained prominence by dint of their willingness to speak openly about sex. The reception of these authors' works (much of it detailed in the chapters of this book) confirms that they had the benefit of being received as men of genius who foresaw a freer future that had not yet arrived and spoke its truths against the repressive mores of their time. In essence, they come to belong more profoundly by exempting themselves from the system to become its masters. This is the narrative of obscene genius.[12]

But this seeming freedom is false, and the reason is that it is part and parcel of how the larger power status quo is maintained. For one thing, as Foucault explains elsewhere, the notion that sex has been solely or even primarily subject to a regime of suppression and repression is itself insufficient. Moreover, figures such as Miller accrue their status at the expense of others—women, racialized minorities, sexual minorities—whose own willingness to break the codes of silence are not as often marked as revolutionary or prophetic but instead frequently construed as confirmation of their marginal status. In fact, this is where my intervention takes off from Foucault's foundation. I argue that the "speaker's benefit" is an exclusive benefit that has the effect of propping up the false binary of repression and incitement that attends sexuality in Western culture, and is *also* an exclusive benefit designed to characterize the system as free and progressive while maintaining the political disempowerment and cultural marginalization of those outside the white hetero-reproductive order.

Specifically, while those who are placed and policed in a position of marginality have some access to the canonization and market success that the narrative of obscene genius includes, they gained such access only by a more fraught path: the narrative of obscene pathology. According to this script, the people of color and LGBTQ+ folk who create sexually transgressive works do sometimes accrue material or cultural capital as a result of their works, but during this period it is not reliably by dint of being deemed geniuses or through recognition of their role transforming the canon—regardless of their innovation, creativity, or transformative work. Their transgressions are not routinely marked as "outside the reach of power." Instead, their transgressions are judged as confirmation of negative stereotypes of deviance already assigned to their social groups and thus reify that power and justify their being pushed into delegitimized cultural zones. These works are read as sociological documents of received truths regarding the social pathology of the author's community, forced to engage with stereotypes that already existed but which are often in search of proof. Such motivated readings negate the artistic innovation of the creators while replacing it with public discourses aimed at confirming or refuting those stereotypes. This reception is in keeping with the long-standing reductive practice of reading minoritarian literature ethnographically, but it also signals how literary reception can play a role in the ongoing marginalization of excluded groups.

Foucault's claim that sexuality has been subject to an incitement to discourse certainly describes the history of obscenity. Calls to silence, suppress, burn, or otherwise neutralize taboo sexual speech have led to its diffusion, celebration, archiving, and canonization, not to mention having produced a wealth of secondary discourses in the courts, in the press, and in the halls of Congress. The discourses thus incited, however, are revealing because their bifurcation demonstrates underlying forces of inequality that would otherwise not have been obvious. That is to say, discourse is not always incited equally. The discourses incited by the transgressions of dominant voice authors tend to elevate their status in the realms of politics and philosophy, while the discourses incited by the transgressions of marginalized people tend to justify their status in the realms of pathology and criminality. This creates an oppressive hierarchy through which marginalization is perpetuated and naturalized. I intend this book as a step in demolishing this hierarchy.

By affording gains in the form of status and market success, the narrative of obscene pathology can create a place for the author within the national community while the fact that the narrative centers negative stereotypes affirms that this belonging is often predicated on condition of lesser status. In these cases, writers of color and LGBTQ+ creators are admitted to the community at the cost of affirming—or at least *centering*—the mechanisms of exclusion that push them out of positions of full equality. An author like Toni Morrison may gain acclaim, become a national treasure, win the Nobel Prize, and so on, but her work is still judged by a white supremacist culture according to the question of how it represents the black community, why she seemed unwilling to write a book with "universal" appeal, and whether her books reify the existing scripts of deviance marshaled by U.S. national mythologies to maintain racial hierarchies. Just as the narrative of obscene genius cements the belonging of those to whom it is applied, the narrative of obscene pathology maintains the marginalization of those to whom it is applied.

I offer these strands as jumping off points for a larger discussion of the inequalities of reception that occur around texts subject to the label of obscenity and the contradictions of moralist discourses around obscenity politics. Certain clear instances of these two narratives do present themselves in the archive, but the binary breaks down more frequently as American attitudes toward race, gender, and sexuality are transformed through the late twentieth century, something I hope to demonstrate in later chapters. Rather than being the definitive condition of reception, they are simply horizons of possibility for the reception of a text. In nearly all cases, what remains most interesting about these tropes or motifs within the literary history is how those subject to them resisted and transformed them. It is also important to stress that these binaries do not represent immanent qualities of the literary artifacts subject to them. They are the expression of pernicious power dynamics that play out as debates over aesthetic value and intellectual cachet.

Similarly, the American canon, it must be acknowledged, is not a simple list of geniuses and their works. I hope my arguments make clear that many factors contribute to the loose collection, never fully codified, that constitutes the books taught, assigned, read, and recognized as literature across the country and the world. The canon has at times lived up to its reputation as the exclusive redoubt of dead white male authors, but recent work has helped to counter this historical trend. Thanks to the important work of ethnic studies, queer studies, and feminist scholars in the past half-century and more, the canon today—and even at the end of the twentieth century—includes a wider range of voices as older authors have fallen out of favor and been replaced with others. In particular, vis-à-vis the current study, Miller, who enjoyed semi-canonical status for a time mid-century, is now seldom read and almost never taught. On the other hand, Morrison, who struggled famously against accusations of simplicity and reductive readings of her novels, is today among the leading figures of American literature with an undisputed place in the canon.

In his comprehensive attempt to describe the American canon, *The Program Era*, Mark McGurl centers the institutional trends that contributed to the accretion of a canon rather than using either a great-works / great-authors model or purely commercial or historical models of reception. Instead, he describes it as "breaking down into three relatively discrete but in practice overlapping aesthetic formations," all of which have roots in the birth of graduate writing programs.[13] These three generic categories (technomodernism, high cultural pluralism, and lower-middle-class modernism) exist more or less alongside each other and are treated by McGurl as "path[s] to literary distinction in the postwar period" that are mostly parallel "though sometimes overlapping" (57). One of these strains, technomodernism, is inhabited by the likes of Pynchon and others thought to be emblematic of the high post-modernist experimentalism of the mid-twentieth century. The strain he calls "high cultural pluralism" represents those works that are also self-consciously literary but which center an experience of racial or ethnic identity. Morrison is a representative figure in this category. The three strains enjoy different levels of prestige in different spheres, but it is worth remembering that none is obviously ascendant or imbued with awe in the sense that one might have spoken of a canon of great books in the past with near-mystical reverence.

Thus, while there may be a tendency to identify certain high-modernist forms and themes as the representatives of the American canon, this is not strictly true but only an effect of the tendency of those genres to be associated with certain prestige discourses because of their affiliation with literary theory and conventionally empowered and centered communities. My purpose here is not to ratify any theory of the shape of the canon, but to discuss some forces that impact how works are produced, distributed, and—especially—celebrated, and through that discussion to highlight that the terms of celebration are different and unequal.

Defining an Obscene Archive:
Shifting Centers and Double Meanings

Titling this book *Obscene Gestures* runs the risk of misleadingly implying that I intend to talk about, say, giving someone the middle finger. There is a rich history of obscene gestures in that regard, and I encourage readers to explore it. However, I should clarify that I do not use the word "gestures" here to refer to the language-like acts one performs with their hands or other body parts as a complement to spoken communication.[14] When I say "gestures," I employ the term figuratively, referring to a course of action meant to express an underlying belief, disposition, or ideology. Giving a thank-you gift was a nice *gesture*, we might say. An obscene gesture, similarly, is not when one extends a particular finger but when one's artwork is interpreted as a giant "fuck you." These gestures can be grand or petty, but they signal more than a single sign transmitted from sender to receiver, instead encompassing rhetorical strategies and content choices that are interpreted as pushing the boundaries of propriety. What I consider, then, too, is broader than any individual work of fiction or drama or photography that contains taboo content, but the larger action of imagining, creating, publishing, and defending those works. I use the word to indicate not only a single expressive act but courses of action undertaken both singularly and collectively, both consciously and unconsciously, as they come together to shape our understanding of what the possibilities of sexual expression are, how they mediate or intersect with other forms of resistance to social power, and what their echoes are today. In this sense, my project will touch on aesthetic ideas but will primarily be concerned with the historical dimensions of certain representations, deeply situating them in a larger cultural politics.

"Obscenity" is also a term with quite specific contextual meanings, some of which I intentionally invoke here. In the legal context, the term's definition is limited narrowly to sexual material of an offensive nature that is not afforded First Amendment protections. In common parlance, the definition is much broader, referring to something that shocks the sensibilities and which the utterer wants to characterize as excessive in a way that offends propriety or morality. When used in this sense, it is not only applied to sexual representations but is metaphorically extended to excess of any kind, especially wealth or pleasure. One routinely hears, for example, of people who are obscenely wealthy or food that was obscenely delicious. Both connotations echo one another in the sense that no matter which way the term is used, it connotes behavior that goes too far and thus is judged by the speaker to violate standards of decency. What constitutes "too far" and what defines "decency," however, are up for debate, and this is true no matter the venue and regardless of whether the debate is between a prosecutor and a publisher or between a preacher and a plutocrat.

The scholarly tradition treating the issue of obscenity tends to engage extensively with the relevant legal history, meaning that the former use (defining "obscenity" narrowly and literally) dominates. This is especially true for studies that deal with the early to mid-twentieth century, because at that time the Supreme Court was concerned very much with defining the term, and so the precision or lack of it in popular usage as well as in legal precedent demanded precise application. Perhaps this semantic focus dominates because the Supreme Court efforts to articulate precisely what the word meant was done in reaction to the term being applied very loosely by would-be censors and very narrowly by free speech activists. Thus, the legal conception of the term was developed to combat the amorphousness of the popular use of the term that prevailed then and that prevails today.

From these distinct ways of talking about obscenity emerges a tension between what is properly, in a legal sense, deemed obscene (which today is an extremely limited category of texts) and what texts have been subject to accusations of obscenity and for which the notion of their *potential* obscenity has influenced reception in meaningful ways (which today is an extremely broad category of texts). Because the current study is more a cultural than a legal history, it is the latter category of texts—those for which obscenity has been a factor in their circulation and canonization—that comprises the archive for this study.

For the sake of convenience, and at the risk that my claims will seem misleading when presented out of context, I have often referred to these texts as simply "obscene," though from the vantage of certain strict definitions this is untrue; none of these texts are *legally* obscene. The alternative is to refer to them using convoluted and often equivocal language that can be just as misrepresentative and is often confusing. In this way, then, I use the term "obscene" in a bracketed sense, always aware that the term's meaning is contested and this contestation is the very issue under analysis. The same goes for my use of the terms "obscene genius" and "obscene pathology." I do not assert, in using these terms, that the authors or works to which they are applied actually represent genius or pathology, but rather that the authors and works are subject to literary-historical and racial-cultural discourses that presume potential obscenity to be an important element of understanding them. Further, the terms "genius" and "pathology" are mis-applied to these works in a motivated way that reflects deeply ingrained prejudices.

Defining an Obscene Act:
Legal Obscenity Discourses in the Twentieth Century

My use of these terms in this way indicates that my manner of engagement is deeply invested in cultural criticism and indebted to theories of racialization and gender and sexuality, which I see as crucial for making sense of the cultural politics that dominate the discourse of obscenity in the latter part of the twentieth century. However, in the preceding decades, the landscape of obscene literature was primarily a legal one. In the United States, restrictive measures owing their origin to the Comstock laws passed before the turn of the twentieth century severely limited the kinds of sexual material one could publish and distribute (the Comstock laws governed the mailing of print materials, and in a pre-internet era this affected essentially all movement of book stocks, magazines, newspapers, and advertisements). Across the Atlantic, however, salacious books were being produced aplenty, including many that are now considered classics, such as James Joyce's *Ulysses* and D. H. Lawrence's *Lady Chatterley's Lover*. Of course, scads of more explicitly erotic and pornographic books were being produced and circulated, such as the works of the Marquis de Sade. These became a prominent factor in U.S. obscenity history when they were imported, and shipments of these books were often impounded, resulting in lawsuits that found their way to the Supreme Court several times. Scholars have already comprehensively detailed these events and the controversies around the works of Joyce, Lawrence, and others.[15] My goal here is not to duplicate their work but to highlight the elements of this history that shaped the literary and political landscape in relation to race and heteronormativity, which will transform obscene literature in the decades to follow.

The ruling Supreme Court precedent on obscenity dates to 1973, when the conservative Burger Court sought to refine prior rulings by the Warren Court, which was famous for progressive decisions, including *Brown v. Board of Education* (1954), *Miranda v. Arizona* (1966), and *Loving v. Virginia* (1967). The Warren Court had played a central role in dismantling Jim Crow and produced important progress on civil rights, and its obscenity rulings can be interpreted in these terms as part of a broader liberalization of culture. However, the Warren Court was also succeeded by conservative backlash that walked back some of what it had achieved, and the push and pull between the courts during this era shed considerable light on the issues I address in this book.[16] Moreover, because of the influence of these rulings, U.S. culture still lives in the shadow of this period of social change, and existing obscenity law signals vestiges of the unfinished work of civil rights and the growth of neoconservatism.

Just a few years after *Brown*, the Warren Court issued their first major ruling on obscenity: 1957's *Roth v. United States*. It is evident in the comprehensiveness of the ruling that the Court sought to settle a wide range of issues related to state oversight of sexual speech. The most significant of these issues was whether the Constitution permitted obscenity laws of any kind. Justice Brennan, writing for the majority, signaled a strong interest in strengthening freedom of expression, arguing that "The fundamental freedoms of speech and press have contributed greatly to the development and well-being of our free society and are indispensable to its continued growth." Nonetheless, despite this and other protestations, the Court ultimately found that "implicit in the history of the First Amendment is the rejection of obscenity as utterly without redeeming social importance," and thus it did not, for the Court, enjoy unlimited Constitutional protection.

Having established that the Constitution does permit censorship of obscenity, the salient question became (and would remain for more than a decade) "what is obscenity?" The legal guideline emerging from *Roth* was that a text was obscene if "the dominant theme of the material taken as a whole appeals to prurient interest" (Roth). This seemed to draw a line between materials that do not have arousal as their primary purpose (though they might include sexual content) and those (e.g., pornography) that are primarily intended for arousal. Going further, the justices tended to affirm that a work must have no social value whatsoever, and appeal *solely* to prurient interest, to be declared obscene. If the term "obscenity" marked off those texts that were "utterly without redeeming social importance," it seemed that the presence of some level of social importance, even nominal, would mean that a text could not be found to be obscene—and in fact this is how the Court's ruling was subsequently interpreted.[17]

The Court attempted to address disparate interpretations of this standard in 1964 with *Jacobellis v. Ohio*, concerning an Ohio theater owner charged with obscenity for showing the French film *Les Amants* (1958).[18] In its ruling, the Court reiterated that "material dealing with sex in a manner that advocates ideas, . . . or that has literary or scientific or artistic value or any other form of social importance, may not be branded as obscenity and denied . . . constitutional protection."[19] Even this was not enough, though, and the Court revisited the issue in 1966, with the case of *Memoirs v. Massachusetts*, which concerned John Cleland's *Fanny Hill, Or, Memoirs of a Woman of Pleasure* (1748). The lower courts had determined that *Fanny Hill* (referred to as *Memoirs* in the legal documents) was offensive and prurient, and that while it might have "some minimal literary value," that "does not mean it is of any social importance."[20] However, the Warren Court disagreed with the balancing test used by the appeals court and took the occasion to state their opinion unequivocally: "A book cannot be proscribed unless it is found to be *utterly* without redeeming social value. This is so even though the book is found to possess the requisite prurient appeal and to be patently offensive" (*Memoirs*, emphasis in the original). The standard reaffirmed by the Warren Court is that *any* social value is sufficient because a text must be "*utterly*" without it to be obscene. This strident affirmation sets a remarkably lax standard, and this is ultimately what the Burger Court sought to overturn, largely because the finding all but entirely negated obscenity statutes of any kind.

The rightward lurch on the Supreme Court that enabled this was a result of Richard Nixon's four appointments and can be seen as a reaction to the progressive action of the Warren Court in other areas. Nixon saw a political opportunity in conservative anger over the actions of the Warren Court. According to Bruce H. Kalk, those who objected to the expansion of rights and freedoms under the Warren Court rhetorically conflated a wide variety of disparate groups (communists, civil rights workers, criminals, publishers) who had been given greater license or protections (262–63). As a result, the Warren Court became a focus of conservative—especially white Southern—dissatisfaction, and this environment presented a political opening for Nixon, whose pro–law enforcement judicial appointees reflected his neoconservative politics.

This ideological shift was felt in the Burger Court's obscenity rulings. The Burger Court revised the *Roth* and *Memoirs* precedents in 1973 with *Miller v. California*. The appellant, Marvin Miller, was convicted of mailing circulars advertising pornographic materials. In the ruling, Chief Justice Warren Burger invoked what he called "the somewhat tortured history of the Court's obscenity decisions" to justify returning to an issue the Warren Court had taken pains to settle.[21] Concerned that *Memoirs* made it difficult for prosecutors to prevail in court, Burger and the majority took it upon themselves to refine the definition of obscenity. The Court established a three-prong test that we now call the "Miller Test" and which is used to this day to define obscene material. According to this test, the triers of fact in these cases must determine:

> (a) whether "the average person, applying contemporary community standards" would find that the work, taken as a whole, appeals to the prurient interest; (b) whether the work depicts or describes, in a patently offensive way, sexual conduct specifically defined by the applicable state law; and (c) whether the work, taken as a whole, lacks serious literary, artistic, political, or scientific value.

Much of the language echoes *Memoirs* but deviates from it in subtle but significant ways. The final prong of the test, for example, requires that the artwork lack "*serious* literary, artistic, political, or scientific value." The requirement that the value be serious as opposed to incidental is key. The court was dissatisfied with rulings on texts—specifically *Fanny Hill*—which it deemed to be predominantly prurient while having only superficial artistic or didactic value.[22]

When it came to obscenity, then, Nixon realized his vision for a court more likely to side with prosecutors than with those who produce and distribute sexual material. Burger led a narrow majority of just five justices—which included the four Nixon appointees—that walked back the more permissive standard of their predecessors, and the new guidelines they set affirmed the importance of community standards in determinations of what is offensive.[23] More than privileging state and local authority against federal oversight, this enabled prosecutorial forum shopping, where material produced in liberal cities, such as Los Angeles, was charged in more conservative communities, such as Kansas and Ohio where the material might be bought or sold. This, then, enabled more contentious prosecutions better suited to symbolic cultural warfare, rather than limited, viable enforcement action.

In practical terms, the Miller test considerably ties censors' hands. Nonetheless, the subjectivity of the term "serious" leaves the door open to selective prosecutions for obscenity because the seriousness of aesthetic value becomes an issue of fact for juries to decide. Thus, obscenity laws remain on the books and prosecutions continue today, though they are less common than they were a century ago. By mid-century, a shift had been set in motion that would result in the question of obscenity ceasing to be a legal one and becoming predominantly a moral and aesthetic one; however, it did not entirely curtail obscenity prosecutions, nor did it head off controversies around and challenges to sexually explicit artworks. If it had, we might not have seen the birth of the Parents Music Resource Center, the prosecution of Dead Kennedys and 2 Live Crew, or the frequent challenges to *The Bluest Eye* when it appears on high school reading lists.

However, in many ways, the end of the legal question of obscenity with *Miller* is the beginning of the cultural question of obscenity, and that is the central question *Obscene Gestures* attempts to address. In this book, therefore, I examine not primarily the legal question of whether certain books crossed historically specific lines of acceptable expression, nor the progressive development of a legal discourse on a specific Constitutional question. Rather, I hope to address the street-level controversies (protests and boycotts) and boardroom decisions (canceling publication contracts, demanding editorial changes) that suggest how and why certain books were targets of obscenity discourses, and what effect that had on their reception and canonization.

Theorizing Post-Legal Obscenity

The shift from a legalistic obscenity discourse centered on the limits of state authority to a sublimated disciplinary discourse limiting the expression of sexual nonconformity in the social sphere is largely in keeping with what Foucault suggests is the result of the transfer of behavior regulation from the singular state apparatus to the diffuse forms of self-regulation that characterize our particular episteme.[24] The shift from state intervention to cultural norms built on modesty and propriety is itself a complex and contradictory process. As Foucault famously contends in *A History of Sexuality*, overt acts of censorship and moralism that appear to stifle sexual expression (whether they are state measures or not) instead result in their multiplication. Similarly, while he warns, "I do not maintain that the prohibition of sex is a ruse" (12), he clarifies that the suppression of sex and sexual expression are only partial explanations and that the mechanisms of suppression do not result in the silence that we assume—and that censors assert—is their goal. Rather, the suppression of sexual expression and the repression of sexual desire serve to channel that desire into other forms that are more socially desirable from the standpoint of the power status quo. Non-reproductive sexualities and sex acts and those outside the familial home, abhorred by a heteronormative order allied with capital, are shunted to "a place where they could be reintegrated, if not in the circuits of productivity at least in those of profit" (4). In these locales, those marginalized acts of non-authorized sex do not recede into silence but become objects of knowledge and power via the modes of the law, sociology, medicine, and politics. They do not become invisible or silent but they are, instead, forced to explain themselves, often against the backdrop of assertions or assumptions of pathology.

Such was and is certainly the case with obscene literature. Though in earlier eras certain regimes of censorship such as the Hays Code and the Comics Code have been more or less effective in changing the horizon of representational possibilities for a time, it is generally understood, and the cases I examine in this book confirm, that efforts to challenge texts on their obscenity in the twentieth century reliably lead to increased interest and greater distribution of the works, not their suppression. Efforts to suppress a work generate debate, archiving, study, and secondary texts that cement the work's place in culture. In explaining the naiveté of assuming that censorship silences or suppresses sex generally, Foucault asks incredulously: "A censorship of sex? There was installed rather an apparatus for producing an ever greater quantity of discourse about sex, capable of functioning and taking effect in its very economy" (22). One might replace the word "sex" in this passage with "taboo representations of sex" or with the name of any particular work that contains such representations (*Ulysses*, for example, or *Tropic of Cancer*), and it would probably describe what actually occurs as an effect of censorship, counter to the intentions of those who seek to censor. Rather than silencing the author or burying the offending material, their challenges produce a wealth of discourse around those representations as prosecutors, courts, readers, librarians, academics, politicians, and others seek to determine whether the representation should be censored, who gets to decide if it should be censored, whether its prestige elements outweigh its offensive ones, whether it might be better to restrict it or ban it outright. . . . In essence, the effort to silence produces a welter of speech, and the effort to push the text to the shadows brings it into the light of analysis. Moreover, this effort enters the text into the economy rather than removing it from it, both because the public attention often stimulates demand, but because the work of determining the appropriateness of censorship engages myriad actors in the public and private sectors, such as lawyers, librarians, lecturers, and list-makers. Ultimately, then, counter to conventional wisdom (and likely to the chagrin of censors), obscenity challenges are hardly a means to silence ideas but are rather part of the larger "incitement to discourse" that turns sex, the law, and identity into technologies of power and production.

In addition to Foucault, I also take critical bearings from Josh Lambert, whose *Unclean Lips* both traces a complex history of obscenity and provides the model for the simultaneous analysis of legal and cultural trends that I hope to mirror in this work, which takes a historicist route. Lambert emphasizes the major role Jews played in the history of obscenity—often as the result of anti-Semitic prosecutorial decisions—as he traces the gradual changes in American culture and Supreme Court jurisprudence. As Lambert notes, Supreme Court decisions in the middle of the century contributed "to the freeing of virtually all literature and most film from obscenity prosecutions by the mid-1960s."[25] This was both a sign of changing national mores and a significant factor in the subsequent development of the sexual revolution in the United States. This is so because Warren Court decisions decriminalized pornography and loosened restrictions on the publication of sexual material. What results, however, is not an open, Wild West–style publishing landscape. Instead, the regulation of speech shifts (incompletely) from government and legal spheres into the spheres of social and cultural morality. Lambert calls this "the American turn from obscenity regulated by law to modesty regulated by participants in the literary system" (21).

What makes this a potent area of cultural analysis is the significant difference between law and modesty as regulatory systems. The law aims at universality and is deeply entrenched in particular theories of textual analysis. It aspires to be unitary and authoritative. In contrast, modesty relies on multiple disparate regulatory systems, each of which aspires to this unitary status, but which together in dialogue become a multi-front conflict among religious adherents, philosophers, libertines, and others. That is, while the law in the United States is a system in which multiple local jurisdictions are subject to the single jurisdiction of the Supreme Court, there is no such unified measure for modesty or authority whose word is final on the matter. Individual religious communities may understand modesty very differently, while secular citizens may define it in still other ways. Moreover, these groups (and the sub-groups within them and individuals themselves) also disagree on whether and to what extent the judgments of their group ought to control the actions of others. The politically active Christian right, for example, argues that its view of modesty is, or ought to be, the national view and seeks consciously to impose it through legislative activism and political organizing, while other groups take a more live-and-let-live approach, respecting that certain people's religious identity demands certain practices concerning clothing, pleasure, and interactions between people of different genders, for example, without seeking to condemn them or limit the freedom of others. Thus, the shift from legal regulation to social regulation of obscenity creates a proliferation of regimes of control rather than a diminution of them. While the threat of legal consequences for publishing sexually explicit works has decreased, the threat of social consequences has increased dramatically and become more amorphous and unpredictable.

Ironically, this proliferation of discourses contributes to market success and enduring demand for obscene works. The most salient examples of the way that obscenity has contributed directly and even deliberately to the market success and canonization of literary texts in the mid-century period come from Grove Press. As Loren Glass lays out in *Counterculture Colophon*, the press began to push the envelope by importing French and other European titles that violated the obscenity standards established during the Comstock era.[26] Some of these works, like Lawrence's *Lady Chatterley's Lover*, made defensible claims to artistic value, and in order to make these claims in court the press solicited a wealth of reviews and testimonials that contributed to the scholarly archive around these works and introduced them into college classrooms at the same time that the GI Bill was helping to balloon university enrollments.

Barney Rosset, the publisher of Grove during its most influential period, more or less made this a marketing strategy but was driven by another more radical purpose, which he later accomplished through successive high-profile court battles. As Glass describes this purpose, Rosset "[took] the avant-garde into the mainstream, helping to usher in a cultural revolution whose consequences are with us still" (4). Doing so required a combination of radical social politics and market savviness:

He intuited that the obscure experimental dramatists whose work he acquired in the 1950s would become steady sellers once their reputations were established, and he realized early that the market for their printed work would be in the expanding American university system. He sensed that the regime of censorship established under the Comstock Act was collapsing and that challenging it could therefore become profitable. (Glass 7)

Though Rosset always felt his primary allegiance was to the works he published—and the fact that he nearly bankrupted the company and spent a multi-million-dollar inheritance defending them in court confirms this—he nonetheless recognized a business opportunity in the controversy that attended these high-profile trials. These twin strains of market success and cultural politics arise in almost all literary obscenity controversies in the United States, and so Rosset's story and that of Grove is representative. Glass encapsulates here how resisting authoritarian and moralist forces was not only an ideological stance, but was—and is—a successful marketing strategy. As Lambert reminds us, "Since antiquity, it has been obvious to just about everyone (except perhaps self-appointed moralists) that suppressed literature has tremendous sales potential" (14).

This is true because efforts like Rosset's entail establishing a foothold in emerging markets, stimulating public curiosity, and cementing the texts in question as historical artifacts. Contributing to all of this is the wealth of critical writings produced in and for the court proceedings that established the works' literary bona fides, but which subsequently also became part of their marketing materials. Glass notes, for example, that Grove used this strategy in its marketing of *Lady Chatterley's Lover*, *Tropic of Cancer*, and *Naked Lunch* (1959) by including court rulings and expert testimony as paratexts in new editions, which were often released following the trials, as well as in promotional materials sent to booksellers (103, 119). As Glass describes it, the effects go well beyond financial success, though: "The obscenity trial in this context functioned as a ritual of consecration whereby modernist texts could be affirmed as 'classics' by experts on literary value" (103) without having to outlive their authors. Glass is describing the establishment of a new script for fast-tracking literary works to prestige status that would obviate the older test-of-time model through which works had historically become classics. This was a boon for publishers seeking to capitalize on the perceived status of their works while retaining the benefits of copyright that attended recently published works and that tended to disappear for books that lived long enough to become classics.

Though some presses were able to cannily capitalize on the obscenity trials of the twentieth century—and such trials and presses have had a lasting impact on the mechanisms of canonization and literary studies—one cannot ignore that obscenity charges do continue to have negative effects on artists, publishers, and producers and maintain broader power hierarchies. This dual mechanism is one of the reasons that obscenity is such a complex subject, but it is complex in ways that are illuminating. Whitney Strub's careful history of pornography in the twentieth century helps especially to shed light on the efforts of moralists to maintain certain exclusions and on how this aspect of obscenity discourse shapes the boundaries of the nation by serving as a proxy for battles over belonging. Strub demonstrates, for example, that the courts have routinely classified material depicting same-sex couplings and desire as inherently obscene, preferentially offering constitutional protection to expressions of heteronormative sexuality while in effect criminalizing representations of same-sex desire using selective enforcement of the same statutes.[27]

The effect is to normalize heterosexual identity and violently marginalize LGBTQ+ identity. Efforts to use obscenity in this way to limit expressions of sexual nonconformity continued even in the era after *Miller*, in which such efforts were unlikely to secure convictions. In fact, as Strub has noted, obscenity prosecutions continued (and were encouraged by activist groups) even when it was known that such prosecutions had no chance of withstanding Constitutional challenges in the hopes that the accused would capitulate in the face of pressure (and under the weight of legal costs) and that others would be discouraged from following in their footsteps (*Perversion*). Such actors realized, like Rosset did, that the new frontiers in obscenity opened up new opportunities. Strub contends that during the 1960s, "Conservative politicians displayed more interest in attracting voters with pronouncements of their piety than in following through with substantive policy, damning rather than damming the 'floodtide of filth' allegedly engulfing the nation." However, this shift to a rhetorical battle actually signaled the shift to a battle over identity and nation that sublimated older racial and ideological antinomies. According to Strub, moralist efforts to suppress sexual speech were "a discursive displacement of the increasingly obsolete conservative tropes of racism and anti-communism" (*Perversion* 2).

It is not only in the post-*Miller* period, however, that obscenity was used as a bludgeon to police the racial and sexual borders of national identity. Lambert sees this as one of its original foundations: "the concept of obscenity evolved in American legal discourse in the late 19th century as a response to fears about the speech and behavior of Jews and others suspected of being insufficiently American and Christian" (3). The Comstock Laws of 1873, the earliest version of widespread obscenity restrictions in the United States, arose out of a culture of anti-Semitism, Lambert argues, and were used extensively to punish those who for political or ideological reasons were outside the mainstream. The use of obscenity as a proxy to condemn those who are viewed as insufficiently loyal or patriotic and those who deviate from mainstream religious affiliations or observances, then, is not new. However, this facet of obscenity discourse becomes more significant in the context of social justice movements in the late twentieth century.

Obscenity debates do not operate in a vacuum, and analysis of them must not slip into problematic habits of considering categories of exclusion in isolation. Rather, discourses of racial exclusion, gender bias, and sexual normativity are comorbid in efforts to suppress sexual expression precisely because they represent intersecting rather than independent systems of oppression. When Roderick A. Ferguson, interpreting Chandan Reddy's "Home, Houses, Nonidentity," remarks that "the decisive intervention of queer of color analysis is that racist practice articulates itself generally as gender and sexual regulation," it goes to the heart of the matter.[28] Racist practice plays out as the maintenance of sexual and gender norms that buttress power inequalities. Because the reception of the texts in this book allows us to track this process historically, Ferguson's work and queer of color critique provide crucial frameworks for what follows, as they reveal how heteronormativity articulates its exclusivity through the pathologization of non-white bodies. In particular, his thinking helps illuminate why the narratives of obscene genius and pathology become increasingly unstable as we consider how race, gender, and sexuality contribute to a multifaceted culture of reception that is seldom reducible to simple binaries.

Ferguson uncovers a shared tendency among historical materialism and neoliberalism to treat heteronormativity as the sign of order and civilization and encode non-conforming sexual and gender practice as signs of disorder and decay. For my work here, the notions of disorder and decay map onto the discourses of pathology that animate the narrative of obscene pathology. In one passage, for example, Ferguson describes how "heteropatriarchy produces the prostitute as the other of heteropatriarchal ideals, an other that is simultaneously the effect of racial, gender, sexual, and class discourses" (9) and notes that the marginalization of prostitutes "denoted the pathologies, disorders, and degradations of an emerging civilization" (10). The result of such marginalization practices was the habitual characterization of racialized people as a threat to the social order through (real or imagined) sexual practices construed as non-normative. Similarly, building on Lisa Lowe's identification of whiteness as the presumed condition of citizenship,[29] Ferguson writes that "As a technology of race, U.S. citizenship has historically ascribed heteronormativity (universality) to certain subjects and nonheteronormativity (particularity) to others" (14). Ferguson thus demonstrates how racist practices around sexuality take for granted the imputed sexual deviance of non-white people and use this as justification for unequal access to civic participation and state protection.

In the obscenity controversies of the twentieth century, we see this process clearly. By constraining the reception of transgressive works by writers of color and LGBTQ+ folks according to the presumption of sexual deviance, one limits their access to universality by assigning them the particularity of historically specific pathologies. It may not matter that the foreclosed universality is a fiction (though certainly it is) because those in power take it to be a prerequisite for and justification of social power. Obscenity discourses, then, take place not as an additive element of the U.S. racial order or a single sphere in which it operates by unequal application of a general law but as a component part of how racialization proceeds generally.

Scholars on the study of ethnic literature have provided additional important insights I hope to build upon, particularly as they elaborate on the notion that works by writers of color are judged first and foremost ethnographically. This results, in part, from the assumption that, as Toni Morrison remarked in the preface to *Playing in the Dark*, "Regardless of the race of the author, the readers of virtually all of American fiction have been positioned as white." She then provocatively wonders, "What happens to the writerly imagination of a black author who is at some level *always* conscious of representing one's own race to, or in spite of, a race of readers that understands itself to be 'universal' or race-free."[30] Morrison is driving at the way that black writers have felt the pressure of a white audience constraining their representations and obligating them to speak to the racial attitudes of whiteness rather than their own concerns or from an authentic perspective. Morrison elsewhere notes that the practice of reading African American literature and art according to notions of it being emotionally moving or "sociologically 'revealing'" are part of a systemic—often pejorative—classification designed to diminish the intellectual weight of African American art as inferior to "Western" canonical traditions.[31] Together, these notions illuminate how the whiteness of literary criticism continues to shape what can be said. Even when criticism seems to allow space for non-white voices, work by non-dominant authors is chained to the center of white perspectives, even if only as the site and catalyst of resistance.[32]

This constraint often consists of various traps affecting what can be represented within works by marginalized people and which works make it to market or gain traction once they do. As Hazel V. Carby explains, for example, African American women writers must contend with "the long history of the exploitation of black sexuality" in ways that force them to either avoid representations of sex and sexuality or run the risk of affirming that history of exploitation: "Racist sexual ideologies proclaimed the black woman to be a rampant sexual being, and in response black women writers either focused on defending their morality or displaced sexuality onto another terrain."[33] Perhaps more to the point, she argues elsewhere that "in order to gain a public voice as orators or published writers, black women had to confront the dominant domestic ideologies and literary conventions of womanhood which excluded them from the definition 'woman'" (6). In this instance, Carby is explaining how black women public figures, artists, and intellectuals historically had first and foremost to contend with racist stereotypes about their gender and sexuality as the precondition for participation in public discourse. As Carby then notes, black women writers resisted these ideologies in complex ways.

What concerns me at present is how racist discourse expresses itself in unequal restrictions on what can be said and the discriminatory ways what is said is received and interpreted, a characteristic of the narrative of obscene pathology that I described previously. This requirement resonates today as it did then, and it is not restricted only to black women but affects other marginalized groups, to whom it is applied in culturally and historically specific ways. I argue that in each of the cases I consider in this book, spanning more than fifty years of the twentieth century, the cost of entry into public conversations for writers and creators outside the mainstream is an engagement with existing stereotypes, as well as racist, sexist, and homophobic ideologies. This engagement may enable resistance for the authors and their audiences and the benefits of obscenity in terms of financial success and canonization can accrue to the creators, but the compulsory engagement itself contributes to maintaining hegemony by centering the concerns of the hegemonic system.

Chapter Summaries

Throughout the book, I explore a handful of cases that demonstrate these principles. Keeping in mind that the book must, of necessity, be only a provocative beginning, I have tended to choose works that were published close in time and that highlight, by virtue of their similarity in content, the diverging paths forced on different authors. For example, because Morrison's *The Bluest Eye* and Pynchon's *Gravity's Rainbow* both contain scenes of pedophilia and incest, Chapter 2 juxtaposes them and heads off the counterclaim that they faced such different receptions as a result of differences in content. Where possible, too, I have attempted to acknowledge the complications with any easy schema to describe what is inescapably an incredibly complex social phenomenon. Chapter 4, in particular, attempts to both account for those texts that do not fully fit the established narratives (like Tony Kushner's *Angels in America* and Robert Mapplethorpe's *The Perfect Moment*) and to consider what other factors contribute to divergent receptions for obscene texts, including regional variations in political ideologies and the influence of different political activist groups whose memberships and coalitions shift over time. Meanwhile, I have had to omit some titles that would productively advance my thesis, such as Philip Roth's *Portnoy's Complaint* (1969) and Burroughs's *Naked Lunch*. Similarly, though they are undoubtedly important, I have not considered works such as Cherríe Moraga's *Heroes and Saints* (1994), which might illuminate how the politics of obscenity is affected by the discourses of ability.

Chapter 1 stages a prehistory of post-1973 obscenity to consider the different fates of Miller's *Tropic of Cancer*, published in France in 1934, and Richard Wright's *Native Son*, published in the United States in 1940. These texts emblematize the counter-narratives of genius and pathology that will re-emerge in subsequent chapters. The reception history of Miller's novel produced the narrative that would later come to characterize the move toward liberalized obscenity laws in the United States, while also providing a script for other beat and counterculture works. Originally banned from being imported into the United States over Miller's explicit descriptions of his protagonist's sexual adventures, the book catalyzed a lengthy legal process that cemented the book's status as a major literary event and played a pivotal role in legal obscenity discourses of the twentieth century. In contrast, Wright's novel had to be expurgated to achieve a similar level of success. In order to make *Native Son* its first work by an African American, the Book-of-the-Month Club required that several passages be removed from the manuscript to assuage concerns over cross-racial desire. The resulting omissions not only diluted the novel's challenge to racialized sexual norms of the time but also diminished important complexities in the psychology of the main character Bigger Thomas.

Considering the two novels through lenses of obscenity and race brings significant differences into focus. Miller's novel championed frank sexuality as a viable means of metaphysical exploration and consequently became a touchstone for the counterculture and the sexual revolution while remaining aesthetically intact. In contrast, Wright's novel had to be expurgated to accommodate white discomfort over African American sexuality, and the resulting changes threatened Wright's ambitious aesthetic goals and risked affirming stereotypes of black pathology and white saviorship that would haunt civil rights activism for decades.

Chapter 2 then moves into the period around the *Miller* decision to explore what was possible in the wake of mid-century legal precedents. In this chapter, I consider Morrison's *The Bluest Eye* (1970) and Pynchon's *Gravity's Rainbow* (1973). Objecting to content that was called obscene, the Pulitzer Prize board chose to issue no prize for fiction in 1974 rather than accede to the jury's unanimous selection of *Gravity's Rainbow*. Frequent charges that the novel contains problematic sexual content are often explicitly weighed against its literary merit in reviews in ways that tend to affirm its place in the canon rather than challenge it. *The Bluest Eye*, on the other hand, is frequently challenged when it appears on school reading lists. In many ways it is the very fact of the book's presence on reading lists that enables such challenges. By comparison, Pynchon's novel is hardly ever taught, and so the relative complexity of *Gravity's Rainbow* has rendered it comparatively uncontroversial, though close analysis reveals real concerns about its content, including the main character's sexual encounters with a child. What makes *The Bluest Eye* comparatively *more* controversial despite its less problematic politics is that it has a more prominent place in classrooms because it is more accessible and representative of a literary movement with more currency in lower grades. The divergent fates of these novels represent the impact of schools as a locus of obscenity challenges after the obscenity trials of the 1950s and '60s. After it becomes impossible to limit the content available to adults, activists and activism shifted emphasis to controlling what is available to children.

The third chapter of *Obscene Gestures* moves into the 1980s. Indicative of the era, the Dead Kennedys' album *Frankenchrist* (1985) and 2 Live Crew's *Nasty as They Wanna Be* (1989) were both subject to prosecution for obscenity during this time, and while these prosecutions certainly resulted in some difficulties for the performers, the sensationalism of the trials propelled them to later fame, mirroring the pattern of artists being catapulted to success by obscenity charges. However, there were also significant changes in feminist organizing, and I turn to Alice Walker's *The Color Purple* (1982) and Kathy Acker's *Blood and Guts in High School* (1984) to explore how the experiences of women of color in the arena of obscenity diverge from those of their white contemporaries. Though

Acker never achieved the fame of other authors I consider, she remains a popular cult figure and this novel, in particular, has remained significant. Walker's novel became much more successful and remains a cultural touchstone, but like *The Bluest Eye* it is also regularly banned from school reading lists. In addition, *The Color Purple* was criticized for seeming to confirm stereotypes of African American pathology. Drawing on the theoretical work of Hortense Spillers and Cherríe Moraga, I confront a history of representational over-determination of sex and sexuality for women of color to show that the privilege to explore transgressive sexual representations was racially coded and that sex and sexuality were not equally open as avenues of liberation. This analysis reveals one way that financial and cultural success for women of color are often attended by the danger that the works may reaffirm the pathologization and pornotroping that are widespread in culture.

Chapter 4 brings the project up to the closing moments of the twentieth century, beginning with Robert Mapplethorpe's final exhibition, *The Perfect Moment*, which traveled the country from 1988 to 1989, and concluding with Tony Kushner's monumental play *Angels in America*, which debuted on Broadway in 1993. The fortunes of these texts reveal the trials and triumphs of representing same-sex desire during the height of the AIDS crisis and so crystallize a major facet of the cultural mechanisms of obscenity where non-normative sexuality is concerned, while also suggesting some of the important limits of the schema I outlined previously concerning genius and obscenity. Mapplethorpe's traveling retrospective, *The Perfect Moment*, was the subject of several controversies as part of the broader culture wars of the moment, and conservative politicians succeeded in getting one of the early exhibition sites to cancel the show. Furthermore, the Cincinnati Contemporary Arts Center was later prosecuted for obscenity when it presented the collection. Kushner faced a different fate with *Angels in America* just a few years later. Though it, too, was protested for its frank discussion of AIDS and same-sex desire, it was also widely celebrated and won both the Tony Award and Pulitzer Prize. Protests were relatively isolated and actually served to galvanize support for the play. What unites these two texts that faced different fates is the recognition of rapid change in LGBTQ+ visibility and equality around this time. In particular, same-sex desire had historically been assumed to fulfill the legal criterion that something be offensive in order to merit suppression, but this was becoming less true. The two stories also highlight the importance of local politics in determining the fate of transgressive sexual representations. Because Supreme Court rulings on obscenity include provisions that works can be banned if they violate "community standards," obscenity prosecutions often do take on such local characteristics.[34] Thus, the causes and legacy of obscenity cases and obscene literature are often too complex to reduce to single vectors or easy racial, gender, or sexual binaries. Finally, the book concludes with a brief epilogue outlining some of the ways these themes echo today despite apparently transformative social events, such as the advent of the internet.

Putatively Political Acts and Possibilities

There are innumerable factors that impact the application of the label "obscene" and the afterlives of texts thus marked. At the end of the day, the operation of obscenity is curiously contradictory. Often those who create transgressive forms of artistic expression see themselves as principled outsiders pushing the boundaries of a society they mean to critique. And yet their transgressions are used to cement the existing structures of privilege and exclusion, including their own. Breaking the rules strengthens the reigning economic and racial systems, which are immensely resistant to change not only by standing firm in the face of challenge, but by co-opting avant-garde and revolutionary movements and by selectively incorporating difference when it cannot be smothered. This is true of those who are marginalized, too, for even when they humanize those who have been dehumanized or complicate the simplistic or aporetic knowledge systems of racism, dominant powers may still tend to pigeonhole their work as only a reaction to these systems of dehumanization and simplification, defined by what they resist rather than what they imagine. Resistance, in this sense, is often twisted to sustain and strengthen the status quo.

I want to return momentarily to Lenny Bruce and Belle Barth, with whom I opened this introduction. It can seem specious to suggest that the mere act of stating a taboo word is a form of political protest as Bruce did. However, as Lambert notes in referring to the legal rulings that make no distinction between merely saying the word "fuck" and saying "fuck the draft," "government efforts to suppress obscene speech mean that all obscenity, however abstract or apolitical it may seem, constitutes a putatively political act" (16). This sentiment drove a lot of mid-century activism in favor of loosening obscenity restrictions, but it cannot be the last word. After all, if all obscenity is "putatively political," then it matters what politics is imputed to the specific act. As Strub has noted, "The notion that obscenity law serves as an enforcing agent of normative sexual regimes carries a certain tautological truth, but its self-evidence has perhaps acted to obstruct investigative efforts at historicizing its operations under specific settings" ("Lavender" 84). Strub is right; as we concede that restrictions on sexual representations often do contribute to norming and abjection, he also reminds us that this should enable deeper investigation of the specific circumstances in which it does this. We must, for example, uncover why Bruce and Barth have left different legacies. For those who come from marginalized groups, the putative politics may be externally defined by stereotypes: the dangers of confirming them and the responsibility to refute them. For authors whose belonging is not questioned on the grounds of social group, their transgressions can capitalize on a different putative politics: the politics of prophetic genius. Thus, what matters is the way that texts are shunted into different spheres of expectations and how authors resist this.

Finally, we should keep in mind that for all the complexities of their reception, these texts and authors do important work. *Angels in America* probably helped significantly to normalize same-sex desire and destigmatize AIDS. *The Bluest Eye* dramatized the human stakes of racialized beauty standards and likely helped fight the psychological damage of that form of bias. *Gravity's Rainbow* probably does draw readers' attention to the web of connection between fascism and the current industrial economy, with the possibility that people become more open to alternative modes of production. Each work is doing good work, but considering them as an archive reveals some of the constraints placed on the work they can do.

1 / Classic Counter-Narratives: Deep Psychology vs. Deep Pathology in Two Early Twentieth-Century Novels

Henry Miller's *Tropic of Cancer*, published in France in 1934, and Richard Wright's *Native Son*, published in the United States in 1940, anticipate and emblematize the counter-narratives of obscene genius and obscene pathology that become prominent after the important mid-century Supreme Court rulings on obscenity. The different fates of the two texts, published close together but taking very different routes to canonization, demonstrate with valuable clarity the racialized disparities in the American publishing landscape that persisted through the rest of the century. These texts, then, provide models of the two narratives by which the narratives of later years might be measured.

On one hand, Miller's *Tropic of Cancer* follows the more general narrative that characterized the lead-up to liberalized obscenity laws in the United States and blazed a trail for other Beat and counterculture works, including Allen Ginsburg's *Howl* (1956) and William S. Burroughs's *Naked Lunch* (1959). Originally banned in the United States over Miller's highly explicit descriptions of his protagonist's sexual adventures, the book later spawned a yearslong legal process funded by Grove Press that exonerated the author and publisher and moved the already-popular book closer to canonical status. Moreover, the legal battle played an early role in an important series of Supreme Court precedents that enshrined First Amendment protections for literary works by 1973. Miller's novel, which treats sexual transgression as a means of individualist self-expression and metaphysical transcendence, thus found its place in American letters secure as a result of Miller's violation of taboo, and though the novel was unavailable in his homeland for nearly thirty years, he benefited from the process without compromising his vision.[1] Miller became an icon of the counterculture, his home in Big Sur a pilgrimage site for beatniks, and his influence on later writers and American culture significant.

In contrast, Wright's *Native Son* had to be expurgated to achieve a similar level of notoriety. *Native Son* was the first work by an African American to be a Book-of-the-Month Club selection, which resulted in widespread distribution and public attention. However, before the book could be published, the Club required the removal of several passages to assuage concerns over its explicit content. This request was problematic because the scenes in question are crucial to the novel's depiction of cross-racial desire as a nodal point of the white anxiety underpinning Jim Crow. The resulting omissions not only diluted the novel's challenge to the racialized sexual order of the 1930s but also diminished the psychological complexity of the main character, Bigger Thomas. As a result of the changes, *Native Son* became more deterministic, less ambivalent, and more univocal. It was thus easier to read the book ethnographically and to conclude that despite its social protest, it reduced the subjectivity of the main black character to a lab rat in the novel's experiment about racism and pathology.[2] Because part of Wright's intention was to create a fully human picture of a social type that was often explicitly dehumanized—the African American juvenile delinquent—the expurgations diminish the novel's political impact and dilute Wright's vision.

The lives of these two novels, then, parallel each other. Both cemented their authors as major literary figures, and both found their way to major status within the canon and commercial success. However, considering the novels through lenses of obscenity and race reveals their significant differences, and the contrasting narratives of obscene genius and obscene pathology provide a framework for explaining why those differences arose. Miller's novel, on one hand, championed frank sexuality as a means of metaphysical exploration and consequently became a touchstone for the sexual revolution while remaining aesthetically intact. In contrast, Wright's novel had to be expurgated to accommodate white discomfort over African American sexuality and the sexual border underpinning white hegemony, and the resulting changes pushed the novel into an aesthetic space that made it vulnerable to stereotypes of black pathology and white saviorship while compromising parts of Wright's artistic vision.

"Obscenity Is Necessary and Prophecy Inevitable"

I turn first to the earlier novel, Miller's *Tropic of Cancer*. The book dramatizes a certain Nietzschean literary fantasy about individuals of genius who are exempt from social norms. These might be characters in the books themselves (as in *Cancer*) or a general principle held by the author that an artist must follow their muse into terrain that polite society might disdain. Works in this category would include such forerunners as D. H. Lawrence's *Lady Chatterley's Lover* (1928) and James Joyce's *Ulysses* (1922). Such is *Cancer*, Miller's sexually explicit fictionalized memoir of the life of an expatriate in Paris during the 1930s.[3] In the passage from Ihab Hassan's *The Literature of Silence* that serves as the title for this section, Hassan encapsulates the sometimes breathless encomiums lavished on such works, claiming that in this sort of boundless searching after the truths of life, "obscenity is necessary and prophecy inevitable."[4] According to this rubric, the artist transgresses social norms because they stand in the way of insight, and what the artist observes or creates on the other side of those boundaries becomes a guiding light for a more liberated future society.

Cancer's route to success, however, was circuitous. It was published in France in 1934 but banned in the United States. It was widely distributed in French editions that were smuggled into the States by tourists and GIs for decades, accompanied by a prominent warning on the cover that it was not to be imported into the United States or Britain. Eventually, in 1961, Grove published a U.S. edition, which led to the Warren Court's 1964 ruling in *Grove Press, Inc. v. Gerstein* that it was not legally obscene.

Criticism of the novel has been understandably varied, but has largely tapered off in recent years as Miller's position in the canon became more questionable. Moreover, criticism of Miller's misogyny has been a more prominent element of criticism since the seventies, and the book has fallen out of favor, though it remains an important artifact of twentieth-century American literature. Dominant strains of this criticism include analysis of the autobiographical elements of Miller's many novels,[5] arguments about his relationship to the canon,[6] explorations of the sexual ideologies of the book,[7] and cultural analyses of the obscenity trials and publishing history of the novel.[8]

In an attempt to encapsulate the whole of Miller's work, Hassan participates in many of these strains. In sweeping prose, he links Miller with Whitman, Emerson, and others often seen as the antecedents of Miller's anti-establishment ethos and individualism.[9] In so doing, Hassan establishes some key concepts for understanding Miller, including notions of prophecy and Messianism and of transgression and rebellion. Prefacing his interpretation of Miller's work, he affirms a particular strand of criticism that was prominent from the time of *Cancer*'s French publication through its later U.S. publication, stating, "The ground of praise has shifted, yet Miller is still placed in the vanguard of spiritual, if not artistic, discoverers" (Hassan 36). Hassan is referring specifically to Lawrence Durrell and Karl Shapiro, but his summary applies generally. Miller was immediately acclaimed as an important new voice signaling a transition away from modernism and toward a visceral realism and was later regarded by many as a revolutionary responsible for a liberalization of sexual attitudes in the United States.

Still, much of the scholarship on Miller attempts to explain away his transgressions as representative of a rebellious strain within the American tradition. Hassan describes Miller as "thoroughly American, even if, like many American artists before him, he is an American against the grain" (46). The paradox here is instructive: classic American art includes a major theme of resistance to America. It seems to me that Hassan is right, and Frederick Turner makes a similar argument about Miller: "He was definitely not a mainstream American, but still he belonged to a strong, colorful countervailing tradition of cranks, crooks, tall-talkers, hucksters, adventurers, outlaws, and utopian dreamers that had its roots deep in the American experience."[10] American literature in the tradition that includes figures such as Whitman and Emerson holds in high regard—perhaps even awe—ideas about individualism and self-reliance, while lamenting the corruption of such ideas through materialism and intellectualism.

Hassan, Turner, and others seek to elevate Miller's place in American letters by explaining that his seeming transgressions are, in fact, recognized elements of a *transgressive tradition*. In so doing, they lend weight to my central claim: that transgression of this kind, paradoxically, works to strengthen one's place in the nation, rather than make one an outcast, because it is interpreted as the expression of an individualist ethic justifying antisocial acts in pursuit of higher principles. This tradition's more paradoxical elements are revealed in Miller's case and similar narratives of obscene genius. Miller's attacks against America—his condemnation of its cheap materialism, philosophical paralysis, and stultifying prudery—form the basis of a script that will lead to his embrace within the nation rather than his rejection from it. While these aspects of materialism, paralysis, and prudery would seem to be at odds with his vision, they actually enable his rise as the foils for his art.

However, reception of the novel has not remained so laudatory, and critics both past and present have noted that celebration of Miller's genius often overshadowed concern over the misogyny and political nihilism of

Miller's vision.[11] As Kate Millet points out, Miller's descriptions and narrative reduce women to bodies or worse, and he and his compatriots in the story understand sex as a game of debasement in which men win by exploiting women without acknowledging their humanity. In this sense, the liberation from puritanical values that Miller proposes is reserved only for men and is built at the expense of women's subjectivity.

In a similar vein, this liberation is reserved for members of the sexual mainstream. As Whitney Strub has chronicled, same-sex desire was often seen to violate community standards *per se*. In this sense, a book like Miller's, full of debasing, abusive, but *heterosexual* sex, found its way to publication, while those that depicted mutually affirming acts between same-sex partners were subject to greater scrutiny and more often came into conflict with local officials, a trend that continued well into the 1980s and 1990s.

Finally, this liberation is not equally available to people of color. Rooted in a libertine tradition out of the wealthy classes of European aristocrats, Miller's vision presumes sexual power is waiting to be seized if one simply overcomes vestigial puritanism. But the history of racialized embodiment faced by people of color alters the narrative possibilities. Ranging from what Hortense Spillers calls "pornotroping" to the legacy of La Malinche described by Cherríe Moraga, to the stereotypes regarding rape foisted on black men that I describe shortly, people of color have dealt with a history that implicates sexual expression in enslavement and cultural betrayal. In these ways, gratuitous sex does not lead in a straight line to liberation from social constraint, but warps around gendered, sexist, and racist stereotypes. Thus, through its omissions and its focus on a white psychology, the novel reinforces the sexual privilege attendant on whiteness.

Tropic of Cancer was the first of Miller's multi-part fictionalized memoir.[12] The book is a loosely structured chronicle of sexual exploits and attempts to scam free meals, smatterings of lyrical descriptions of Paris, and philosophical ruminations. Artistically, the book is of a piece with Dostoevsky's *Crime and Punishment* (1866). Both emphasize a Nietzschean conception of the empowerment of the individual who explores the darkest reaches of experience to enable a testing of human potential. While I will not deal extensively with the extreme individualism Miller espouses, the issue demonstrates how the prerogatives arrogated by such characters and the obscene texts they inhabit operate in relation to existing structures of power.

One of the key characteristics of Nietzsche's *übermensch* is that he opts out of the social contract and exceeds the bonds of the state.[13] Nietzsche's Zarathustra says, "There, where the state ceases, only there does the human being begin who is not superfluous" and "There, where the state *ceases*—cast your glance over there, my brothers! Do you not see it, the rainbow and the bridges of the Over-human?"[14] In essence, this passage identifies the *übermensch* as the figure by which the bonds of the state fall away, and at this point bridges appear, suggesting that the *übermensch* leads the way toward another way of being.

As an aesthetic program, this notion obliges the author to smash the state, dismember culture, and sear the eyes of the masses with unvarnished truth. This is quite explicitly the ethos of *Tropic of Cancer*. Miller's narrator/surrogate states:

> Who that has a desperate, hungry eye can have the slightest regard for these existent governments, laws, codes, principles, ideals, ideas, totems, and taboos? If anyone knew what it meant to read the riddle of that thing which today is called a "crack" or a "hole," if anyone had the least feeling of mystery about the phenomena which are labeled "obscene," this world would crack asunder. It is the obscene horror, the dry, fucked-out aspect of things which makes this crazy civilization look like a crater. It is this great yawning gulf of nothingness which the creative spirits and mothers of the race carry between their legs. When a hungry, desperate spirit appears and makes the guinea pigs squeal it is because he knows where to put the live wire of sex, because he knows that beneath the hard carapace of indifference there is concealed the ugly gash, the wound that never heals. And he puts the live wire right between the legs; he hits below the belt, scorches the very gizzards. It is no use putting on rubber gloves; all that can be coolly and intellectually handled belongs to the carapace and a man who is intent on creation always dives beneath, to the open wound, to the festering obscene horror. He hitches his dynamo to the tenderest parts; if only blood and pus gush forth, it is something. The dry, fucked-out crater is obscene. More obscene than anything is inertia. More blasphemous than the bloodiest oath is paralysis. (225)

Miller's polemic against "inertia" and "paralysis" resonates as a critique of convention and conformity while demanding a liberation rooted in filth and transgression.[15] According to this ideology, the mandates of good taste—the requirement that we refrain from mentioning genitalia and excreta and keep mum about erotic desire—serve only to keep us from seeing society for what it is. For Miller and those who share this worldview, it is incumbent on the superman or the artist—the figure of genius in either case—to shock us out of complacency so we can live more authentically.

Underpinning this notion is the sense that the mandates of taste and propriety are in league with the status quo of state and economic power, an argument that has been put to more egalitarian use since the mid-twentieth century by thinkers such as Cherríe Moraga and Gloria Anzaldúa, not to mention Michel Foucault, Roderick Ferguson, and others. For Miller's speaker, though, the urge is still primarily individualistic, dripping with scorn for the masses who remain beholden to puritanical norms, capitalist longing, and staid aesthetics. In his view, real knowledge and power are only found when one throws off the rubber gloves and goes looking where we are told not to. The underlying ideology, then, places sex and arousal in privileged positions as means to social revolution.

And yet Miller presents a contradiction. He values sex, and his works will later inspire the counterculture celebration of pleasure for its own sake, but at this moment, he pointedly does not advocate for arousal as a good in itself. In fact, as scholarship on *Cancer* often points out, Miller's protagonist is critical of those who pursue pleasure for its own sake. Instead, Miller's persona grapples with sex and taboo in pursuit of deeper understanding and spiritual transcendence. He contemplates "the obscene horror" because it allows him to see that "this crazy civilization look[s] like a crater." He "dives beneath" because he "is intent on creation." Hassan, for example, points out that in Miller's work, "the physical body of men and women is anatomized only to be finally transcended" (37). The body here is not a source of pleasure but a waystation on the route to transcendence, a sentiment echoed closely by Durrell, who writes that in his pursuit of spirituality, Miller "dismantles and shreds up the physical body in order to transcend it" (Durrell 16). By thus rendering sex as a means to an end, sex is instrumentalized in pursuit of a retrograde metaphysics of body and spirit.

This binary and the instrumentalization of sex by which it is reified are pertinent to the legal fate of the novel. When the book was ultimately declared not obscene by the Supreme Court, the justification hinged on the artistic and social value of the book.[16] In essence, the potentially offensive sexual elements are redeemed by the fact that they contribute to important social ideals or knowledge. Thus, the juxtaposition of Miller's novel and the Supreme Court jurisprudence on obscenity reveals that literature and the law work in seemingly divergent ways toward parallel purposes. Both reject sex and arousal as vestiges of a bestial past, but admit its utility in pursuit of higher aims. While they were at odds in Miller's case for more than thirty years, they ultimately converge via their mutual participation in the persistent ideology privileging the mind and abstraction over the body. What we would do well to remember is that this facet of culture, casting a long shadow over the twentieth century, has historically been exclusive, and it remains so even when it aims toward—and seems to produce—freedom for some.

Having identified this particularly enduring cultural formation, I want to gesture toward the political limitations of such a vision. On reflection, it is not at all shocking that an icon of the counterculture and a major institution of the U.S. state would share a worldview in which sex operates primarily as the baser pole of a metaphysical dualism of body and spirit. This is true despite Miller's ostensibly antiestablishment impulses. Antiinstitutional sentiment driven by hyperbolic possessive individualism is consonant with the metanarratives of American identity that undergird the institutions of the state. Despite its seemingly contradictory nature, this sentiment is well understood already. Its application to Miller's particular case is illuminating in part because he serves as an early forerunner of a cultural trope that will become prominent in the mid-century period in other narratives of obscenity that echo this rhetoric of genius.

The obscenity of Miller's texts is part and parcel of his artistic vision, as is often attested to by the author himself and by his critics. However, the obscenity of the work was also explicitly a factor in its financial and institutional success. Hassan notes, for example, that the original French edition of *Tropic of Cancer* was selling briskly during the years after its release and long before it was available in the United States. This was in part because of its salacious content and status as forbidden object, and he writes that during this time "*Tropic of Cancer* was going through five editions, some of which had been pirated and were selling hugely at black market prices" (Hassan 41). The novel that was selling so well on the Continent earned Miller both financial success and fame as an author during the 1940s and early '50s, as Hassan further attests: "Meanwhile, his fame was spreading wildly among cultists, and his accumulated royalties for the French edition of his earlier works were becoming huge" (43). Thus, Miller achieved fame and fortune as a direct result of his works. Perhaps most germane here, the efforts at suppression themselves contributed to this success, as Hassan highlights when he notes that in the late 1950s, "his reputation was on the upsurge; and the censors, who attacked the Grove Press edition of *Tropic of Cancer* (1961), *Tropic of Capricorn* (1962), and *Black Spring* (1963), contributed to his wealth" (Hassan 44). Similarly, Frederick Turner argues, "By the 1950s, *Tropic of Cancer* had acquired a folkloric status while its author wore with an increasing unease the shadowy reputation as a writer of truly 'dirty books'" (5). In simple terms, then, Miller's case exemplifies a narrative that will play out again and again later in the century, whereby an obscene text rides the wave of public excitement to commercial success while seeing its cultural status elevated as part of the deal. The obscenity is hardly an impediment to this, and instead drives the process along.

The viability of this narrative can be traced partially to Grove's deliberate legal strategy as they defended Miller in the many cases that followed the U.S. publication. In *Counterculture Colophon*, Loren Glass describes how obscenity trials in the first part of the twentieth century played a crucial role in the formation of the post-war canon by providing a new mechanism through which modernist texts could have their bona fides established:

> The obscenity trial in this context functioned as a ritual of consecration whereby modernist texts could be affirmed as "classics" by experts on literary value. It enabled an alliance between publishers, lawyers, and literary critics that was crucial to providing mainstream acceptance for modernism by replacing the test of time with the patina of professionalism.[17]

This process was begun with the trial of Joyce's *Ulysses* and includes work on behalf of the book and publisher by literary experts who testify to a book's merit, quickly producing a discourse and an archive that attests to a book's literary merit. Because this merit was grounds for overturning an obscenity finding, it made it possible to publish the book at the same time that it created a market for that book.

Glass confirms that this was not only a legal strategy but a marketing one as well: "Over the next few decades, it became the job of literary critics to affirm the category of the 'modern classic,' which Grove used both in its legal defense and in its commercial promotion of *Lady Chatterley's Lover*, *Tropic of Cancer*, and *Naked Lunch*" (103). This strategy applied to Miller's novel, but also to works both before and after. Moreover, as Glass notes, it became a routine method for ensuring the canonization of a book at the same time that it could be used to establish copyright and drive public interest. Glass describes how, Barney Rosset, Grove's owner and editor, "used these expert opinions, as well as the ultimate decision of the Massachusetts Supreme Court, to leverage sales of *Naked Lunch*, as he had done with *Lady Chatterley's Lover* and *Tropic of Cancer*" (119). Following this path, Miller's text could reach commercial success *as a result of*, rather than in spite of, the controversy over its transgressive sexual elements.

The paratexts published along with the 1961 Grove Press edition of *Cancer* reveal that a part of this strategy was an attempt to demonstrate that the author was a particular kind of genius, which characterizes one set of tropes for obscenity discourses. The edition opens with an introduction by Shapiro revealingly titled "The Greatest Living Author." In the essay, Shapiro marks Miller as unique, noting that Miller has in the past given himself the sobriquet "the Patagonian," asking "What is a Patagonian," and then offering the reply, "I don't know, but it is certainly something rare and *sui generis*" (vi). He does so in order to advance the thesis that Miller's work makes him a "*sui generis*" figure who breaks from preceding traditions to produce something entirely new. Setting aside Shapiro's credulous indulgence, as we read on we see that Shapiro works to canonize Miller by appeals to the authority of his compatriots, and he scrupulously catalogues the other respected artists who admired or accepted Miller. He notes especially William Carlos Williams as well as an essay in which George Orwell compares Miller to Céline and Whitman. This gesture seems designed to ensconce Miller among those figures on syllabi and best-books lists in the manner of Grove's larger strategy of defending the book's academic and artistic chops while advancing the cause of canonization.

The unique greatness of Miller, Shapiro avers, is rooted in his transgressions and the obscenity issues surrounding his novels. Shapiro contrasts Miller's work with Joyce's *Ulysses* and Lawrence's *Lady Chatterley's Lover* and finds the older works too obsessed with sex to throw off their puritanism. Shapiro weaves a contrast that elevates the American by association before flatly declaring his work superior:

> Miller undoubtedly profited from the mistakes of his predecessors; his aim was not to write about the erotic but to write the whole truth about the life he knew. This goal demanded the full vocabulary and iconography of sex, and it is possible that he is the first writer outside the Orient who has succeeded in writing as naturally about sex on a large scale as novelists ordinarily write about the dinner table or the battle field. (xvi–xvii)

According to this interpretation, Miller's work is inherently taboo-breaking in a way that frees him from previous constraints that limited titans like Joyce and Lawrence. More than merely defending Miller against charges of empty prurience, Shapiro claims Miller is entirely unburdened by sexual morality. He is unique among the greats, exceeding them, benefiting not from their inspiration but from their mistakes. Other compatriots of Miller's echo this sentiment. In correspondence with Alfred Perlès, for example, Lawrence Durrell makes essentially the same argument about Miller and de Sade, contending that both authors "dismantled the morality of their ages, but Henry's intention was to question it and reformulate his own. He progresses, grows, exfoliates as a personality. De Sade stays put like an electronic device which has got stuck" (16).

The preface to the edition continues in this vein. It was written by Anaïs Nin, who had been Miller's lover and patron and who was instrumental in funding the 1934 edition with money she secured from her analyst Otto Rank. Nin assesses the value of the work and the genius of Miller in part by justifying its taboo sexual representations—for most of the novel's apologists, its transgressions are a feature, not a bug. She writes, "In a world grown paralyzed with introspection and constipated by delicate mental meals this brutal exposure of the substantial body comes as a vitalizing current of blood. The violence and obscenity are left unadulterated, as manifestation of the mystery and pain which ever accompanies the act of creation" (Nin xxxi).[18] Nin's assessment is similar to Shapiro's and others—and even to currents of Miller's own thinking as expressed in the novel itself. In essence, she argues that the power and value of *Cancer* abides in its "unadulterated" engagement with sex, bodies, obscenity, and other aspects of life that propriety has put off-limits.[19] His genius as an author, then, is indissociable from the obscenity of his work, and his imagined sexual romps are a kind of realism of the underside that true artistic spirits grasp and can convey without vestigial guilt or fear.

Like Shapiro, Nin compares Miller to Céline, to Joyce, to Lawrence, only to find that he has surpassed them. He stands equal to recognized giants, but his work is "a swing forward into unbeaten areas" (Nin xxxii); that is to say, he is moving recognized tendencies into unexplored regions and his novels, *Cancer* in particular, represent important progress. Like Shapiro, she is orchestrating a twofold defense. She links Miller with works against which it can be compared to rebut claims it is beyond the pale or without precedent. Then she contends that it exceeds the accomplishments of these antecedents in order to argue that it is necessary and innovative. Underlying this is the insistence that Miller is a writer of particular genius.[20] This kind of talk contributed to the general sense that Miller was an outlaw genius following his muse where American prudishness forbade and leaving in his wake a transformed culture.

Texts and authors in this tradition proclaim their independence from social norms in the interest of a larger individualist project. Their rebellion is of a piece with a larger individualistic spirit that characterizes the American national myth, and it is more consonant with major figures of American letters than against them. In the early twentieth century, this tradition of rebellion was channeled into challenges to First Amendment restrictions and obscenity laws. These works flesh out the narrative by which the transgressive acts of dominant-voice authors are interpreted as an indication of their special election, insight, or greatness—particularly through their fealty to first principles of American identity and willingness to go against social norms in their advocacy for them. Rather than being shunting out of the community as rule-breakers, authors of such texts are lauded as visionaries.

This process, especially the role of Grove Press in promoting and defending many of these books, has been admirably catalogued by Glass. The new terrain I hope to examine concerns texts that offer alternative visions, using extreme depictions of sex and violence to offer inclusive visions or contest exclusive cultural formations. They, too, resist the imperative to remain silent on the subject of sex and pleasure; they, too, break with laws and social norms about the depiction of sexual acts and sexualized violence. However, they do so to promote egalitarian visions of society. Alice Walker's *The Color Purple* (1982) (see Chapter 3) and Tony Kushner's *Angels in America* (1993) (see Chapter 4) are particularly good examples of this kind of work, and both were banned or protested over their representations of sex.

These works dramatize the abjection of groups who are disempowered because of their sexuality or who face trauma, discrimination, or oppression that is explicitly sexualized. Their transgression, then, is more communal in nature, in part because they are transgressing the norms of a culture that they take for granted to be oppressive. *Obscene Gestures* juxtaposes these types of works to reveal how the various scripts imposed on them indicate racial disparities in publishing and marketing, as well as in national metanarratives of belonging.

"An Obscene Joke Happening amid a Colossal Din of Siren Screams and White Faces"

Richard Wright's *Native Son* is emblematic of the remarkably different fate of taboo-busting works by authors of color, and the story of its fate in the publishing world highlights how cultural narratives of racialized sexuality operate to maintain inequality.[21] Analyzing what that fate was and how it came to be brings into view the narrative of obscene pathology that I outlined in the introduction. Specifically, Wright's novel faced a more fraught route to financial success and canonization because his work had to negotiate existing cultural narratives about the pathology of African American sexuality as well as broader white supremacist notions of deviance. While taboo content could still shock readers and drive public discussion—resulting in public interest and sales as it did for Miller—in order for the novel to secure its place in a white-dominated publishing landscape, Wright had to tack close to existing scripts governing the representation of racialized sexuality. As Roderick Ferguson points out, Wright's interest in Chicago School sociology ensured this would be the case; *Native Son* was already set to be a sociological exposé of the deplorable conditions African Americans were subjected to under Jim Crow. However, the history of its censorship reveals much about how this came to be and signals how other artworks by authors of color might be received when they contest norms of sexual propriety.

Native Son was originally scheduled to be published by Harper and Brothers in the fall of 1939, but the influential Book-of-the-Month Club expressed interest in making it the first book by an African American to be selected for distribution to its members. As Arnold Rampersad recounts in his notes on the restored text, Wright's manuscript had already been edited and scheduled for publication, but the Club's deliberations about the manuscript held things up. Eventually, they requested excisions before they would proceed with the selection. Wright assented to their wishes, and the book was published as the Club's selection for March of 1940.[22] As further detailed by Rampersad and others, the specific material removed largely addressed complex issues of sexuality and race, and the result of the removal was a book that was less unsettling to white audiences.[23] The bowdlerized edition was a smash hit and sold nearly 215,000 copies within weeks.[24]

As Charles Sumner notes, one effect of the expurgations was to further amplify the objectifying tendencies of the novel's Naturalist mode. Sumner argues that the Naturalist aesthetic relied on an educated narrator who exposes for his similarly situated readers social conditions that limited the options for the marginalized people whose plight is dramatized (135). The resulting dynamic objectified the subjects of the text, who were portrayed as unable to advocate on their own behalf. One of racism's primary modes of functioning is just this kind of paternalistic objectification, which robs racialized subjects of the agency to narrate their own lives. Cognizant of this, Wright sought to obviate this tendency by giving greater weight and narrative space to his protagonist's thoughts within the narration.[25]

In rendering Bigger as a complex individual, the novel makes it harder to view him as beast, thus offering a more nuanced counterpoint to racial stereotypes. The difficulty of synthesizing Bigger's contradictions is, in part, what vexes readers, teachers, and scholars about this book; we are impelled alternately to recoil from Bigger and to understand his feelings as deeply human, a shuttling back and forth that will be identified by many readers as a hallmark of obscene texts. And yet, for all Wright's care in rendering Bigger as more than a specimen in a laboratory, this interpretation still dominated reception of the novel, a fact that was exacerbated by its route to publication via the Book-of-the-Month Club.

As Sumner describes, the instrumentalization of Bigger as the subject of novelistic social experiment was amplified as a result of the removal of the selected passages. Dorothy Canfield Fisher provided an introduction to the 1940 edition in which she suggests the kind of scientific, abstracting frame of reading that is similarly suggested by the sociological approach of Wright himself.[26] According to Hazel Rowley, Canfield Fisher's "introduction made it clear that the value of Wright's novel was as a sociological case study" (628). Wright and the Book-of-the-Month Club settled on a marketing strategy that downplayed Wright's stylistic innovations but emphasized the book's role as a sociological revelation and exploration of the psychological impacts of racism that encouraged the reader to see Bigger as different, as other.[27]

Wright's assent to the changes was likely under pressure from his publisher and his lack of power in the publishing industry. As Rowley notes, "It was the white literary establishment that accepted or rejected his manuscripts" (627) and "he almost certainly underestimated [the problem] that his fighting words had to pass muster in what was then the all-white territory of book publishing" (626). In this sense, the fact of Wright's willingness to make these changes at the request of the Club was not entirely voluntary, and so he can't be considered to have collaborated with them.[28] As Rowley notes later in her essay, he pushed back more persistently on such changes with his later book *Black Boy* at a time when he was more empowered within the publishing world.

Lawrence Hogue offers a valuable reading of the novel that unpacks Bigger's psychological complexity and attempts to place it in a suitable political framework by analyzing how the construction of subjectivity affects power relations. This was Wright's motive, too: to use fiction as a means for understanding and then communicating the manner in which social conditions stemming from unequal power relations create and foreclose different intellectual and existential avenues of being. In this sense, Hogue's question of whether Bigger, as the subaltern, can speak is also a question of whether murder and rape are forms of speaking and whether we can simultaneously admit that they are reprehensible and admit the responsibility of society at large in calling them into being. When such questions arise in an analysis of obscenity, they highlight how the shadow of pathology hangs over certain representations and the moral ambivalence such texts often create in readers.

The roots of *Native Son* go back to Wright's early life. Wright describes the Bigger Thomases of his youth as people who consistently defied the mandates of Jim Crow society because of their refusal to submit their dignity to it. He describes them in contrast to himself and others like him who "were more willing to tighten our belts than risk conflict" (Wright, "How Bigger," 435). And while these men were, he says "shot, hanged, maimed, lynched, and generally hounded until they were either dead or their spirits broken," at the same time there was a humanity in them and they inspired a kind of reverence. Wright is keen to note that it was society that produced these figures, and he warns the reader against "the impression that they were essentially or organically bad" ("How Bigger," 437). Seeking to explain and clarify what he imagined Bigger to represent, Wright expresses his intention to make Bigger real and human, sympathetic and at times noble, but also unable or unwilling to adapt to a white supremacist society and therefore prone to unpredictable acts of daring and unchanneled resistance expressed as violence.

Regarding those, like James Baldwin, who panned the book claiming that one problem with rebellion of this kind is that it tends paradoxically to reinscribe patriarchy and white values while sneering in their face—offering resistance without revolution—Wright seems to offer a rebuttal, noting about Jim Crow that

> because the blacks were so *close* to the very civilization which sought to keep them out, because they could not *help* but react in some way to its incentives and prizes, and because the very tissue of their consciousness received its tone and timbre from the strivings of that dominant civilization, oppression spawned among them a myriad variety of reactions, reaching from outright blind rebellion to a sweet, other-worldly submissiveness. ("How Bigger," 438, emphasis in original)

Wright's description of the depth of psychological interpellation of Jim Crow suggests that his portrait of Bigger's abortive rebellion was not intended to offer Bigger as a model of effective revolution, but rather to show how a figure like Bigger arises and how his desire to rebel and the manner of that rebellion are conditioned by the psychological structures of white supremacy—something that is strikingly parallel to the way Wright's resistance was constrained by the white-dominated publishing landscape.

Responding, also, to the anticipated critique that his novel would be mechanistically sociological, Wright avers, "I don't mean to say that I think that environment *makes* consciousness . . . , but I do say that I felt and still feel that the environment supplies the instrumentalities through which the organism expresses itself, and if that environment is warped or tranquil, the mode and manner of behavior will be affected toward deadlocking tensions or orderly fulfillment and satisfaction" ("How Bigger," 442). Wright's mission was to do what he is alternately castigated and celebrated for, which is to render a distinct psychology as the result of a distinct society. This method allowed Wright to criticize the racism of American society in the 1930s and '40s, emphasizing unequal housing restrictions, paternalistic philanthropy, red-baiting, sham criminal prosecutions, and racialized sexual norms. In effect, Wright holds Bigger Thomas up as the inevitable result of these things, and calls out the hypocrisy of blaming him for such behavior. The indictment is prescient, anticipating later theories about how a well-ordered society produces its own abject others and naturalizes its control through violence against them.

As Rowley recounts, the resulting book was often disliked and even reviled by African American scholars. She explains some of the reasons for this:

> Bigger played into the stereotype of the semi-socialized black man who threatens the established order of white civilization. . . . On the surface *Native Son* appears to confirm the very prejudices with which white supremacy propped itself up: here was a black man ready (it seemed) to rape a white woman, kill her and chop her body into pieces to stuff her into a furnace. Here was a brute prepared to pulverize his black girlfriend with a brick, then pitch her body down an airshaft. (Rowley 626)

This concern, which she notes was expressed by figures as prominent as David Bradley and Langston Hughes, dogged the novel, though it appears not to have bothered Wright. Nonetheless, the novel's reception has been characterized by these feelings of ambivalence over the potential such a representation might have to inadvertently confirm white supremacist notions of pathology, despite Wright's forceful efforts to undermine those prejudices.

Baldwin was one of the most outspoken critics of the novel. In "Everybody's Protest Novel," Baldwin reminds us of the danger of a certain kind of novel that rages against racial injustices simplistically and thereby undermines its own politics.[29] He warns that in being too satisfied with bold, definitive pronouncements, such novels might "reinforce . . . the principles which activate the oppression they decry" (Baldwin 14). Baldwin highlights how a critique of the immorality of slavery that itself emerges from mechanistic ideologies of the European Enlightenment might rely on the very binaristic moralism that is the structure of colonialism and racial hierarchy, reifying hierarchized dyads such as "inside/outside" and "white/black." Thus, it may attack the symptoms of white supremacy while shoring up its epistemologies. Baldwin ascribes this tendency not only to the popular protest novel writ large, but to *Native Son* specifically: "Below the surface of this novel there lies, as it seems to me, a continuation, a complement of that monstrous legend it was written to destroy" (Baldwin 22).

It is particularly relevant that Baldwin decries aesthetic projects that envision their characters as case studies of the society from which they emerge, bemoaning how such works reduce the human being's philosophical vitality:

> We have ... attempted to lop this creature down to the status of a time-saving invention. He is not, after all, merely a member of a Society or a Group or a deplorable conundrum to be explained by Science.... In overlooking, denying, evading his complexity—which is nothing more than the disquieting complexity of ourselves—we are diminished and we perish; only within this web of ambiguity, paradox, this hunger, danger, darkness, can we find at once ourselves and the power that will free us from ourselves. (Baldwin 15)

Baldwin's primary concern about novels that treat their characters like sociological case studies is that they dehumanize them in service to the production of surplus capital, and that they do so in ways that mirror the logic of racism. After all, racism functions in part as an adjunct to the labor needs of capital, abetted by narratives of dehumanization. Baldwin also contends that by palliating the revolutionary spirit, such ostensibly resistive works actually do much to reinforce fundamental exclusions:

> The "protest" novel, so far from being disturbing, is an accepted and comforting aspect of the American scene, ramifying that framework we believe to be so necessary. Whatever unsettling questions are raised are evanescent, titillating; remote, for this has nothing to do with us, it is safely ensconced in the social arena, where, indeed, it has nothing to do with anyone, so that finally we receive a very definite thrill of virtue from the fact that we are readings such a book at all. (Baldwin 19)

By satisfying the progressive spirit prematurely, the protest novel puts the spirit of revolution to bed while the house burns. Baldwin's harsh critique emphasizes that what this kind of novel wins through psychological perceptiveness it sacrifices by its satisfaction with the mechanistic epistemologies of contemporary society.

Ralph Ellison is somewhat more generous. Writing in response to the publication of Wright's memoir *Black Boy* in 1945, Ellison argues that the important tradition informing Wright's art was the blues, and that as a folk tradition, "The blues is an impulse to keep the painful details and episodes of a brutal experience alive in one's aching consciousness, to finger its jagged grain, and to transcend it, not by the consolation of philosophy, but by squeezing from it a near-tragic, near-comic lyricism."[30] Ellison's notion that philosophy's consolations might not be the native mode of *Native Son* is meant as a rebuke to those who found *Black Boy* lacking, but much of the essay speaks to Wright's opus more broadly. His point is that there is another mode of aesthetic that speaks from and returns to an African American tradition, and that when Wright's work is subjected to this more relevant lens, some criticisms might fade away.

In defense of Wright, Ellison takes issue with the notion that laying bare the social conditions of Jim Crow and their psychological impacts is insufficiently radical. He writes of *Black Boy*, rather, that "in it thousands of Negroes will for the first time see their destiny in public print," and he claims that, through this visibility, "he has converted the American negro impulse toward self-annihilation and 'going-under-ground' into a will to confront the world, to evaluate his experience honestly and throw his findings unashamedly into the guilty conscience of America" (Ellison 74). This impulse to come out of the shadows becomes an important move toward social justice, as well as a catharsis. Yes, a protest novel may not be focused on ontological development, but it can have profound significant effects.

What I hope to add to the rich discussion of *Native Son* is a more developed understanding of the racial-sexual history the novel illuminates, particularly as it applies to the publication history. The recent restoration of the text and more contemporary theoretical work by figures like Roderick Ferguson and José Estéban Muñoz can help us to understand the novel as offering an important window into the sexual aspects of race in U.S. culture, and its publication history—comprising the expurgations, its reception, and the eventual restoration—can show us how the narrative of obscene pathology haunts American letters.[31]

In *The Novel and the Obscene*, Florence Dore links the novel's exploration of rape as a cultural trope to the shifting discourses around obscenity in the early twentieth century. She argues that *Native Son* is important in this regard, because it "demonstrates that the very possibility of sexual purity—and therefore the very possibility of American obscenity standards—rests upon the symbolic absence of the African American man."[32] Dore reveals how the impulse to reestablish the social order in

Native Son by expunging Bigger from society and defining his behavior as aberrant—a narrative impulse as well as a cultural one—is an extension of both racial and sexual logics operating in tandem. The novel crystallizes that aspect of American national mythology that relies on an ideal of purity in order to justify exclusions, exclusions that abet the unequal allocation of resources and freedom. This false ideal of purity is overlaid onto white women, while its manufactured aberrant other is overlaid onto African American men.

For Dore, the representations of sex in *Native Son*, which would have been considered shocking to readers at the time, play an important role in Wright's project of racial progress, rather than being ancillary or simply gratuitous.[33] She contends that Wright is attempting to fight back the racist presumption undergirding American obscenity discourses, suggesting that "Wright flouts obscenity restrictions in order to challenge the stereotype of the African American man as a 'bestial monstrosity'" (Dore 96). Dore is probably right in the sense that Wright does attempt to humanize Bigger by insisting on his psychological complexity, a complexity that emerges in part through his sexuality. Dore's argument is useful because it echoes the kinds of justifications that were given for Miller's obscene transgressions. Both authors, we can conclude, used shocking sexual content as a vital part of their aesthetic and political projects, rather than gratuitously.

My analysis of the effects of the censorship of *Native Son* hinges on two scenes that were altered at the request of the Book-of-the-Month Club. The first concerns Bigger and his friend Jack in a movie theater after they have planned, but before they have executed, a robbery. The second occurs later that night just before Bigger kills Mary Dalton. In the restored version of the earlier scene, Bigger and Jack are killing time before a planned robbery. They head to the theater where they masturbate in the dark before the film starts, egging each other on. A newsreel then comes on that features celebrity-gossip–style footage of Mary Dalton cavorting with her boyfriend Jan in Florida. After the film, Bigger and Jack leave and part ways to grab their guns before meeting up for the robbery. The Book-of-the-Month Club requested that the scene be removed entirely, and their request gives us a provocative window into their motives and the forces affecting what could and could not be published in novels by and about African Americans. Since the sex act depicted in this scene so dramatically pales in comparison to those in Miller's novel, it is especially telling as evidence of radically different racialized possibilities.[34]

Bigger's and Jack's masturbation has often been interpreted as an expression of arousal related to the newsreel, specifically to Mary Dalton—

and the prosecutor explicitly makes this false connection in the novel.[35] However, it is clear in the novel that for Bigger the impulse to masturbate in the theater stems from a need to release a tension that was stimulated earlier in the pool hall during his interaction with Gus, another member of his gang. The violence Bigger commits against Gus there is itself a sublimation of his desire to strike back against white society. Bigger is angry with Gus because Gus is afraid of robbing a white man, but Bigger is also afraid of the same thing, and so he is acting out this fear against Gus to deflect from his own fear (Wright, *Native Son*, 25). Once Gus agrees to participate in the robbery, thus proving that he is unafraid of robbing Blum, Bigger is outraged.

In the following moment, Bigger has fantasies of hurting Gus, hitting him with a pool cue, cutting him, tripping him, and so on. But he does not act on them. Instead, the fourth member of the gang, G. H., ushers Gus out of the pool hall, leaving Bigger with this pent-up tension. This tension is a mixture of fear and resentment toward white society, feelings of inadequacy in the face of Gus's courage, and a boiling desire for violence. Faced with no ready outlet, he thinks about things that he might do: having sex with his girlfriend, Bessie; reading a detective story; and others. Among these options is going to a movie. He seeks a cathartic experience to calm his nerves and sublimate this urge to violence, and the options he comes up with from his experience dealing with such feelings are sex and movies.

He and Jack then go to the movie theater, where they masturbate. Ferguson argues convincingly that the masturbation is not in response to the image of Mary Dalton and that for this reason the elision of this scene at the request of the Club was not necessarily a result of worries about a black man having desire for a white woman—Bigger's masturbation is not spurred by desire for Mary. However, the masturbation scene occurs in the same location as the image of Mary Dalton, which is eroticized by Bigger and Jack when it appears. Thus, the most we can say is that Bigger's and Mary's sexuality are associated; as Sumner notes, the scene exposes them both as sexual beings close together in the narrative frame. Thus, to borrow phrasing from Ferguson, the two images are adjacent enough to create discomfort in readers anxious about miscegenation, even if the act and image are not joined by narrative causality.[36]

For Ferguson, this scene is, rather, a figure of non-mainstream sexual expression. He argues that "Bigger and Jack . . . do not masturbate to the image of the idealized white woman presented later on screen. Rather, they masturbate simply as part of their fraternal bond."[37] This is likely true, and it is important to interpret this scene in ways that account for the simultaneity of their masturbation and their jocular competitive approach. The two characters come together through self-pleasure without anxiety or compunction. Earlier, they expressed some concern about being caught by theater attendants, to be sure, but they are not concerned with hiding their pleasure from each other. Rather, experiencing this together adds to their excitement and cements their bond.

However, it is crucial to recall that the impetus for this expression was delineated pages before. We do not have to speculate about the urge that drives Bigger to masturbate in this scene; he described his feelings in the pool hall:

> Bigger felt an urgent need to hide his growing and deepening feeling of hysteria; he had to get rid of it or else he would succumb to it. He longed for a stimulus powerful enough to focus his attention and drain off his energies. He wanted to run. Or listen to some swing music. Or laugh or joke. Or read a *Real Detective Story Magazine*. Or go to a movie. Or visit Bessie. All that morning he had lurked behind his curtain of indifference and looked at things, snapping and glaring at whatever had tried to make him come out into the open. But now he was out; the thought of the job at Blum's and the tilt he had had with Gus had snared him into things and his self-trust was gone. Confidence could only come again now through action so violent that it would make him forget. (Wright, *Native Son*, 29)

What led Bigger and Jack to the theater and to masturbate there is not a desire to see a particular image of a woman, and the feeling of sexual arousal was not foremost in Bigger's consciousness. In this sense, the act of masturbation that ensues is not driven by desire at all. It is rather a need for release, a search for something to "drain off his energies." The act of masturbating is driven more by Bigger's feelings of impotence in the face of white racism than about any object of desire.

Bigger is frustrated that his typical defense mechanism of surly indifference has faltered, and he needs substantial action to reestablish his scoffing indifference. We should make no mistake that this is a desire to reestablish the uneasy stability he found in coping with the mandates of white-dominant society. It is inherent in his cynical joking with Gus during their discussion of why he is unable to be an airplane pilot, and in fact here he notes that joking and laughing would be a suitable outlet. But it is also to be found in popular entertainments, and in a visit to his girlfriend, Bessie, presumably for sex, something that Bigger does wish for in passing while he masturbates in the theater.[38]

And so, Wright is offering a kind of explanation for a constellation of behaviors that includes losing themselves in lowbrow media, immoderate humor, non-conforming sex, and violence—essentially for the stereotyped pathologies of the juvenile delinquent. His desire for sex and movies is linked to the pent-up tension that came about in his fight with Gus, a fight that was more or less explicitly about his anger at white society limiting his options in the world. Thus, this scene of masturbation is one in which Bigger's act of public perversion is driven by the compression of his world caused by white racism. In this way, the scene is continuous with other readings of the novel that ascribe to it Wright's desire to dramatize the links between racism and social deviance, between limited options and transgressive behaviors.

This reading, too, intersects with my argument that novels like this tend to be read in this era as more or less faithful dramatizations of social processes. Ferguson's tracing of the influence of the Chicago School on Wright's artistic vision applies because it suggests that the narrative of obscene pathology is in complex tension with Wright's deliberate artistic efforts. He meant the novel to shock white readers with the aberrant behavior of black juvenile delinquent characters in order to frame a critique of the racist social order that produced such behaviors. Interestingly, the expurgation of this scene actually serves to diminish the portrait of pathology. Still, as Ferguson suggests, the removal also eliminates potentially pluralizing depictions of sexuality not bound by white middle-class norms. The removal of an aberrant act here sanitizes the image of society, even as it leaves in place other key elements of the picture of pathology.

Importantly, we must interpret the masturbation as an indictment of white society, which limits options for African American men as much through state violence and police enforcement as it does through paternalistic philanthropy. In this sense, then, the removal of the material also limited the novel's critique of white saviorship and white society more generally. Once this passage is removed, Bigger remains boiling over with animosity toward white society after the incident with Gus, but he is also depicted as having no sustaining outlets. His later acts of violence, then, exist in continuum with the scene at the pool hall and serve as the outlet for them, rather than those impulses being temporarily vented through the theater masturbation. With the theater scene in place, Bigger's frustration finds some release, and the intervening experience where Jan and Mary ignorantly provoke Bigger places more blame on them for her death.

The other expurgated scenes are more obviously fraught with cross-racial desire that would have stood out as unacceptable in conventional ways, stimulating fewer polymorphous fears and provoking readily available scripts of suppression related to rape. Abdul R. JanMohamed provides an analytic of racialized sexuality that helps to reframe the material that the Book-of-the-Month Club requested removed, and doing so lends credence to the idea that the effect was to diminish Bigger's humanity in order to reify the fictions that maintain racial borders. While acknowledging Foucault's important insights in *The History of Sexuality*, JanMohamed critiques his argument for its neglect of the distinctive contours of sexuality in the context of racial politics. Foucault's argument is that sexuality, while often accompanied by taboos, shame, and veiling, has actually been attended by a multifaceted discourse of revelation.[39] Sex has been made an object of knowledge and investigation, driven into greater and greater discursive production, even as people are ostensibly discouraged from speaking about it in certain settings marked as public. JanMohamed argues that while this may be the case for white, middle-class sexuality, the opposite tendency has dominated discourses about sexual contact along the color barrier. There, he argues, silence reigns because the current power hierarchies are more effectively maintained by refusing to acknowledge kinship between people of different races. Whereas certain kinds of sanctioned sex and sexuality are characterized by incitement to speak, silence and interdiction attend those sex acts that remind us that people of different races share common humanity.

In his discussion of *Native Son*, JanMohamed finds that the central figure of this disavowal is rape. He writes that "Wright characterizes sexuality in general and rape in particular as the paradigm of all modes of crossing the racial boundary."[40] To clarify, he is arguing that both in *Native Son* and in American history, rape is the figure of racial crossing in dominant discourses of power because contact between African Americans and whites has been construed in ways that delegitimize sexual encounters between people of difference races. As JanMohamed describes, the shared humanity implicit in cross-racial intimacy must be anxiously disavowed, and the sign of this fiction is the illegitimate sexual act, an act energized by unequal power relations and always coordinate with violence: On one hand is the white master's quite real rape of the Black enslaved woman, and on the other is the invented rape of the white woman that became the justification for the lynching of Black men. He concludes that, for Wright, "Rape, thus, subsumed the totality of force relations on the racial border, which is in fact always a sexual border" (JanMohamed 109).[41]

In *Native Son*, Wright grapples with this racist myth in a way that makes its impact harrowing and highlights its deep psychological penetration. After Bigger runs from the Dalton residence when Mary Dalton's bones are discovered, Bessie warns him that he will likely be accused of rape, simply on the presumption that the presence of a Black man and a white woman in her bedroom would entail rape. Bigger turns Bessie's words over in his mind, thinking:

> Had he raped her? Yes, he had raped her. Every time he felt as he had felt that night, he raped. But rape was not what one did to women. Rape was what one felt when one's back was against a wall and one had to strike out, whether one wanted to or not, to keep the pack from killing one. He committed rape every time he looked into a white face. He was a long, taut piece of rubber which a thousand white hands had stretched to the snapping point, and when he snapped it was rape. But it was rape when he cried out in hate deep in his heart as he felt the strain of living day by day. That, too, was rape. (Wright, *Native Son*, 228)

Bigger, like JanMohamed and Wright, extends the notion of rape beyond narrow definitions to see rape as a broader sign of his transgression. Every way that he acts out—theft, anger, theater masturbation—is a kind of rape because under Jim Crow and white supremacy, this is the single crime that subsumes all others. It becomes the cause of extrajudicial killing, but is also explicitly wrapped up into those criminal proceedings that follow the "legal" institutional procedures—often gratuitously so, as in the case of his later trial in the novel, where the rape of Mary Dalton is invented as a prosecutorial strategy intended to demoralize Bigger and whip the white jurors and press into a frenzy.

In describing how Bigger "putative[ly]" rapes Mary, JanMohamed stresses that white society needs to find Bigger guilty of raping Mary in order to justify its bringing the force of state violence against him (110). While the rape of his girlfriend, Bessie, a black woman, does not seem sufficient to justify this, the prosecutors invent the rape of Mary in order to do so.[42] Here, JanMohamed provides the springboard for a revealing analysis of some of the expurgated material. If white society needs to understand Bigger as having raped Mary or perhaps simply needs to see any sexual contact between a black man and white woman as the result of coercion or violence—and emphatically *not* as the result of shared desire—then the requested expurgations reveal that the Book-of-the-Month Club was attempting to shift the novel in this direction.

Though Rampersad describes the changes to the scene of masturbation in some detail, in regards to other changes he merely remarks that "Other changes were also requested: toning down explicit sexual language, altering details of plot, and shortening the speeches of Bigger's lawyer and the district attorney" ("Notes," 486). Of course, my primary interest is in what was meant by "toning down explicit sexual language." Sumner notes that one of the passages in question was this one:

> He eased his hand, the fingers spread wide, up the center of her back and her face came toward him and her lips touched his, like something he had imagined. He stood her on her feet and she swayed against him. He tightened his arms as his lips pressed tightly against hers and he felt her body moving strongly. The thought and conviction that Jan had had her a lot flashed through his mind. He kissed her again and felt the sharp bones of her hips move in a hard and veritable grind. Her mouth was open and her breath came slow and deep. (Wright, *Native Son*, 84; qtd. in Sumner 138)

As Sumner points out, the original version of the scene seems to depict desire from both characters. Contemporary readers will acknowledge that Mary is incapable of consent because she is, as her mother later notes with grim irony, "dead drunk" (86). In this sense, Bigger's actions are assault, but Wright seems to have been careful to include signs that Mary was reciprocating Bigger's actions, even if there is some ambiguity in the depiction and considerable ambivalence in our reception.

The initial kiss is described such that when Bigger moves his hand, Mary seems to respond to his movement: "her face came toward him and her lips touched his." In this part of the sentence, Mary's body is the acting agent, a gesture that might signal her participation but is somewhat vague. Later, when Bigger "kissed her again," he encounters a clearer response: "the sharp bones of her hips move[d] in a hard and veritable grind." Her movement here suggests that she is reciprocating. And yet, the qualifier "veritable," like the earlier phrase "like something he had imagined," make it difficult to know if Mary's actions are being interpreted as desire by Bigger or represent it as a fact within the text. Rowley contends, however, that the actions are quite conscious and that the intentional nature of them is central to Wright's vision. She argues that while Wright's original version supposed Mary to be a willing partner, in the expurgated version of this scene, "the white woman's hips have been stilled. She is pure passivity, as limp as a rag doll, scarcely conscious," whereas "Bigger has become the archetypal black beast pawing the sleeping beauty" (Rowley 631). In this scene then, and in others, we can see that Mary is expressing some desire for Bigger. This scene is not the rape it will be made out to be, even if Bigger later considers it to be so figuratively, and even if it would certainly be so now.[43]

Dore argues that what makes the scene distinctive is that Bigger's actions are pointedly unseen. One danger of the obscene from the standpoint of American legal and political discourses is that it presents for audience consumption something that should be hidden from view. In this moment, the presence of the blind Mrs. Dalton suggests that Bigger's action is off-limits; it should not be seen. For Dore, this is a weakness in Wright's challenge to sexual norms. The representation of Bigger is resistive, but not as much as it could be because, she argues, Bigger is not only unseen, but his power is erased; specifically, that "In the scene between Mary and Bigger . . . there is a symbolic collapse of arousal and fear that erases Bigger's phallus" (Dore 99). Dore is right to suggest that Bigger's invisibility recapitulates the logic that disarms him, but the textual dynamics in play are complex enough to admit further interpretations.

Yes, Bigger is unseen by Mrs. Dalton, but the reader sees him. His mimetic invisibility (within the text) exists alongside his diegetic visibility (between the text and reader). This renders the blindness of Mrs. Dalton the important fact. More specifically, Mrs. Dalton serves as a representative of the broader "seeing" practices of white society. Though Mrs. Dalton is physically blind, it is her general practice of making assumptions about life based on race and class that makes her unable to perceive the situation accurately. That is to say, she could physically perceive Bigger any number of ways. But these avenues of perception are pre-empted by her assumption that a black man would never be in the room. She relies on the assumption that racial divisions are total, that the Jim Crow society is seamless. In so doing, she is unable to even entertain the possibility of Bigger's presence.[44]

The novel offers substantial support for this indictment in those passages where Bigger reminds himself that as long as he behaves according to white expectations, he will not be suspected of having committed any crime. Bigger trusts he can perform the proper role of submissive black man and thus avoid being seen for what he is: a killer and an individual, someone freed from social norms. Dore brings the argument home in a way that is compelling. She points out that in the scene between Bigger and Mary, Bigger's erection and any potential orgasm have to be removed from view. This is true for American society at the time, and the text recapitulates this in a way that dilutes its resistive politics. Dore then contrasts this with the scene in which Bigger rapes Bessie, a scene with an African American victim in which Bigger's arousal is described fully, and in which he reaches orgasm in a way that is insistently visual. In rendering his arousal with Mary unseen and his arousal with Bessie explicitly, the text reifies the taboo around sexual encounters that cross the color boundary. *Native Son* suggests the dangers of this border and calls our attention to the absurd violence that polices it, but the novel is itself unable to cross it.

The Club's expurgations support this reading because they also diminish Bigger's sexual agency. When the passage in question is removed, not only is the explicit sexual language toned down as the Club ostensibly wanted, but Bigger's actions become more violent and less reciprocal, thereby diluting the resistance the novel offers to these damaging tropes. Rowley argues that:

> If Wright was to challenge this racist stereotype rather than reinforce it, it was crucial that his readers understood that Mary Dalton desired her black chauffeur every bit as much as he desired her—if not more so. The build-up of Mary Dalton's somewhat wanton sexuality is every bit as important as the build-up of Bigger as a highly libidinous young man. By modifying what they called Wright's "savage frankness" when it came to sex, the Book-of-the-Month Club judges upset the novel's delicate boundary. (629)

By removing signs of Mary's desire, the Book-of-the-Month Club is replicating the actions of the white prosecutors to construe Bigger's sexual encounter with Mary as rape, even when the signs in the original were ambiguous. Moreover, this is accomplished by way of compelling the removal of the scene of cross-racial desire. These elisions explicitly recapitulate the logic of silence that attends sexual encounters across the racial boundary by insisting that they simply not be represented.

The very act that Wright seems to condemn is the action the Club undertook: They seemed to take for granted that the cross-racial encounter ought not to imply the consent or participation of the white woman. As JanMohamed suggests, and as I would concur, the reason for this is likely that the danger of miscegenation and cross-racial desire is simply too great for the racialized order of differential power allocation. Admitting the possibility of racial kinship would undermine the polymorphous structures of control that maintain the color barrier as an effective fiction.

This suggests the removal of the passage is energized by much more than concerns over sexual propriety; instead, it crystallizes the anxieties of racialized, sexualized power by instating a stereotype of violent pathology where there had been a complex portrait of conflicted desire. Further, it produces much more than a sanitized text; it produces a text in which the main character is less human, more violent, less a fully realized subject and more a monster, and it simultaneously solidifies the damaging myths around rape and interracial sexual contact. When this move happens as the result of market-driven censorship, it begins the process through which the novel's canonization can rest more firmly on its reification of stereotypes of pathology. In this case, then, *Native Son* demonstrates that texts containing transgressive sexuality authored by people of color or addressing issues related to race run the risk of being shunted into narratives of obscene pathology on their way to commercial success and canonization.

Even in the expurgated Book-of-the-Month Club edition, there is an element of transgression to the novel because of the sheer weight of Bigger's violence and the explicit descriptions of both violence and sex. The scenes would have been shocking and unsettling in their time because those descriptions evoked very potent contemporary fears, as Hogue notes: Bigger "is a black man in the room of a white woman alone at night with socially constructed, repressed desires to have sexual relations with her, which is the ultimate taboo in American society in the 1930s" (18). In this scene, Wright is provoking the anxiety of white dominant society by staging the scene it perceives to be the biggest threat to its order. In itself, even absent the expurgated elements, the book violates taboos insistently.

The fact that the book remained shocking does not mitigate criticism of its censorship. The history of censorship in the United States is more complex than banning books that depict prohibited acts. In more sophisticated censorship regimes (such as the Hays code and Comics Code Authority), the treatment of dangerous subjects was as important as their mere presence. That is to say, violence might be presented if it served to discipline wayward subjects. Here, then, the presentation of taboo content is not in itself an unforgivable transgression from the standpoint of dominant ideology; what matters is the manner in which it is portrayed and the interpretations it might lead to. When Bigger is functionally alone in this scene, with Mary unconscious, the scene reinforces dominant ideology. It is taboo but not a threat to the underlying cultural logic of oppression. But if the scene suggests that cross-racial desire can be mutual and reciprocal, that white women can have active desires, that their coupling with African American men might be something other than rape—this brings down social opprobrium more reliably.

Native Son is widely read and often studied. And while it is not quite so frequently *taught* because of difficulties instructors face getting student readers to appreciate the complexity of Wright's vision, it is unquestionably canonical. In these ways, the novel tracks along the first part of the obscenity narrative I outlined. The controversy over its taboo content, some of it sexual, contributed to its success both in its moment and through subsequent generations.

However, the success found by the novel confirms the common scripts for transgressive works by writers of color. *Native Son* was a success in part because it confirmed existing dominant notions about African American pathology. While Wright's idea was to produce a work that unmasked the social conditions that led to the symptoms of social pathology, the work's legacy is mixed. The image of Bigger Thomas can be twisted to reify, rather than resist, the narrative of delinquency and violence, and this might seem to confirm the racist stereotype that the African American in the inner city was a brute and a threat to the social order. Wright himself was keenly aware of this danger. Writing in "How Bigger Was Born," he describes how he faced an internal censor bearing on his work whispering things like: "What will white people think if I draw the picture of such a Negro boy? Will they not at once say 'See, didn't we tell you all along that niggers are like that? Now, look, one of their kinds has come along and drawn the picture for us?'" (Wright, "How Bigger," 448). The critique is apt; Wright knows that Bigger's criminality and bestiality, his cunning and violence, will be used as confirmation of existing stereotypes of black men and that his own status as a voice from the African American community will seem to lend truth and authenticity to the picture.

Yet Wright worries not only about those "reactionary whites who would try to make of him something I did not intend" ("How Bigger," 448) but about liberal whites, a group with which he was intimately aware and whose views he represents incisively in the novel. Wright expresses disdain for improvement programs funded by wealthy whites in "How Bigger Was Born." Working at the South Side Boys' Club in Chicago, he felt that "those rich folk who were paying [his] wages did not really give a good goddamn about Bigger, that their kindness was prompted at bottom by a selfish motive. They were paying [him] to distract Bigger with ping-pong, checkers, swimming, marbles, and baseball in order that he might not roam the streets and harm the valuable white property which adjoined the Black Belt" (Wright, "How Bigger," 453–54). For my reading, the confirmation of certain ostensibly progressive biases is just as important as the confirmation of more obviously racist ones. That is because some interpretations of the novel offer support for both paternalistic attitudes and confounded inaction.

However, when Wright expands on what he hopes will be the main contribution of the novel, he expresses little fear of this and describes a pathology that might be embraced both by the white reactionary and the white liberal for different reasons. He describes "what *I* felt was the moral—the horror of Negro life in the United States" (Wright, "How Bigger," 461). This phrasing, "the horror of Negro life," leads just as easily to vitriolic condemnation as to objectifying sentimental saviorship or even to paralysis caused by the institutional nature of the problem, which seems bigger than any one person and which encourages the reader to be skeptical that individual action—such as those Jan and Mary engaged in—will be helpful. Even more striking, the passages that were removed from the novel at the request of the Book-of-the-Month Club make this tendency more pronounced. The expurgated novel appeals more effectively to white audiences, both progressive and regressive on issues of race. For all this, it must be acknowledged that Wright was thoroughly aware of the danger of the narrative of pathology of which the narrative of obscene pathology is an offshoot. Wright's novel does not offer a simple picture of Bigger's pathology, as we have seen, nor does it leave that narrative itself unanalyzed, and the complexity of his vision shows how authors resisted these imperatives.

For example, after Bigger has been captured, he reads in the newspaper a particularly salacious example of this false narrative. The article, after characterizing Bigger's physiognomy as apelike, continues "it is easy to imagine how this man, in the grip of a brain-numbing sex-passion, overpowered little Mary Dalton, raped her, murdered her, beheaded her, then stuffed her body into a roaring furnace to destroy the evidence of his crime" (Wright, *Native Son*, 279). The newspaper's rhetoric recapitulates the stereotypical narrative applied to Black men in manifestly over-the-top terms, and several phrases inform the reader that the report is speculative and sensational, including "it is easy to imagine" and "though the Negro killer's body does not seem compactly built, he gives the impression of possessing abnormal physical strength" (275), which implies he does not fit the physical type they are after but that they are content to overlay it on him nonetheless. In this passage, Wright is calling attention to the falseness of this narrative and the tendency to privilege the social script over the facts on the ground. From this and other evidence we know that Wright was specifically resisting just this narrative, that he wanted to combat this exact element of white supremacist culture. And yet the narrative of obscene pathology persisted alongside other modes of reception despite its direct rebuttal in the novel.

We may conclude that this is due to Wright's admirable insistence on complexity. One of the factors underlying the ambivalence many readers feel about the novel is precisely this refusal to entirely rebut this narrative. For Wright, there was a greater truth that existed in a not entirely dialectical relationship to the white supremacist fictions, what Bigger identifies as "a figment of that black world which they feared and were anxious to keep under control" (276). For proof that he is not engaged in a point-by-point rebuttal of the racist fantasies of white society, we can re-examine the newspaper account. Certainly we acknowledge that Wright is critiquing yellow journalism intended to sell papers while reifying racial hierarchies, but he does not call it out as wholly false. The news report conjures a litany of crimes, asserting that he "overpowered little Mary Dalton, raped her, murdered her, beheaded her, then stuffed her body into a roaring furnace to destroy the evidence of his crime." Some of these elements are true, others partially true or exaggerations. Only one item in the list is wholly false: the rape.

As others have noted, it is the rape that the white society Wright is analyzing desperately needed and anxiously invented in order to sustain the fixity of the racial border. In fact, the newspaper story in question goes on to lay that bare in stark terms while also suggesting that the lynch-mob vigilantism of the South is only a more overt form of the hegemony exercised institutionally in the North. What is useful in this report for understanding Wright's engagement with these public narratives is that the image that emerges here is not one in which white racist fantasies are wholly fabricated, but rather one in which they are part false and part self-fulfilling prophecy. This seems in part to be a call to avoid seeing figures like Bigger Thomas as proof of the false narrative, but this is a sometimes subtle point to make.

One important explanatory element of the story is missing here: the way that Bigger's actions were compelled by his place in Jim Crow society. Bigger had to murder Mary to cover up the crime of his being present in her bedroom. In this way, Bigger is less responsible for the crimes. However, his diminished responsibility is also a dilution of his autonomy; he becomes more a cog in the machine, more of what he wonders about as he sits in his jail cell. He suspects on some level, that "Maybe he was just unlucky, a man born for dark doom, an obscene joke happening amid a colossal din of siren screams and white faces and circling lances of light under a cold and silken sky" (Wright, *Native Son*, 275). In this mechanistic vision of his place in the world (paired with strikingly sensitive description), Bigger might not be the vicious beast of the crass white culture represented by the police and newspapers, but he may still be the victim of a genteel white progressivism represented by Jan and the Daltons.

It is this genteel dehumanization, this ethnographic objectification, that echoes one strand of the reception of the novel, and though it is dressed in good intentions, we do well to remember that this narrative of objectification is itself an appendage of a white supremacist society, not its antithesis. As Bigger himself remarks, despite their generosity and commitment to social programs, the Daltons represent "those whose hate for him was so unfathomably deep that, after they had shunted him off into a corner of the city to rot and die, they could turn to him, as Mary had that night in the car, and say 'I'd like to know how your people live'" (240). Wright attempts to resist this patronizing dehumanization just as Bigger does and carves out a place for his art and its critique.

For these critics, the deep subjective constraints placed on Bigger by his environment are determinative, just as Wright's text operates generically at the level of social protest characteristic of naturalism. Ian Afflerbach describes this reception narrative as one in which "Bigger [is] an exemplary victim of reprehensible social conditions and *Native Son* [is] a seminal case study of literary naturalism."[45] The other strand is represented by critics for whom Bigger's struggles take on universal subjective dimensions, placing Wright's novel more in the tradition of philosophical literature and the tradition of existentialism (Afflerbach 91). Afflerbach's schema usefully highlights what seems to be happening here: For reasons both personal and aesthetic, Wright's novel resonates both with social protest literature and with existential literature of the period. The division of criticism into competing strains unfortunately represents the creation of false dichotomies for such works in which the work of protest (denigrated as formulaic, superficial, or transitory) is seen as being in competition with the work of psychological or metaphysical depth (celebrated as innovative, deep, and universal). Generic and disciplinary impulses to divide and categorize are undoubtedly at work here, but so are the forces of racism, which offer reductive readings of works (as *only* protest) and preferentially apply them to works about race, often missing the work's complexity and the author's innovation.

Moreover, Wright began to conceptualize *Native Son* with the express intent of fighting narratives of victimization. In "How Bigger Was Born," for example, he writes of his previous book *Uncle Tom's Children*: "I found that I had written a book which even bankers' daughters could read and weep over and feel good about. I swore to myself that if I ever wrote another book . . . that it would be so hard and deep that they would have to face it without the consolation of tears" ("How Bigger," 454). The next book he wrote, of course, was *Native Son*, and he faced it with the determination that sentiment wouldn't play a role in expiating the sins of American society or comforting those among his readers who were complicit in them. From the outset, then, he was determined to resist this narrative of pathologization.

In the end, Bigger does ultimately evade and perhaps exceed the reductive narratives offered to him and even thrust upon him, never allowing himself to become that pitiable victim others want to see him as. Moreover, he is not fully restricted to the environment that created him and is imbued with existential potential that he only belatedly realizes. At the close of the novel he refuses the expiating discourses of religious and sociological confession. Instead, he blames Mary Dalton for her naiveté about race relations that sparked the whole series of events because she believed that her good intentions and kindness would somehow erase segregation and its insidious effects, while they instead put him in greater danger (Wright, *Native Son*, 350). As his lawyer, Boris Max, attempts to cajole Bigger into a more complacent state of mind and to encourage him to blame society for his dashed hopes, perhaps to show some contrition, he refuses, instead asserting, "Maybe they going to burn me in the electric chair for feeling this way. But I ain't worried none about them women I killed. For a little while I was free. I was doing something. It was wrong, but I was feeling all right" (354). He flatly rejects the conscience-clearing of confession or even feigning guilt. Instead, he says what he truly feels, that the murders were the only time he felt powerful and free. He refuses to change his revolutionary perspective for one that would re-integrate him into the narratives of confession and repentance, even on pain of death. Instead, after Max leaves he pursues internal reflections that provide him insights about the dark reality of humanity's hate and the subjective deprivations of segregation. In essence, his refusal to accept the simplistic narratives of pathology and sentiment are the catalyst of a deeper and more authentic understanding of life.

Revolution versus Revelation: Figuring Divergent Paths

There are important distinctions between the afterlives of *Tropic of Cancer* and *Native Son*. At root, they demonstrate how narratives of obscene genius and obscene pathology can influence the reception of artistic works and thus provide a preview of later developments. For Miller, an obscene text leads to market success and canonization while cementing the author's image as a genius. For Wright, an obscene text leads to market success and canonization, but provokes and must navigate a fraught engagement with social stereotypes of racialized pathology and deviance in ways that leave the novel's and the author's legacy conflicted and ambivalent.

On one hand, Miller did not have to alter his novel to achieve commercial and artistic success. Admittedly, as Glass has catalogued, it took a concerted effort, to say nothing of the expense, to bring the book to the United States. The novel did not simply land on the scene, sell hundreds of thousands of copies, and transform Miller into a celebrity, but Miller did find success with the novel immediately on its release. The novel was widely read across Europe, and the salaciousness of its content and its status as a forbidden text contributed significantly to that success. The English ban was one cause of its popularity in France, and the American ban caused the controversy and court cases that ensured its prominent place in American culture. In fact, the plodding pace of legal battles kept the novel in the American consciousness for nearly thirty years, a lifetime of relevance. Similarly, Miller himself was mythologized as a result of his storied refusal to compromise his vision.

On the other hand, Wright achieved immediate U.S. success and the novel has maintained its relevance, but success required the alteration of Wright's artistic vision, and *Native Son* retains a split and ambivalent reputation. The decision by the Book-of-the-Month Club to publish *Native Son* undeniably increased its profile and broadened its distribution, leading directly to its financial success and popularity. And the subsequent controversy over its taboo content *and* intellectual disagreements about its merit as a work of art produced a wealth of literary and scholarly ephemera that have served as the foundation for college courses, academic articles, and lengthy analyses (such as this one). In this way, the censorship of the novel contributed to its market success and canonization, just as it had for *Cancer*. Still, while many controversial passages remained, Wright had to dilute his vision to achieve the kind of success that Miller did while tenaciously refusing to compromise, only later achieving a similar level of artistic autonomy with later books.

Once success was achieved, the afterlives of the texts diverge in ways that are even more revealing and more racially charged. Whereas Miller's novel was credited with starting a revolution in culture, Wright's is presumed to be a *revelation* of culture.[46] Miller's work is often claimed to have changed the culture in which it appeared. Advocating a radical change in ideas and in public morality, *Cancer* became a touchstone not because it reflected or exposed the culture it stemmed from but because it changed that culture. Along these lines, Hassan remarks, "Small wonder that Miller continues to perplex us; his work, in a particular sense, is revolutionary" (Hassan 36). Hassan argues that Miller's role is that of intervening, of being a force for change, of altering the course of history. His status as a genius carries with it the sense of transcending the culture and envisioning its future.

Hassan goes further, using apocalyptic metaphors that cement the image of Miller leaving behind an old order and contributing to the rise of a new one. For example, he describes Miller's deliberate violation of taboo by saying, "The violence of obscenity destroys and creates anew," and continues by saying, "The obscene objurgations of the artist who sees himself standing among the ruins of social and literary forms are invocations of rebirth" (Hassan 37–38).[47] By consciously describing Miller's intervention in "social and literary forms" using images of total ruin alongside religious iconography and notions of rebirth, Hassan cements the idea that Miller's place in American literary history is one of tectonic change.[48] Finally, Hassan affirms Miller's role in creating a new strain of American literature: "It is important to dwell on the affinity of Henry Miller for the country he abused with passion and humor, not because his present stature may tempt us to claim him as authentically American, but simply because a whole new stream of literature derives from the source that Miller has tapped" (Hassan 48). Though Hassan might be the most fervent advocate of this position, it reflects a dominant strain among critics who saw Miller's value as primarily in his effort to transform culture, over and above realism or even artistic merit.[49]

In contrast, Wright's work has been interpreted as a *revelation*, not a revolution. That is to say, his work reveals what the culture was doing at the time he was writing, perhaps constrained by its boundaries. As JanMohamed argues, "*Native Son* turns out to be a profoundly *specular* novel; it *holds up a mirror to* the structure and economy of phallocratic society, but it is unable to escape or undermine them" (111, emphasis added). According to this strain of criticism, Wright's contribution lies in insightfully showing us what is already there, not in changing what is possible. Ralph Ellison sounds similar notes when describing Wright's intention as an author as "To *discover* and *depict* the meaning of Negro experience and to *reveal* to both Negroes and whites those problems of a psychological and emotional nature which arise between them when they strive for mutual understanding" (Ellison 61, emphasis added). Ellison describes Wright's work as an author primarily in terms of framing difficult problems for analysis. Wright has a knack for understanding them, for seeing their ramifications. He is able to "reveal" the social conditions resulting from racism and depict them in ways that move readers toward deeper understanding. This description is not meant to be derogatory. In fact, Ellison finds cause to praise Wright in strong terms shortly after this passage, contending that "Wright is an important writer, perhaps the most articulate Negro American, and what he has to say is highly perceptive"

(61). Yet Ellison does not contend that Wright has invented something fundamentally new, only that his work adroitly displays what was already there. He is not imaginative, but perceptive.

Wright's status as an author then—at least for some critics—becomes a derivative one compared to the way Miller was celebrated as something radically new. Wright is construed as merely an interpreter of history or culture, not its agent. While these strains of criticism do not exhaust the meaning of these texts or their history, they do demonstrate something important about long-standing racial tropes that influence reception. Authors, whether members of dominant groups or minoritized groups, have different possibilities that track along with their real social power. The contrast between narratives of genius/revolution and pathology/revelation also reflect and reinforce the assumptions about social power that accompany the tendency to read the work of writers of color through sociological frames. Dominant voice authors are not only given power in real terms, but the conditions of their appreciation and their reputations of authorial accomplishment carry the connotations of agency that attend having cultural shifts attributed to their work. In contrast, minoritized writers contend with social scripts that stem from the tendency to read these works ethnographically. Their work is read as a revelation, not a revolution, and so even the meta-scripts of their power tend to obscure agency and individual greatness.

2 / Geniuses Abroad, Deviants at Home: Racial Counter-Narratives of the Global and Domestic

> *I am particularly alarmed when I compare the differences in society 20 years ago and today regarding a fundamental breakdown in values. I first noticed these differences when I returned to American society after more than 7½ years as a prisoner of war in North Vietnam.*
>
> *Things that were considered totally unacceptable for public presentation when I left, were common sights when I came home.*
>
> —JEREMIAH DENTON, Senate Hearing on the Cable-Porn and Dial-a-Porn Control Act

> *Americans regard the public schools as a most vital civic institution for the preservation of a democratic system of government. It is therefore understandable that the constitutional prohibitions encounter their severest test when they are sought to be applied in the school classroom.*
>
> —JUSTICE BRENNAN, *Abington v. Schempp*

In the statement from the 1985 U.S. Senate hearing regarding the Cable-Porn and Dial-a-Porn Control Act, Senator Jeremiah Denton reflects on American culture in 1973, the year of his release from a North Vietnamese prisoner-of-war camp. Denton's decision to make these remarks at hearings about pornography implies that changes in sexual mores are his chief concern, yet his ambiguous phrasing obscures a deeper truth. He bemoans "things" that were not seen in public in 1965 but which had become common by 1973, but these "things" reflect not only changes in sexual culture, but also toward gender and racial equality. During this period, social norms, national identity, and political power were being contested profoundly. The Voting Rights Act of 1965 was passed a month after Denton was captured in July and Malcolm X had been assassinated in February; 1967 saw the Summer of Love and *Loving v. Virginia*; and Robert Kennedy and Martin Luther King were assassinated in 1968. In the early 1970s, the Watergate scandal reached its apex, and 1973 brought the Burger Court ruling in *Roe v. Wade*, a ruling that came down the month before Denton was released. Just two weeks after he was released, federal agents engaged in an armed standoff with members of the American

Indian Movement at Wounded Knee. Nineteen seventy-three also saw the signing of the peace accord in Vietnam, the withdrawal of American troops, and Operation Homecoming, which led to Denton's release. Literarily, it is also a significant moment: 1973 was the year Pynchon's encyclopedic *Gravity's Rainbow* was published and the year the Burger Court set the reigning precedent for obscenity in *Miller v. California*.

Senator Denton's yoking together of the war in Vietnam and concern over the distribution of sexual material instantiates a long-standing metaphorical slippage between violence and sexuality in the public imagination that has often abetted the censorship of images of war.[1] Such was nearly the case of a famous photo from the year before Denton's release. On June 8, 1972, South Vietnamese jets accidentally dropped napalm on civilians in Trangbang. Associated Press photographer Huynh Cong "Nick" Ut's Pulitzer Prize–winning photo of the incident titled *The Terror of War* (commonly referred to as *Napalm Girl*) was published across the United States the next day.[2] The image shows a group of children running from the site of the bombing, smoke and fire visible in the background. In the center, nine-year-old Phan Thi Kim Phúc runs naked and screaming in pain and terror; she has torn off her burning clothes (see Figure 1).

Ut's photo rendered visible the monumental price paid by civilians and highlighted the tragic impossibility of making war precise or ideologically pure. Like other critiques of the war that attempted to highlight its inextricably human cost, such as the Academy Award–winning documentary *Hearts and Minds* (1974), Ut's photo put a human face on the destructive technology of the war in a way that enshrines it in American memory of the conflict.[3] However, because of Kim Phúc's nudity, *The Terror of War* faced hurdles to publication stemming from concern that her nude body might violate decency standards. In this way, the image crystallizes the aesthetic politics of the moment in which the chilling effect of moralist outrage props up the power status quo.

At first, photographers and correspondents were unsure whether to transmit the photo over the wire from Vietnam to New York. They were concerned that the mere presence of a nude body might be objectionable on its face, regardless of context or importance. Joe McNally and Janet Mason reported in *Life* in 1995 that the photo almost was not published because "An Associated Press staffer thought newspaper editors would find the girl's nakedness offensive."[4] Similarly, on initial inspection, an AP deputy editor rejected the photo because of the nudity, though this decision was later overturned.[5] Hal Buell, head of the Associated Press at the time, conceded that there was concern about public reaction. He notes that "there was a discussion before it went out, because of the fron-

FIGURE 1. *The Terror of War* (*Napalm Girl*) by Huynh Cong "Nick" Ut, 1972 © Associated Press. Used by permission.

tal nudity," though he downplays concern, saying, "We would discuss any photo that might be controversial."[6]

Contrary to Buell's contention, the responses of other news agencies indicate that the image came dangerously close to violating taboos. NBC, which had cameramen present at the bombing, destroyed its footage of the incident because of Kim Phúc's nakedness (Westwell 409), though they ran a cropped version of Ut's photograph (411). Similarly, John G. Morris recalls that the decision to place the image below the fold on the front page of the *New York Times* was due to concern over the nudity (qtd. in Winslow 20). Thus, while it was decided that the photo was sufficiently newsworthy that it should be published, concerns over its potential to offend impacted *how* it was published.[7]

The nudity in *The Terror of War* is simultaneously incidental and central to the image's social value. To elaborate, the discussion of potential objections by publishers invokes the specter of sexualization of the suffering body in the image, a sexualization that is particularly troubling because the image is of a child. Westwell points out that technical manipulation was undertaken to reduce the possible interpretation of the photo as representing an adolescent or adult, a move designed not only to avoid sexual suggestiveness, but to alter the photograph's meaning by emphasizing the innocence of the war's victims (410).[8] Anne Higonnet argues that the anxiety we feel over this image's openness to sexualized readings grows not only out of a need to protect children from harm, but out of a deeper historical attachment to children as repositories of communal innocence.[9] This deep-seated anxiety often authorizes the demonization of certain groups by representing them as potential threats to that innocence, for example the LGBTQ+ community.

In this case, the trope is used to condemn the war. The image of a child subjected to physical harm and robbed of modesty is used against the ideology that enabled these twin violations. Ut's photo uses figures of threatened innocence for political purposes. Thus, the nakedness of the body is part and parcel of the power of the image, not for sexual purposes but because Kim Phúc's nakedness is an index of her suffering. She is in such pain and terror that standards of modesty—particularly valuable because of Kim Phúc's age—have been superseded by immediate material concerns: tearing off her napalm-covered clothes that are literally burning her alive. This image, then, reveals the privileged underpinnings of a cultural insistence on modesty because it can operate in situations where the possibility of violence is remote—and all of this militates against the simplistic narratives justifying the war.

Further, centering discussions of propriety often short-circuits more important considerations. Sylvia Shin-Huey Chong points out that a concern for the obscenity of the image misdirects attention from the violence and allows the reader to mistake its full import (116). Again, then, the nudity of the central subject is hardly beside the point—it is precisely the point, because it is by virtue of the nudity that attention is directed away from more important considerations. The challenge this photo launches at existing structures of power is jeopardized by a moralist discursive trap. Because the discourse of obscenity regulating the creation and distribution of images of the body—especially nude and wounded—permeates culture, the power of this image might have been suppressed and can still be mistaken. Here, the image was not restricted, but it is instructive that questions about public objections prompted journalists to police their own actions because concern over the possible impact of nudity was so pervasive.

In this chapter, I consider this moment's obscenity politics through Toni Morrison's *The Bluest Eye* (1970) and Thomas Pynchon's *Gravity's Rainbow* (1973). Though these two major novels were published much later than *Native Son* and *Tropic of Cancer*, they provide a bridge between my analysis in Chapter 1 and later concerns for two reasons. First, they stage their plots retrospectively in the 1940s, contemporaneous with both Wright's and Miller's novels.[10] In this sense, they share a concern for early twentieth-century metanarratives of American identity that played out in the later part of the century. Second, both benefited from the altered publishing landscape *Tropic of Cancer* made possible, in that both works were spared costly legal proceedings because of the more liberal legal possibilities resulting from *Grove v. Gerstein*. Thus, they share a legal/literary/historical genealogy with Wright's and Miller's novels.

Pynchon's novel is set in Europe and the Allied Occupation Zones around the end of World War II, a setting that allows him to trace the interwoven fates of techno-capitalist enterprises in a post-national space and thus take on themes in keeping with what McGurl calls technomodernism. Morrison's work is set on the home front where she might address issues of racism and poverty, and in this way her novel suggests the beginnings of political motivations and stylistic turns that McGurl associates with high cultural pluralism. In this way, they reflect a common practice during this period of examining the early roots of late-century upheaval. Within McGurl's framework, each author is an iconic representation of a distinct strain of American literary production in the program era,[11] and yet juxtaposing them (as I do here) rather than siloing them (as is often done), offers the possibility of drawing conclusions from their very different fates.

Each novel uses extreme representations of sexuality to complex ends. *Gravity's Rainbow* allegorizes Vietnam-era concerns and broader issues of social organization by drawing connections between sexuality and industrialized warfare—in addition to indicting global corporate structures in the perpetuation of violence across the world. Morrison's novel uses its depictions of incestuous rape to communicate the dense web of psychological destruction wrought by a culture of white supremacy. Both novels use sexual and violent imagery to advance arguments about the cruelty or voraciousness of the will to power during this period as well as its deep imbrication with sex and taboo. Their particular concern is, respectively, the epistemological conditions of international warfare and the perpetuation of inequality through the enforcement of body, gender, and sexual norms. Each was challenged for the extremity of its sexual content, and for this reason, they represent important examples of both obscene political work and the cultural environment in which they circulate.

Both novels were found objectionable by some readers because of their explicit depictions of taboo sex acts. Objecting to content that was called obscene, the Pulitzer Prize board chose to issue no prize for fiction in 1974 rather than accede to the jury's unanimous recommendation of *Gravity's*

Rainbow. The documents of this controversy reflect the tendency to weigh the novel's shocking and unsettling elements against its literary merit in ways that tend to affirm—rather than challenge—its place in the canon and which have largely lost their urgency since the novel's debut. In contrast, *The Bluest Eye* is still frequently challenged when it is assigned to high schoolers, because of its explicit portrayals of rape and incest (both of which are also present in *Gravity's Rainbow*). In many ways, it is the very fact of the book's presence on reading lists that enables such challenges. By comparison, Pynchon's novel is hardly ever taught because of its length and opaque prose, as well as the extensive background necessary to make sense of its allusions. Thus, the relative complexity of *Gravity's Rainbow* has also rendered it relatively uncontroversial. What makes *The Bluest Eye* comparatively *more* controversial is that it has a more prominent place in classrooms.[12] The divergent fates of these novels in part represents the impact of schools as a locus of obscenity challenges following the obscenity trials of the 1950s and '60s. It is only after it becomes impossible to limit the content available to adults that activists and activism shift emphasis to controlling what is available to children. This new legal reality begins in the 1960s and continues into the 1980s with rulings by the more conservative Burger Court and the agitation of public groups such as the Parents Music Resource Center.

While part of my goal is to explore this new formation, I will also examine how the narratives of obscene genius and obscene pathology play out in the literary afterlives of these two novels. Going further, this juxtaposition demonstrates that the international political sphere is a privileged sphere for the narrative of obscene genius, while the domestic is the sphere into which the narrative of obscene pathology is shunted. This fact both ratifies and extends already-existing false dichotomies such as those between international/domestic, public/private, and male/female. In this case, it appears that transgressive representations that fit into the first three categories redound to the author's credit, while those in the latter categories run greater risks.

"Carried On under a Sentence of Death": Globalized Sexual Transgressions in *Gravity's Rainbow*

The January 1973 signing of the peace accord in Vietnam and the withdrawal of American troops that March signaled the end to a contentious war, if not the contentiousness of American politics. *Gravity's Rainbow*, published between these events just as it was published between arguments and decision in *Miller*,[13] crystallizes American anxieties and fascinations about power and the obscene through its sexualization of war and its encyclopedic treatment of the entanglement of capitalist enterprises, science, and human devastation. Though the novel is set during World War II, its indictment of the corporate entities that profited from the industrial mobilization that enabled both World War II and the war in Vietnam forces us to attend to its implications for circumstances contemporary to its publication.

Generally considered Pynchon's magnum opus, *Gravity's Rainbow* was criticized for its difficult prose and sometimes objectionable content, notably instances of BDSM, erotic urophagia and coprophagia, and a number of explicitly described sexual encounters, some involving adolescents. The mixed reception is demonstrated by the novel's unsuccessful journey toward the Pulitzer Prize in 1974. The Pulitzer Board rejected the fiction jury's unanimous recommendation of *Gravity's Rainbow* for the prize and instead issued no fiction award, describing the novel during their debate as "unreadable," "overwritten," and "obscene."[14] Pynchon's style pairs historical and technical minutiae with cinematic description and absurd humor; Louis Menand calls him "a writer of postmodernist high-tech, a literary encoder of scientific arcana," and declares that "on one level his stories slosh merrily along from one farcical-tragical episode to the next, while on another level an enormous web of symbolic implication is continually being woven and unwoven. It is as though the story of Popeye the Sailorman had fallen into the hands of Richard Wagner."[15] In *Gravity's Rainbow*, this combination of epic and inane mirrors and in some respects explains the pronounced disconnect between enthusiastic responses both positive and negative that characterized the novel's initial reception while also echoing the grand rhetoric of initial reviews of Miller's *Tropic of Cancer*.[16]

Most scholars stress the novel's critique of scientific ideologies that have eclipsed the human reality they once served, a process embodied in the arc of the rocket: gravity's rainbow. As Staes puts it, "*Gravity's Rainbow* hints at an ongoing historical process typified by the transformation of nature into a web of domination."[17] To enable this political analysis, many scholars turn to Herbert Marcuse's *Eros and Civilization* to flesh out the novel's sexualized representation of war and capitalism, which suggests a psychological connection between the two.[18] This by no means exhausts the possible lenses through which to read Pynchon's novel. Slade traces Pynchon's critique of Protestantism and Calvinism through his anti-empiricist projects. Michael Harris and Menand both read Pynchon as concerned with the effects of colonialism. Pynchon's conception of World War II as a moment of transition for, rather than *terminus of*

European colonialism is also highlighted by Harris, who notes, "Pynchon insists that we understand colonialism not only as a political-historical-economic phenomenon but also as a way of seeing the world and experiencing life."[19] I would read this alongside Jodi Y. Kim's assertion in *The Ends of Empire* that the Cold War represents not so much a series of international events, but as a hermeneutic that explains and represents the world. Pynchon's novel, then, speaks to the fallout of World War II and the continuity of colonialist and Cold War hermeneutics.

Despite Pynchon's meticulous reliance on tropes and metaphors from the 1940s (avoiding historically specific references from his own era), scholars locate suggestions within the text that the war in Vietnam forms part of the relevant background. Slade notes that the experience of the South African Herreros in the novel may be resonant with the imposition of Western epistemologies in Vietnam during the years Pynchon was composing the novel. And Slade remarks on "the hints that the narrator of *Gravity's Rainbow* is a Vietnam veteran strung out on mysticism and dope."[20] A still more compelling overlap emerges in the aesthetics of the novel; Chong notes, "The Vietnam War instigated the development of televisual and filmic representations of explicit violence in a quantity and with an immediacy lacking in previous newsreel coverage of the Second World War and the Korean War" (19), which suggests the importance of Pynchon's imagining of World War II through the cinematic mode more associated with the Vietnam era.[21] Similarly, Christina Jarvis argues that, along with Kurt Vonnegut's *Slaughterhouse Five*, *Gravity's Rainbow* participates in a larger cultural project she dubs "the Vietnamization of World War II," by means of which the previous war's moral clarity was contaminated by new understandings of its fallout.

The novel is set in Europe during the closing days of World War II. A huge cast of characters (most estimates put the number over three hundred) engage in clandestine, occult operations for the various combatant governments and extra-governmental agencies, both for the Axis and the Allies, not always sure which and possibly both. As Germany's defeat seems imminent, the Allied powers seek to secure the Reich's technologies, especially Germany's V2 rocket. One aspect of Pynchon's critique aims at the subsequent impact of these efforts on the ensuing Cold War—the V2 would become the basis for space exploration and the Intercontinental Ballistic Missile. The plot also traces the historical connections between Western industrial corporations and the Nazi war machine. In *Gravity's Rainbow*, these corporations are beginning to eclipse national states, and thus the novel historically situates—and thus denaturalizes—economic globalization, as well as reminding us that globalization is intrinsically related to colonialism and warfare. Pynchon's exhaustive demonstration of these connections is made more resonant by the involvement of, for example, Dow Chemicals in the development of Napalm B and Agent Orange, both of which were being used in military operations in Southeast Asia at the time the novel was published. Pynchon's thematization of the unchecked pursuit of economic opportunity at the cost of massive human suffering allows us to see the continuity among World War II, Cold War military actions, and globalization.

The primary character, an American Army lieutenant named Tyrone Slothrop, largely wanders through the novel searching for information to explain his bizarre arousal patterns. Slothrop is not always aware of what turns him on or why. Gazing on the streak of a rocket's trail across the sunrise horizon early in the novel, he marvels to himself, "There is in his history, and likely, God help him, in his dossier, a peculiar sensitivity to what is revealed in the sky. (But a *hardon*?)."[22] In fact, what causes him to become erect is one of the driving mysteries of the novel, both for the reader and the other characters. The locations of Slothrop's sexual liaisons in London map onto the location of German rocket attacks that follow a few days later. Slothrop, a romantic, meticulously records his encounters at the bidding of ACHTUNG, the cooperative Allied unit concerned with arcane operations. Tracing the correlation between his sexual liaisons and the rocket strikes is part of a larger effort to decode the strikes and hopefully prevent them. Paranoid theories abound, including Slothrop's own suspicion that the rockets are tracking him personally. This part of the novel's plot explores the possibility of free will in a hyper-determined world, as well as allegorizing the larger cultural tendency to sexualize violence and technology. As Slade puts it, "Slothrop can apparently convert disorder—in the instance of rocket explosions—into order—in the instance of sexual potency" (173). Anxious rewriting of the chaos of war into linear narratives of battles and victories parallels this process while sublimating its sexual component.

The possibility of agency in a world of psychological, atomic, and metaphysical determinism bears directly on a scene of child sexual exploitation in which Slothrop is involved. The child, Bianca, performs a Shirley Temple routine in front of a group gathered for an orgy, which follows. Slothrop later finds himself alone with Bianca, and the two engage in intercourse that, while ostensibly consensual, emphasizes Bianca's physical youthfulness (in contrast with her adult cynicism). Though the act is repugnant, Slothrop's Pavlovian conditioning causes us to be unsure of his level of responsibility. In fact, as he reaches orgasm, Slothrop is described as "helpless here in this exploding *emprise*" (Pynchon 470); his ejaculation is then linked to the German missile technology he is investigating through metaphors of rockets and detonation (470). This moment of violation coincides with Slothrop's loss of control over his actions. While the scene is troubling, it attempts in part an indictment of the way sexuality is conditioned by technology, whether in the form of missiles or mass media or psychoanalysis. The implication is that even the most congenial among us (like Slothrop) might be made complicit because of our interpellation into an exploitative system of knowledge and commerce. The scene then is not one in which a sympathetic character engages in a heinous act, but a demonstration of the repugnant consequences of social and empirical determinism.

In addition, the novel includes depictions of incest. A German rocket engineer named Franz Pökler has lost his wife and child to concentration camps. As he works on the rocket program, Pökler carries on a periodic liaison with a young girl (also a camp prisoner) that is the same age as—and who may *be*—his daughter. She is sent to Pökler each summer for a brief period as part of an inscrutable psychological game played by Pökler's overseer, an SS officer named Weissmann (also known as Captain Blicero in other parts of the novel), in which the young woman is offered as comfort, compensation, and incentive for his work on the rocket. Through Pökler's incestuous feelings, the novel dramatizes the way that the victims of the camps were pawns in a game of symbolic exchange between German men that incorporated war, sexuality, and patriarchy.

The incest itself highlights the deep moral corruption of the Zone while the instrumentalization of such corruption indicates that moral concerns are subordinate to technological ones in this image of Western civilization. The act (or possible act) of incest *is* condemned in the novel, and Pökler is seen as a wretch, but the reader is also reminded that in times of war, even repulsive behavior finds expression because morality is displaced. The voice of a German administrator reassures Pökler's handler that the scientist's corruption has to be tolerated because he is useful: "Yes, yes, we know it's disgusting, one never can tell what they have locked up in there with those equations, but we must all put off our judgments for now, there'll be time after the war to get back to the Pöklers and their dirty little secrets" (Pynchon 420). Here, taboo and transgressive behavior are tolerated because the minds that produce them also contain scientific value that takes precedence; Pökler's fantasies are "locked up in there with those equations," and the fantasies must be indulged to profit from the technological knowledge.[23]

The novel ascribes Pökler's fantasies to delusion and manipulation at the hands of the Nazis; like Slothrop, he is less than fully responsible. We read even, that "It was not, in fact, even clear to him that he had made a choice" in the matter (Pynchon 421). Further, like most of the characters living in the lawless post-war period of the novel's later sections, Pökler is never punished for his transgressions. As an image of the war, *Gravity's Rainbow* makes the taboo acts it depicts part of a larger war-mania that crosses national borders and erodes conventions of morality, but it does not usually condemn that mania in particular instances. In fact, the descriptions of non-mainstream sexual behavior—including BDSM and coprophilia—are carried out in much the same language as the more conventional sexual encounters between Lieutenant Slothrop and his many lovers around Britain and Europe—encounters that would probably not meet the standard of "patently offensive." These other scenes are portrayed as a part of war and of human behavior, part of the ongoing drama of human life and a ubiquitous—even mundane—part of adult interactions.

Still, all sexuality in the novel is enmeshed in a practice of pushing against taboos, a form of social transgression if not always resistance. In fact, Slade contends, "Sadomasochistic acts are common in *Gravity's Rainbow* as attempts by characters to break through the boundaries of the individual self and to reestablish the sense of community that an impoverished spirituality has forestalled. . . . In a rationalized culture, only sex and death remain mysterious. Aberrant behavior links the two under the banner of rebellion" (189). In this sense, "sexual aberrations, though frequently distasteful, are more human than alien" (Slade 192). They represent an effort to de-sublimate the repressed potential and will-to-life that has been channeled into the paradoxically destructive organization of society. This alignment of transgression with the potential for utopic revolution makes clear the novel's ethics and the purpose of its representations: It violates taboos in order to critique the system of repression they underwrite and which produced the mechanized destruction of World War II.

Ultimately, the scene of pedophilia, the invocation of incest, and Slothrop's Pavlovian sexuality all veer toward the same theme. In *Gravity's Rainbow*, war is an all-consuming social upheaval, one that displaces the logic that ostensibly spawned it. In the novel, World War II is not fought for nationalist or political reasons. Those directly involved, both the planners and the combatants, think only of prolonging the war for their own purposes. Some of those purposes are economic, some are scientific, some are sexual; some are ideological while others are paranoid. Nonetheless, the purpose of the war is these other impulses, not any proximate historical event or teleology of mankind. War becomes nothing more than—and as much as—the most productive theater for the pursuit of economic and political advantage without the conventional restraints of morality or society, and those who recognize this are most able to not only adapt but profit.

Importantly, the goals being pursued by those in the Zone are those that produce civilization, not those that tend toward its destruction. While there is looting and random violence, more common in *Gravity's Rainbow* is the maniacal pursuit of a goal associated with progress: science, commerce, reproduction. The German rocket commander Weissmann/Blicero's attempts to perfect his rocket through the exploitation of novel polymers and increasingly precise engineering serve as one example of such a goal. Pointsman's efforts to confirm the binary operation of the brain are another. The novel seems, in this manner, to underscore Marcuse's argument about society's fundamental organization: the repression of instinctual drives that promotes activities that tend toward greater complexity is based on violence that this structure fails to contain.

The fact that Pynchon was aware of Marcuse's work supports the suspicion that the novel's overall critique is in the revelation that society at its most orderly is firmly grounded in destruction and chaos. Marcuse suggests the reason why:

> [T]he very progress of civilization increases the scope of sublimation and of controlled aggression; on both accounts, Eros is weakened and destructiveness is released. This would suggest that progress remains committed to a regressive trend in the instinctual structure (in the last analysis, to the death instinct), that the growth of civilization is counteracted by the persistent (though repressed) impulse to come to rest in final gratification. Domination, and the enhancement of power and productivity, proceed through destruction beyond rational necessity. The quest for liberation is darkened by the quest for Nirvana.[24]

It is evident to Marcuse that current models of (Western) society are predicated on an uneasy structure of repression that can never be complete. The repression of the id progresses in a fashion that necessarily produces "destruction beyond rational necessity." After the equation of culture is computed, we are left with a remainder of destruction—and this violent remainder indicates the instability of the structure. Moreover, because that destruction exists not in the abstract but as expression, that destruction has a victim; thus, the system is not only unstable, it is unjust.

Pynchon seems profoundly skeptical of the possibility of escaping the structures Marcuse identifies.[25] In *Gravity's Rainbow*, society has effectively been smashed by war, and the opportunity to found a utopia not predicated on the repression of sexual and destructive impulses has arrived.[26] And yet, what obtains is not a cooperative society but a chaos of self-interest and an orgy of violence. Moreover, *Gravity's Rainbow* reveals the misdirection performed by metanarratives of politics and nationalism. The narratives of national unity and of political allegiances that make war possible and inevitable are merely a way of mobilizing the massive forces necessary to radically transform the rules of the game, to allow for the transgression of laws and the abuse of humans and resources to satisfy the desires of scientific curiosity, personal gratification, or economic accumulation.[27]

The novel, then, is not obscene for no reason, but one must grapple with the nature of an aesthetic project that transgresses the boundaries of representation in order to make this point. The novel suggests why this method is necessary in a brief moment where the text muses on the nature of representation. Pausing in its discussion of what is described as a "really offensive and tasteless film," which is mostly nonsense, the narration gives way to exposition on the fundamental flaw in efforts to judge the morality of any text. The novel admits that representations can be offensive, but claims that

> the alternative is to start keeping some out and not others, and nobody's ready for that.... Decisions like that are for some angel stationed very high, watching us at our many perversities, crawling across the black satin, gagging on whip-handles, licking the blood from a lover's vein-hit, all of it, every lost giggle or sigh, being carried on under a sentence of death whose deep beauty the angel has never been close to. (Pynchon 746)

According to the voice of the narration, what is offensive to some is nonetheless a part of existence, and the function of artistic representation is to uncover it, not judge it. Certainly, the text concedes, there could be censorship. But the faculties necessary to make decisions about what is suitable are available only to angels—a figure of the impossible virtue humans do not possess. Moreover, the fallibility of humans—their degradation—is part of their humanity. It is wrapped up in their "sentence of death," an element of life that cannot be understood by those who would exempt themselves from its horrors.

Thus, presenting child sexual exploitation and incest without critical or moralizing language that might negate the contaminating effect of such a representation forces a reader to grapple with the obscenity as part of a larger project, rather than dismissing it. In this way, it crystallizes the questions addressed in, if not resolved by, the Warren and Burger Courts' obscenity decisions. The novel undoubtedly concerns ideas of significant social import (free will, the proliferation of international corporate conglomerates not answerable to national governments,[28] the suspension of morality that attends war) but these ideas are furthered by its taboo content. *Gravity's Rainbow*, then, performs some of the same work and encountered some of the same problems as Ut's photo, *Terror of War*. The two works condemn the epistemologies of war on the grounds that they erode morality and destroy lives, and in both cases, potentially obscene material is central rather than incidental to that project.

Pynchon's defense of artistic transgression is also woven into its literary afterlife. Just as with Miller, the narrative of obscene genius provided a reception script that could justify the novel's obscenities while cementing its place in the canon. Pynchon's role in American letters is often marked by his reputation as a recluse and by testaments to the density of his prose. *Gravity's Rainbow* in particular is sarcastically known as a book many people start but few people finish.[29] The mystery generated by the author's refusal to give interviews, coupled with the reputation of his prose to be difficult, erudite, and encyclopedic, contribute to a reputation as a unique genius with a distinctive vision of Western society.

As I stated in the introduction, one of the recurring themes in the narrative of obscene genius is the establishment of the author as surpassing precedent to the extent of giving the lie to the comparison. This is prominent in contemporary reviews of *Gravity's Rainbow*. For example, James R. Lindroth wrote in *America Magazine* that "only two other books, James Joyce's *Ulysses* and Herman Melville's *Moby Dick*, provide the reader with the proper perspective on its complexities" and W. T. Lhamon Jr. wrote in the *New Republic* that "Only three American novels of the last seven or eight years even approach *Gravity's Rainbow* in ambition, chutzpah and achievement: Norman Mailer's *An American Dream*, Pynchon's own *The Crying of Lot 49*, and E. L. Doctorow's *The Book of Daniel*."[30] In both cases (as in others), massive canonical works are used as the frame of reference. It is *also* typical for reviewers to find that Pynchon surpasses these impressive benchmarks. For example, Lhamon declares that Pynchon exceeds even himself, declaring, "Each pales next to this massive, mind-blowing, stomach-turning, monstrously comic new milestone in fiction" (Lhamon 24), while Simmon contends that Pynchon exceeds the most relevant frame of reference, as he "moves beyond Joyce,"[31] and one of the Pulitzer jurors is said have recommended the novel to the board because "No work of fiction published in 1973 begins to compare in scale, originality and sustained intellectual interest with" *Gravity's Rainbow* (qtd. in Kihss). More than the others, Robert K. Morris is loath even to attempt a comparison in his review for the *Nation*, referring to Pynchon's skill at constructing and interweaving different sociological elements by saying, "How he goes about conveying all this amounts to a literary feat for which literary comparisons may not be at all apposite."[32] Despite feigning concern that Pynchon's work is beyond compare, he continues with a grandiose comparison to Wagner's *Ring of the Nibelung* and, just like Lhamon, Morris, and other reviewers, Morris concludes that Pynchon exceeds Wagner, in this case by plumbing an abyss even Wagner shrunk from: "Pynchon, however, sees beyond Wagner's twilight into the void" (Morris 53).

Growing naturally out of the conclusion that the novel brooks no comparison, reviewers tend to assert that it represents a watershed event. Simmon calls the book "innovative and unique" (Simmon 55); Lhamon claims, "This novel is going to change the shape of fiction, if only because its genius will depress all competitors" (Lhamon 24); and Lindroth concludes, "Pynchon has created a watershed for the literary currents of several decades" (Lindroth 446). Morris is even more apocalyptic (in examining apocalyptic aspects of the novel): "It is no easy job to annihilate 3,000 years of culture by means of language and technique alone. Pynchon very nearly does it; and consequently, this big, and in places overblown novel operates in super-spheres of difficulty. . . . Yet his formal pyrotechnics are not gratuitous. The technical perfection of *Gravity's Rainbow* in itself establishes the novel's controlling idea, just as it allows Pynchon to break from the dominating cliché of even the best apocalyptic literature" (Morris 53). Morris mixes his statements of *Gravity's Rainbow*'s watershed status with direct celebrations of Pynchon's genius, but each reviewer, explicit or not, constructs Pynchon as a literary genius.

The strongly positive rhetoric of these reviews is perhaps consistent with the style of the time, but it can be striking, nonetheless. It is notable, too, that reviewers worked to establish Pynchon as a genius of a particular kind. That is, he is not a genius who uses obscenity like any other material, but rather he is a transgressive genius whose greatness is rooted in that very act of transgression, for he exceeds the boundaries that limited lesser artistic lights (such as Joyce and Wagner). Lhamon, for example, reminds us that all of Pynchon's alchemy is conducted with obscene materials; that is, this is not simply a narrative of genius, but *obscene* genius:

> Out of that excrement loam under the rose and beyond the broadcast, Pynchon brings us all the news that's unfit to print, and that printing can't make fit. Among the heralds of this news are: leftist Jews demonstrating and German Wobbly printers hiding; a "family" composed

of Hansel, Gretel and witch, and another of light bulbs (Byron, Benito, Bernie and Brenda Bulb); a tribe of African Hereros reconstructing the V-2 rocket after the war; several episodes of scatological "fun 'n' games" that make earlier decadent fiction look like a meeting of the DAR in Stoney Lonesome, Indiana; a coven of assorted mediums and general mindfreaks; lovers who mostly get screwed; movie addicts, excrement addicts, cocaine sniffers, reefer tokers, benny poppers; dodo exterminators, dog experimenters, a lemming lover. (Lhamon 24)

Lhamon's laudatory review, then, is a good example of this type of reception for obscene texts, comprising as it does both ringing endorsements of the novel's greatness and of its shamelessness. The two are linked explicitly in his note that Pynchon channels the "excremental vision from Swift and Burroughs" before remarking "both of whom he surpasses here" (Lhamon 26).

Simmon argues that what Lhamon calls Pynchon's "excremental vision" is central to the aesthetic and political project of the novel. He writes, for example, "One cannot come to grips with the vision of *Gravity's Rainbow* without facing the implications of a scene where [Brigadier Ernest] Pudding's perversions are represented" (Simmon 58). Pudding is the submissive in the referenced scene of BDSM coprophagia, and so Morris is contending that this scene—which Simmon speculates was a reason the novel was rejected by the Pulitzer board—is not incidental or antagonistic to Pynchon's revelations, but central to them.

The result is not, as the Pulitzer board concluded, unreadable. For many reviewers, the novel is a testament to Pynchon's skill and expansive knowledge, and that knowledge requires knowledge of taboo material in order to seem complete.[33] Thus, his particular brand of genius—encyclopedic genius—nuances the narrative of obscene genius. Reserving judgment, Pynchon records in a manner that understands all parts of human behavior as worthy of examination, even advocating for a fuller, less prudish understanding of human psychology in order that we might avoid the dangerous conflagrations that result from our incomplete knowledge of ourselves and our natures.

As those reviewers who celebrate the work see it, then, Pynchon's mission in *Gravity's Rainbow* and his skill as a novelist are linked inextricably with the repressed corners of human behavior. In addition, they take pains to provide the literary bona fides of the author and novel in much the same way that critics and scholars did for Miller's *Tropic of Cancer* in the years between the publication of the two novels. Unconsciously following the script laid out by Grove Press, reviewers and advocates worked to establish that Pynchon was a literary genius, that comparisons could be made to other recognized works of genius, that he exceeded those forerunners in ways that made his work unique and important, and that what made his work distinct was rooted in its fearless engagement in taboo sexual representations. Rather than having to contend with obscenity as a negative characteristic making his work suspect or dangerous, his transgressions elevate the work, spur critical production, and move it closer to canonization.

"Too Obvious, Almost Obscene, in the Joy It Promised": Moynihan's Pathologized Domesticity in *The Bluest Eye*

In a scene from Cholly Breedlove's childhood in *The Bluest Eye*, Morrison describes the shining, juicy heart of a watermelon as "too obvious, almost obscene, in the joy it promised (135).[34] The phrasing recalls the book's previous chapter, which ended with a lush and densely symbolic description of the pleasure Cholly's wife, Pauline, used to experience during their lovemaking. However, the novel's "almost obscene" joys— Pauline's rich physical pleasures, for example—are almost universally overshadowed by its obscene pains: those moments where sex is part of abuse and violation. In *The Bluest Eye*, sexual joy and pain sit side-by-side, presenting a complex picture that has proven difficult for readers and is perennially controversial.

To delve into why this is, I first turn from Pynchon's novel and the flood of war images to the more relevant historical frames for *The Bluest Eye*: *Brown v. Board of Education* (1954) and the Moynihan Report of 1965. Engaging with this history of the home front, Morrison traces the genealogy of late-century racial dynamics with an eye toward what kinds of psychological and affective logics might produce a more equal society. Jennifer Gillan notes that by setting the novel the same year that the United States went to war in Europe, Morrison is able to give the lie to the national rhetoric of equality that underwrote the push for war, which distracted attention from ongoing racial injustice at home.[35] Thus, *The Bluest Eye* counters American national mythologies that emerged at this time and that shift attention to the racist ideologies of others (like the Nazis) while speciously glossing the nation's problematic past and present.

As Morrison performs this reversal of priority, she works through two dominant strains of thinking about race from the mid-century and seeks to complicate them. On the one hand, she tells the story of a black girl whose sense of self is destroyed by beauty standards that privilege white phenotypic features. This story of Pecola Breedlove's self-hatred draws extensively on the social psychology of Kenneth B. Clark and Mamie Phipps Clark and their doll tests, which contributed to the watershed Warren Court ruling in *Brown v. Board of Education*. In these tests, the Clarks presented children with dolls that were identical except for the color of their skin. The children were then asked to point to which doll represented certain character traits, including being "good" and "pretty." According to the Clarks' interpretation of the results, children of all races more frequently ascribed positive qualities to the white dolls. The doll tests played an important role in undoing one of the most toxic legacies of racial inequality in the United States, and Morrison's novel testifies to their cultural impact through its engagement with racialized beauty standards.[36]

Though interpreted as demonstrating the harms of segregation, the underlying logic of the doll tests has since been deemed problematic. The tests are dramatic, the links between racial preference and self-esteem intuitive, and the legal strategy they supported produced valuable social change. And yet, as Gwen Bergner demonstrates, by promoting images of pathology and low self-esteem for African Americans, the doll test contributed to a dangerous narrative.[37] The concept of psychological damage that underwrote the NAACP strategy in the *Brown* case was adopted by conservative voices resistant to race-aware social justice measures. The reason for the shift was the slippery slope from psychological damage and cultural pathology to blame-the-victim mentalities that shifted responsibility for a lack of social mobility to those who suffered it.[38] This is typical of the misdirection that characterizes what George Lipsitz calls the "possessive investment in whiteness," whereby "Americans produce largely cultural explanations for structural social problems," which results in "a discourse that demonizes people of color for being victimized by [de-industrialization], while hiding the privileges of whiteness by attributing them to family values, fatherhood, and foresight."[39] Even at best, the notion that the problem was cultural, rather than legal, presupposes that the solutions ought to be private and individual, rather than public and communal. This co-optation demonstrates the difficult racial situation a novel like Morrison's must navigate as it becomes a cultural artifact confronting the flexible mechanisms of racism.

On the other hand, there is the story of Pecola's rape by her father, Cholly Breedlove, which roots his behavior in a personality deformed by encounters with racism.[40] The exploration of psychologies and family structures warped by false comparisons with middle-class norms calls to mind the logic of the infamous Moynihan Report, which explains economic inequality as the result of cultural differences in black communities. The report blames slavery and racism for these differences and attempts to avoid blaming African Americans, but pathologizes (and essentializes) black culture in ways that later served anti-equity measures while centering white middle-class family structures as the societal norm against which others are measured. Thus, the novel seeks—as did the Clarks, the NAACP, and Moynihan—to ameliorate social injustices, but must contend with narrative and dramatic logics that later served to undermine such efforts at racial justice in the years following the novel's publication.

This multiple bind that warps the landscape for the work that Morrison can accomplish through her novels highlights the similar situation faced by many transgressive works by writers of color and demonstrates the insidiousness of long-standing racial hierarchies in art. White supremacy co-opts the epistemologies of resistance and corrupts them. This is one aspect of the narrative of obscene pathology, which does not always restrict canonization, but complicates it in ways that tend to diminish authorial talent and demean artistic value, preferring to see such works as cultural artifacts. This narrative takes on particular vectors with Morrison's work. Stylistic features of the novel, especially its accessible prose and child characters, make it more likely to provoke opprobrium than Pynchon's novel, while complicating its politics. Moreover, its engagement with racism and the family shunt it into devalued narratives of the domestic.

Morrison has been seen as part of a literary moment marked by the ascendance of influential African American woman writers and what Cheryl Wall calls "the shift in the locus of African American literature from the preoccupation with the conflict between black and white men."[41] As Morrison's earliest work, *The Bluest Eye* inaugurates what Malin Walther Pereira has identified as her struggle to undermine and cast off white ideologies as part of a larger aesthetic decolonization.[42] In this novel (and successively through her next three novels, Pereira avers), the characters labor under the weight of dominant ideals of racial beauty. Thus, as her first novel and a representative of major themes in her oeuvre, *The Bluest Eye* remains an important site for understanding Morrison's career.

A common strain in criticism of *The Bluest Eye* addresses Morrison's representation of childhood.[43] Such analyses include explications of facets of the Clarks' doll test in the novel, of black girlhood, how racism affects coming of age, and of the use of children as representations of the nation. As Wall puts it, the dominant theme of *The Bluest Eye*, as it is for the other influential texts by African American women in that moment, is that "in a society ordered by hierarchies of power based on race, class, and gender, no one is more powerless, and therefore more vulnerable, than a poor black girl" (797).

Related to this, of course, is the question of this novel being *for* children, as opposed to *about* children. That is to say, a major element of the novel's scholarly afterlife has to do with its place in high school classrooms, and there is a large body of writing addressing if and how to teach the novel and what it has to say about literacy and education.[44] Since the mid-1990s when the book began to be regularly taught in schools, there have been dozens of bans and challenges in states from Alaska to North Carolina and California to Massachusetts.[45] In fact, the American Library Association ranked the book the second most challenged book of 2013.[46] The fact that the Common Core began including the novel in its recommended reading for eleventh graders in 2013 is likely the reason for the surge that year and ensures ongoing controversy. This inclusion also means that more jurisdictions will produce challenges to the book as part of broader resistance to Common Core, which some see as encroaching on local autonomy.[47]

Of the 2013 challenges, one of the most remarkable is the uproar caused when the president of the Ohio State Board of Education—Morrison's home state and the setting for the novel—attempted to have the book removed from school curricula statewide. The rhetoric of the objections was almost comically extreme, with one member of the Board of Education referring to the book as part of "an underlying socialist-communist agenda" (qtd. in Milhoan) and the Board president herself calling the book "pornographic."[48] Though usually reluctant to address specific controversies over her books, Morrison felt compelled to tell the local NBC affiliate, "I resent it. I mean if it's Texas or North Carolina as it has been in all sorts of states. But to be a girl from Ohio, writing about Ohio having been born in Lorain, Ohio. And actually relating as an Ohio person, to have the Ohio—what, Board of Education?—is ironic at the least" (qtd. in Gates). Morrison's personal resentment reflects a sense that the state ought to be more sophisticated or more generous with her as an Ohioan. Ultimately the ACLU became involved, and the Board of Education decided to retain the book. In all, the controversy lasted hardly over two weeks from beginning to end, but lives on as part of the larger pattern of periodic challenges.

Disagreements arise not only between educators and communities, but among educators themselves, as emblematized by a series of articles in *The English Journal*, a publication of the National Council of Teachers of English that emphasizes pedagogical strategies for middle and high school teachers. An initial article by Missouri English teacher Carolyn P. Henly in 1993 was met with strong reactions from other educators. Henly recounts her internal conflict over the novel, concerned as she was about "the rawness of the language and graphic sex," and worried over "visions of parents lined up outside my classroom demanding to know why I was teaching a class of seventeen-year-olds a book which implies, among other objectionable ideas, that one character prefers sexual gratification from her cat 'squirming in her lap' to normal conjugal relations with her husband."[49] Henly's fears reflect those of many teachers, who know that the novel's explicit representations of taboo material will be difficult for students to experience and concerning for parents interested in managing their children's exposure to some subjects. Because of these fears, teachers feel they need thoughtful approaches to the text to attend to student discomfort and concrete defenses for parental challenges.

The journal chose to follow Henly's essay with responses from contributors who objected to some part of Henly's approach. One of the respondents, Sandra Stotsky, worried that the novel is divisive, inspires white students to feel guilty, and undermines "that sense of shared citizenship and mutual empathy that a multiethnic nation requires" (Randall et al. 21).[50] Stotsky's essay reveals what is insidious about the colorblind multiethnic ideal that she espouses. For example, she worries more about the guilt white students might feel over the structural racism the novel addresses than the experience of students of color who are subject to that racism, and she laments that "The most striking feature of this novel to me is its consistent negative portrayal of white people" (Randall et al. 20). Stotsky's essay emblematizes the kinds of pushback the novel received; moreover, critics did not need to prove their claims by demonstrating, for example, that white students really *did* feel guilty (and that such guilt was inappropriate). Rather, they simply had to generate the sense that texts like *The Bluest Eye* were divisive. Risk averse school systems would then simply opt for less controversial texts.

To some extent, conventional battle lines appear. Some parents object to the book's content, and then school boards facing pressure from free speech activists and social conservatives convene hearings at which angry parents, teachers, and librarians rehash debates over the book's literary merit. Half-measures are enacted, tending to retain the book in libraries and on reading lists but often with alternative texts offered that may not cover the same issues, such as William Faulkner's *The Sound and the Fury* (1929), Jane Austen's *Pride and Prejudice* (1813), and Zora Neale Hurston's *Their Eyes Were Watching God* (1937). Finally, the school promises to communicate more clearly about texts, justifications, and parental rights, and the involved parties let the incident fade into the background while the activists on both sides gird for a similar fight in another locale. No matter the underlying merit of such challenges, stakeholder risk-averseness enables a broad chilling effect that limits the circulation of taboo texts, especially in schools, even in the absence of formal governmental restrictions. As Linda M. Christensen offers in her response to Henly, "Sometimes it's the specter of a finger-shaking mama and papa that keeps us from taking risks. Sometimes it's our misunderstanding of our students' or our own capabilities" and that, as a result, as a friend reminds her, "our greatest censors live in our own heads" (Randall et al. 22).

While some objections to the novel used overheated rhetoric, the novel really does contain a wealth of strong sexual content and difficult themes. The novel features a pedophilic character and his apostasy,[51] multiple frank and extended descriptions of sexual acts, and the clear implication that a woman in the novel derives sexual pleasure from her pet cat. The most contentious scene, though, is the rape of Pecola by her father, which is more integral to the plot and character development than these while also being described in graphic terms. In the 1950s and '60s, such scenes and characters would have been grounds for censorship, but by the time Morrison was writing, obscenity standards were more permissive—at least for content aimed at adults. Nonetheless, in an era of more subtle forms of censorship, it is the most commonly cited reason to restrict access to the book.

Local debates follow a script necessitated by the *Miller* ruling in which a reader/parent/activist objects to the presence of *individual* taboo elements and free speech activists respond by championing the merit of the work *as a whole*. However, discussions of just what the whole of the book is like are often—ironically—elliptical. Defenders of the book point to Morrison's prestige as an author; the book's notable aesthetic elements; its important themes of decolonization, colorism and racism; and so on, while avoiding sustained analysis of the difficult portions themselves. Still, rigor demands treating the taboo representations not as offset by other redeeming qualities of the book from which it is fundamentally distinct, but as interwoven with the other elements in ways that shape their meaning.

As readers, we are repulsed by the scene of the rape of eleven-year-old Pecola by her father and horrified at her victimization. Readers might wish to rush on and simply take the fact of the rape as a plot point without needing to experience it in narrative time, and yet Morrison lingers for over two pages, describing the event step-by-step, not as a datum we might situate and control, but as a story we suffer through. Morrison, for example, runs through Cholly's thoughts not as a list but as a progression, telling us, "Cholly saw her dimly and could not tell what he saw or what he felt. *Then* he became aware that he was uncomfortable; *next* he felt the discomfort dissolve into pleasure. *The sequence of his emotions was* revulsion, guilt, pity, *then* love" (Morrison, *Bluest Eye*, 161, emphasis added). The temporal markers (*then*, *next*, and so on) emphasize that we are not being given a reflective, synthetic description of feelings felt simultaneously, but a series of actions, occurring in time, from which we cannot escape (save to close the book). Instead, we must move through them at Cholly's pace, which heightens our discomfort and mirrors Pecola's victimization. There is more here than the mute fact of the rape, and Morrison compels us to find it.

Similar to how Richard Wright worried that *Native Son* would be interpreted as proof of the racist stereotypes of African American sexual and familial pathology, so, too, was Morrison's novel subjected to concern that Cholly's reprehensible behavior would tend to authenticate, rather than contest, the imputed (but false) pathology of African American fathers. Some readers worried that Cholly's drunkenness, sexual deviance, and his eventual absence from the home would reify existing stereotypes of African American men in American society at large. Morrison's novel, however, offers several rebuttals to such claims. One of the most problematic ways the novel does this is by deeply humanizing its characters—including Cholly—through rich backstories that encourage us to see their malignancies as multifactorial, not entirely their own, and part of a complex human with merits as well as flaws. We are simultaneously compelled to see them as like us and repelled from them, perhaps even more repelled by their very humanity, which makes it hard to reject their failings as completely alien.

Cholly's backstory is central to this dynamic. As a young man, Cholly is in the midst of his first sexual encounter when he is interrupted and confronted with racism. This links his sexual identity with racialized self-hate in ways that make him seem psychologically damaged as a result of unjust forces outside his control. The chapter opens with a description of Cholly's difficult past, which included being abandoned by his mother when he was four days old. Because his father is absent, his great-aunt raises him, but even she leaves him alone when she dies, and, cheated by the insurance and overcharged by the undertaker, he winds up without family or property. In the midst of this sad situation, Cholly experiences a tender and even joyful moment of intimacy with a local girl named Darlene. He and a cousin walk her and another young woman around his deceased aunt's property during the funeral banquet. In a compellingly wrought scene, the four of them get lost in a playful reverie, savoring unripe muscadines that serve as a metaphor for sexual pleasure that comes more from anticipation than from richness of pleasure (Morrison, *Bluest Eye*, 145). As Cholly and Darlene get separated from the others, their interaction becomes tender and playful as they engage in foreplay and then intercourse, and the scene would be deeply endearing if it were not cut short.

Cholly nears climax in a foreboding double entendre—"Just as he felt an explosion threaten"—when he is brought back to himself by Darlene's startled cry at the sight of two white men armed with rifles and laughing at them. Cholly tries to dress, but one of the men lowers his gun and says, "Ged on wid it nigger" (Morrison, *Bluest Eye*, 148). Distraught, wracked by hate and fear, Cholly attempts to simulate sex with Darlene, but the men, shining a flashlight on the scene, gleefully complain that he "aint doing nothing for her" (148). The moment sours for Cholly and the man's flashlight "wormed its way into his guts and turned the sweet taste of muscadine into rotten fetid bile" (148). The transformation of the pleasure and tenderness into hate and resentment is deeply hurtful. Like Cholly, we are shocked and saddened by the incident while Morrison also undoes the stereotype of the black brute by portraying Cholly as deeply vulnerable.

It is an artfully rendered moment rich with complex symbolism, and it has a lasting impact on Cholly. The next day, he transmutes his feelings of impotence at the white hunters into hatred for Darlene. We read that "Sullen, irritable, he cultivated his hatred of Darlene. Never did he once consider directing his hatred toward the hunters. Such an emotion would have destroyed him. They were big, white, armed men. He was small, black, helpless" (150). His impotence has been transformed into anger at Darlene, the black girl whom he was with, because that is its only outlet. The book makes explicit that this hatred is misplaced for a reason beyond his control: If he had hated the white hunters, it "would have destroyed him." Morrison continues, "His subconscious knew what his conscious mind did not guess—that hating them would have consumed him, burned him up like a piece of soft coal, leaving only flakes of ash and a question mark of smoke" (150–51). In this situation, Cholly's hatred of Darlene becomes an expression of his impotence as a black man/child in a white supremacist world.

I think we must link this scene to Cholly's rape of Pecola. His hatred of Darlene is described in terms of her "baby claws" and other symbols of her innocence, such as the mussed blue ribbon in her hair. In addition, when he is developing his hatred of her, Darlene is described as "the one whom he had not been able to protect, to spare" (151). When Cholly rapes

Pecola, we encounter a similar mix of hatred and tenderness that implies continuity between the scenes. In the early phases of grappling with confused emotions before the rape, he wonders to himself:

> What could he do for her—ever? What give her? What say to her? What could a burned-out black man say to the hunched back of his eleven-year-old daughter? . . . How dare she love him? . . . What was he supposed to do about that? Return it? How? What could his calloused hands produce to make her smile? What of his knowledge of the world and of life could be useful to her? What could his heavy arms and befuddled brain accomplish that would earn him his own respect, that would in turn allow him to accept her love? (161–62)

The guilt that he seems to feel emerges from his lack of self-worth and mirrors his feelings about the incident with Darlene. He doesn't deserve her love in part because he cannot effectively provide for her and because he cannot respect himself, which Morrison construes as a necessary precondition for reciprocal love. Morrison construes this abasement as deeply racialized; Cholly refers to himself as a "burned-out black man." Morrison's novel, then, presents us with a compelling picture of a child rapist that makes it more difficult to write off his crimes and forces us to grapple with them. With luck, this will be more productive in the end, as we are forced to contend with the wider social forces that cause such traumas, rather than taking bitter solace in a "one bad apple" explanation.

The fact that the novel humanizes Cholly makes it difficult for us to re-enact the logic of expulsion in which he is simply an aberration to cast out. Though we find his behavior repellent, we understand that it is fostered by a white supremacist culture that has stunted his development and burdened him with limited self-worth and a lack of power in his public and personal lives. The pathological behavior we observe in him becomes more than an indictment of him as an individual, but also a marker of the corruption of the system of racism Morrison is attacking. In fact, Morrison is clear that this was part of her vision, stating in the foreword that she endeavored "to avoid complicity in the demonization process Pecola was subjected to. That is, [she] did not want to dehumanize the characters who trashed Pecola and contributed to her collapse" (xii). Morrison seems particularly concerned with not offering readers an easy out by providing monsters to cast blame on—the very process of racial demonization she seeks to reject. Instead, she teases the raw wounds of society, which implicate us all.

In parallel to Slothrop's entanglement in the psychological determinism of empiricism, Cholly is enmeshed in the psychological determinism of white supremacy. Though Cholly is the agent of terrible things, we don't see him as fully agentive. However, this understanding of Cholly is problematic if carried to the level of the social. Specifically, this is the logic of the infamous *Moynihan Report* (officially titled *The Negro Family: The Case for National Action*). The report was issued in 1965 by the Office of Policy Planning and Research of the U.S. Department of Labor, which was then led by future UN Ambassador and U.S. Senator Daniel Patrick Moynihan. Arguing for the need to redress the negative economic and social legacies of slavery, the report suggests widespread Federal action "designed to have the effect, directly or indirectly, of enhancing the stability and resources of the Negro American family."[52] The goal of giving direct and indirect assistance to African American families in order to undo the structural burdens held over from slavery, Reconstruction, and Jim Crow seems laudable, but for several drawbacks.

First, the report enthusiastically advocated state surveillance of and intervention in families in communities of color. Though Moynihan and those aligned with him viewed their work as an important extension of civil rights, the report and the actions it encouraged were intrusive and paternalistic.[53] In fact, they participate in a larger ideological project of misidentifying difference as pathology—paving the way for state intervention in the lives of already marginalized people.[54] Moreover, as Roderick Ferguson demonstrates, this move was invested in restrictive forms of normativity: "Moynihan's text ... enabled a nationalist discourse that understood non-heteronormative racial difference as deviant. Moreover, the discourse of black matriarchy justified and promoted the regulatory practices of the state and the exploitative practices of global capital" (Ferguson 111). Ferguson is working through the ways that well-meaning progressive efforts to advance equality often relied on ideological groundings that propped up the larger capitalist system that generated these exclusions.[55] Thus, though ostensibly arguing for what later becomes known as Affirmative Action, Moynihan relies on a deeply heteropatriarchal logic of exclusion that pathologizes female power, non-normative kinship structures, and reluctance to participate in capitalist economic modes.

The report's most notorious section is devoted to what Moynihan labels the "tangle of pathology" afflicting African American families. His comments on matriarchy, in particular, stress the need for aggressive norming underlying the report.[56] Though noting, for example, "There is, presumably, no special reason why a society in which males are dominant in family relationships is to be preferred to a matriarchal arrangement," he goes on to conclude that assimilation to the norm is desirable—is cause for action—because: "It is clearly a disadvantage for a minority group to be operating on one principle, while the great majority of the population, and the one with the most advantages to begin with, is operating on another" (Moynihan 29). Despite protestations against normativity, then, Moynihan clearly constructs a notion of the appropriate family structure, and it is modeled on middle-class white families. The report implies that it should be patriarchal,[57] heterosexual, and two-parent; its male members should serve in the military;[58] and it should encourage enthusiastic dedication to American civic, economic, and religious institutions.[59] As Berger points out, the Moynihan Report signals a change in U.S. racial politics.[60] For some on the left, it was intended as the foundation for progressive policies extending the work of civil rights. As Moynihan himself writes, its intent was to move beyond legal assurances of liberty and promote the establishment of equity. However, it also shifted the blame for a lack of equality from institutional discrimination to imputed failings within communities of color themselves.[61]

More importantly for my analysis here, by centering perceived cultural deviations within African American communities as a primary factor in economic inequality, the report reified white notions of African American pathology. The victim-blaming inherent in Moynihan's use of the phrase "tangle of pathology" becomes starkly clear when we compare it to Patricia Hill Collins alternative "matrix of domination."[62] Both phrases suggest overlapping regimes that call for new and complex solutions. However, while Collins's use of "domination" suggests regimes of power and historical injustice while calling for resistance, Moynihan's "pathology" suggests personal failures and the threat of infection while underwriting calls for surveillance. Such a distinction recalls Rose M. Brewer's reminder that while on the one hand "Most analyses of the underlying causes have been filled with normative assumptions about what is proper and improper familial behavior, and, consequently, social scientists have labeled the family formation practices of the black population 'inappropriate,'" on the other hand, "such empirical findings and analyses lack critical perspectives on the political and economic structures that provide the milieu for family formation strategies and emphasize the human capital disabilities of the black population in general, and of black women specifically."[63] Brewer's formulation mirrors the division between the assumption that any deviance is inherent and detrimental and the opposite assumption that would locate any perceived deviance from normative standards within a larger framework that accounts for a history of racism and other intersecting factors, including class and gender.

The report was widely criticized, and those critiques are well catalogued; however, it makes sense to note here the work of Hortense Spillers, which bears on how Morrison's work fits into the larger themes I'm addressing. Spillers argues that Moynihan takes for granted and perpetuates an epistemology under which "ethnicity" and similar markers of cultural belonging/non-belonging become signs of absence or difference from an established norm.[64] This is borne out in Moynihan's assertion that it is not matriarchy *per se* that causes social ills for African Americans, but the distance from the white norm. Spillers's second point is one that I have outlined previously: The report justifies intrusive state intervention. For Spillers, Moynihan is only representative of a deeper tropological vein in American culture: "Moynihan's 'Negro Family,' then, borrows its narrative energies from the grid of associations, from the semantic and iconic folds buried deep in the collective past, that come to surround and signify the captive person" (Spillers, "Mama's," 69). Spillers's description of the means by which U.S. culture others the victims of its exclusions echoes the situation of Wright: both *Native Son* and *The Bluest Eye* demonstrate that the web of symbolic captivity has many filaments. Not only are individuals subjected to this logic and public policy driven by it, but symbolic representations must be crafted to negotiate this discursive background in order to effect political ends. In effect, the Moynihan rule, as Spillers phrases it (66), ensures that efforts to decolonize U.S. culture or those marginalized by it run the risk of deep interpellation within the discursive system of white supremacy.

Scholars have interpreted Morrison's work through the lens of the Moynihan Report before, notably Eden Osucha (*Paradise*), James Berger (*Beloved*), Ferguson (*Sula*), and Gillan (*The Bluest Eye*). Many see the Moynihan Report as directly relevant because those novels often grapple with the issues of race, family structures, and the legacies of slavery that Moynihan also wrote about, and because her novels are historically coincident with the period when Moynihan's report carried the most cultural weight. Moreover, the situations of her stories seem frequently to overlap with the matriarchal family structures described by Moynihan and to explore the relationship between the legacies of slavery and continuing inequality. However, most critics find that Morrison's novels do not recapitulate Moynihan's logic, but rather correct it by offering alternative vectors from the same point of departure.

Osucha notes that early reviews of *The Bluest Eye* tended to view the novel as historical record or sociological tract rather than a work of art. These early reviews took the situations in the novel for granted as being realistic rather than imaginative, a reflection of the habit of readers to treat ethnic fiction as representative of marginalized lifeways instead of as imaginative exploration of possible lives.[65] They seemed to recognize and reify the stereotypes that form the backdrop for Morrison's novel while failing to see how she shifts and undermines those stereotypes. In the end, Osucha sees *Paradise* as a novel that corrects the story Moynihan tells about the condition of racial inequality by offering an alternative social arrangement in the women from the Convent. Like Osucha, Ferguson notes that Morrison's earlier novel *Sula* seems on the surface to recapitulate the black matriarchy discourse that Moynihan encapsulates, but that it also "suggests alternative readings" (Ferguson 125). Ferguson is primarily interested in demonstrating how black feminists were able to use *Sula* to envision non-normative modes of being. Applying similar readings to *The Bluest Eye*, Gillan examines Pauline Breedlove to demonstrate economic forces that held white family structures off-limits for African Americans while still insisting on them as cultural norms; she considers Cholly Breedlove to unpack the hypocrisy of expectations about how African American men should perform patriarchal masculinity given the systematic rape that attended slavery; and she interprets Pecola Breedlove as an example of the scapegoating inherent in the Moynihan Report that would mislay the blame for these apparent failures. These critical analyses confirm that the Moynihan Report is a background element in the racial politics Morrison dramatizes. In all of these cases, Morrison emerges as an author deeply conversant in the rhetoric of pathologization, but who seeks to overturn it in complex ways.

One of the main points of the report is that matriarchy contributes to economic inequality for African Americans. Moynihan writes, "In essence, the Negro community has been forced into a matriarchal structure which, because it is so out of line with the rest of the American society, seriously retards the progress of the group as a whole and imposes a crushing burden on the Negro male and, in consequence, on a great many Negro women as well" (29). This seems to be echoed in an early passage from the novel. Pecola has come to stay with the MacTeers because Cholly has burned down their house. His failure as a father, leaving his children un-provided for and un-sheltered, makes him the subject of unsparing criticism in the community. Morrison writes in the voice of Mrs. MacTeer,

> [T]hat old Dog Breedlove had burned up his house, gone upside his wife's head, and everybody, as a result was outdoors.
> Outdoors, we knew, was the real terror of life. The threat of being outdoors surfaced frequently in those days. Every possibility of excess was curtailed with it. . . . To be put outdoors by a landlord was one thing—unfortunate, but an aspect of life over which you had no

control, since you could not control your income. But to be slack enough to put oneself outdoors, or heartless enough to put one's own kin outdoors—that was criminal. (Morrison, *Bluest Eye*, 17)

Cholly's actions are described in terms that clearly put the blame on him—regardless of the awareness of unequal economic conditions that might cause one to become bereft. After all, the black characters in the novel "could not control [their] income" and are at the mercy of Lorain's white society. The fact of the family breakup—as Pauline goes to live with her employers and the two children are sent to live with other families in the community—is inseparable from Cholly's crime. Moreover, Pauline then takes over the role of breadwinner once the family is reunited.

In this section, the novel links the home and the family structure to physical and economic deprivation. The MacTeers are relatively stable both as a family and an economic unit. In contrast, Cholly's act splits the family and puts economic burdens on others. This seems to create a community ethic where the failure of the family structure or of the father in particular is seen as having a direct correlation with the economic well-being of the family members. Cholly is castigated ruthlessly, in fact, for this failure: "Cholly Breedlove, then, a renting black, having put his family outdoors, had catapulted himself beyond the reaches of human consideration" (Morrison, *Bluest Eye*, 18). The novel, then, begins by staging the community as grappling with the economic and heteropatriarchal logics of the Moynihan Report: Families with failed fathers are a symptom and sometimes cause of economic hardships faced by the black community. At first, at least, rather than attack the economic inequalities ("since you could not control your income"), vitriol is directed at the family and those within it.

However, the novel also indicates that it is myopic to blame the traumatic events of the novel solely on the community or individuals. In one of the novel's important early passages, Claudia MacTeer describes how she and her sister Frieda reacted when their marigold seeds (planted as a magic ward to protect Pecola's unborn baby) failed to sprout:

> Quiet as it's kept, there were no marigolds in the fall of 1941. We thought, at the time, that it was because Pecola was having her father's baby that the marigolds did not grow. A little examination and much less melancholy would have proved to us that our seeds were not the only ones that did not sprout; nobody's did. Not even the gardens fronting the lake showed marigolds that year. But so deeply concerned were we with the health and safe delivery of Pecola's baby we could think of nothing but our own magic: if we planted the seeds,

and said the right words over them, they would blossom, and everything would be all right. (5)

In this passage, Claudia and Frieda blame themselves for the failure of the seeds and by extension the failure of "everything [to] be all right." And yet, she reproaches her younger self for her limited perspective that circumscribed the blame too narrowly, saw only their own failings and not the broader world's. It was not only their own marigolds that failed to bloom; nobody's did. This includes not only their neighbors and other black families, but the "gardens fronting the lake," where the wealthy white families in Lorain live. In this metaphor, then, it is incorrect to look only to yourself or your community for blame when things like this go wrong; it is more appropriate to recognize that the corruption runs far and wide. That is, society as a whole bears the blame. In this sense, Morrison is refuting the victim-blaming logic of the Moynihan Report and those who would co-opt it through a sophisticated staging and reversal of these assumptions that requires careful reading (often re-reading) to piece together.[66]

Morrison's effort to implicate us in Cholly's transgressions were conscious and deliberate. In fact, in remarking on the intimate tone of the passage above, Morrison wrote that

> the intimacy I was aiming for, the intimacy between the reader and the page, could start up immediately because the secret is being shared, at best, and eavesdropped upon, at the least. Sudden familiarity or instant intimacy seemed crucial to me then, writing my first novel. I did not want the reader to have time to wonder, "What do I have to do, to give up, in order to read this? What defense do I need, what distance maintain?" Because I know ... that this is a terrible story about things one would rather not know anything about.[67]

This lengthy passage provides multiple insights that give the lie to the narrative of obscene pathology and suggest that readers selectively refused to apply the narrative of obscene genius to Morrison. Note, for example, that Morrison adapts her artistic choices (shaping diction and tone achieve an effect that she calls "conspiratorial" [147], for example) specifically to the knowledge that her subject is taboo. In that way, the form of the novel is linked intricately with its obscene content. There is more than a simple coexistence of virtuosic literary ability and repulsive material; the material is part of the virtuosity. This would seem to make Morrison a prime candidate for that component of the narrative of obscene genius. And yet, while Morrison's simple phrasing was meant by her to create that conspiratorial feeling and thus shock readers more profoundly, it was taken as a mark of underdeveloped literary talent.

Therefore, despite the seeming overlap with Moynihan's logic, *The Bluest Eye* works from this early moment to complicate the pernicious pathologizing discourses of the late 1960s. Cholly's pathology is explained and humanized as the result of a number of factors, each of which can be ascribed to individual bad actors (the white hunters, his father) or to random fate (the death of Aunt Jimmy) or to social forces beyond individual control (lack of economic opportunity). The narrative of his development is not easily distilled to a single ailment corresponding to a single balm. Cholly's young life and adult transgressions enact the broad pattern Moynihan attempts to describe, and yet we are not able to easily return to the generalizing abstraction of sociology. The novel believes in more complicated notions of cause and effect.

In this context, Morrison's refusal to make Cholly an easy scapegoat even for acts he commits himself is precisely the intended project both aesthetically and politically. In fact, Gillan argues that "Contrary to the Moynihan Report's claim that it is the matriarchal structure of the black family that imposes a 'crushing burden on the black male,' Morrison demonstrates that it is the attempt to embrace patriarchy that crushes Cholly's spirit" (292). In this sense, African American matriarchy is not the reason Cholly fails as a human being, but rather, he fails because of the insistence on certain racialized performances of masculinity that are foreclosed to him. By refusing us the easy comfort of blaming a single individual, Morrison also puts off-limits the habit of emphasizing individual culpability and blaming members of marginalized groups for moral failures. Instead, through the characters' psychological complexity and the multifaceted role social forces play in their behavior, Morrison forces the reader to contend with broad social and institutional forces. This redirection of attention is what the Moynihan report no doubt attempted to do, anxiously reassuring readers that the legacy of slavery, Reconstruction, and Jim Crow were to blame and not African American individuals themselves.

This is the complex bind that the narrative of obscene pathology presents for writers of color. Morrison's novel engages with culturally salient problematic epistemologies of race and sociology, but its insightful complication of those logics requires careful reading and attention to be enumerated, while the novel's obscenity controversies tend to stifle the sustained, deliberate analyses necessary to do this—as well as distracting from Morrison's multifaceted narrative. In this way, the story of Pecola nearly parallels that of Kim Phúc in Ut's photo. There, as here, discomfort over possible obscenity distracts audiences from the victimization being revealed, highlighting how discourses of morality serve to prop up a violent status quo.

First, in the narrative strand that explains Pecola's self-hatred, Morrison engages in the incomplete—if productive—logic of the Clarks' doll tests, which contributed to the end of segregation but also created a harm-mentality legacy that has been used to falsely pathologize African Americans and justify individual, rather than structural, approaches to social justice. Second, in the story that traces the causes of Cholly's actions, Morrison takes on the logic of the Moynihan Report, which sought to ameliorate economic inequality, but ended up creating justifications for racialized austerity. Thus, both major lines of the narrative dramatize narratives of racial justice that were in vogue at the time of the novel's publication, but which have since been deemed problematic.

This problematic nexus of competing liberal, New Left, and neoconservative politics undoubtedly plays a role in the continuing controversies over the novel in schools. One suspects that if the book presented a more simplistically affirmative image of African American family life *or* if it provided easier solutions to thorny racial issues, it might be better received. Berger argues that Morrison's *Beloved* "revives the liberal position of Frazier, Myrdal, and Moynihan" during the late 1980s, when they had been largely eschewed, and *The Bluest Eye* is often erroneously assumed to be doing something similar in the early 1970s, when the Moynihan Report and its pathologization of black communities was viewed negatively by the New Left and Black Nationalists.[68]

The reception of Morrison's novel seems to echo the primary narrative of obscene pathology that I suggested affected *Native Son*. Her novel was controversial because of its sexual representations, and these controversies have tended to obscure the important political message of the novel. This is due to a number of factors, but one is simply that a large number of casual readers (and critics) tend to approach Morrison's work with overly reductive assumptions about the content of her novels. What I mean to evoke here is a tendency in popular criticism of work by this particular Nobel Prize–winning novelist that supposes it is sufficient to know that her books are about race in some way and not necessary to know more particularly that, for example, *The Bluest Eye* is about beauty standards and colorism, that *Beloved* is about slavery and motherhood, or that *A Mercy* (2008) is about the birth of legal hierarchies in colonial-era America. Stripped of specificity, then, each novel is even more apt to have meanings imposed on it from without and even more likely to be subject to suspicion and sanction based on what it *might* mean or what it is *supposed* to mean, rather than what interpretations the text itself privileges, enables, or justifies.

As Osucha reminds us, contemporary popular reviews of *The Bluest Eye* "index the broad cultural impact of the Moynihan Report in its era, suggesting how *The Negro Family* reinforced a literary discourse of racial authenticity by linking it to the report's discursive authority" (Osucha 263). In other words, reception of Morrison's first novel tended to center on a strain of racial thinking from literary studies in the mid- to late century that imagines all literary work by writers from marginalized groups as being first and foremost a sociological documentation of life in those communities, with their merit as works of literary merit judged according to the extent to which they match existing notions of those communities. Morrison's novel, then, was judged on the grounds that it appeared to recapitulate dominant understandings of African American families that could be traced to the Clarks' doll tests and the recently released Moynihan Report. Importantly, though, Morrison was empowered, through her hard-fought place in the American literary world, to push back against these narratives while consciously seeking to free her own artistry from these narratives imposed from without, as well as to free future generations of writers to do the same.

Conclusion

As with Wright's and Miller's novels, *Gravity's Rainbow* and *The Bluest Eye* represent major literary works that evince similarities in content but divergent fates in terms of censorship and controversy. Both texts include scenes of pedophilia, rape, and incest, and both novels make it difficult to condemn the perpetrators of these acts by densely embroidering their histories to demonstrate their interpellation into broader structures onto which blame is partially deflected. Reflecting the racial divide at the root of the narratives of obscene genius and pathology, rather than experiencing parallel literary afterlives, Morrison's text is subject to more frequent and more multifaceted challenges. The reasons for this are varied, ranging from the almost mundane to those with deep cultural significance.

Earlier, I referred to McGurl's schema for post-war literature that included the category of technomodernism (into which he classes Pynchon's work) and high cultural pluralism (into which he classes Morrison). In describing how an author might make their mark on American Literature in either vein, McGurl echoes the notion of divergent paths I have described:

The high cultural pluralist writer is additionally called upon to speak from the point of view of one or another hyphenated population, synthesizing the particularity of the ethnic—or analogously marked—voice with the elevated idiom of literary modernism. Thus, while one path to literary distinction in the postwar period has been to assert the themes of technomodernism, another, though sometimes overlapping, path has been to forge a career in literary cultural pluralism.[69]

In this passage, McGurl is describing dual paths to "literary distinction," what I have discussed primarily as canonicity. It's worth noting that he says these authors are "called upon" to speak for their racial or ethnic communities. We can infer that the larger bifurcation is an involuntary one for writers of color and those from other marginalized communities. Essentially, McGurl's schema acknowledges that the high cultural pluralist tradition, while afforded the prestige of high modernist (or postmodernist) modes, is nonetheless a space into which writers are involuntarily thrust and from which position their work is forced, required, or expected to engage directly with issues of identity and representation specific to their communities. While writers like Pynchon are given the privilege to speak for the nation from the perch of technomodernism, writers like Morrison struggle to be taken seriously against the erroneous notion that they are writers of little more than stylized ethnographies. McGurl will later argue that high cultural pluralism combines both the imperative to speak for one's identity group associated with multiculturalism and the pressure to establish individual genius that characterized modernism and late modernism (58–59). This suggests that he sees figures like Morrison as blurring the distinctions between the paths, and he later argues that technomodernism and high cultural pluralism are complementary, rather than diametrical.

For reasons that require careful parsing, however, the works of high cultural pluralism are much more often taught in schools, a factor that contributes to their being banned and challenged more frequently. McGurl notes, for instance, that minoritarian literature finds its way into the curriculum more readily: "Categories that more obviously split the national culture into smaller units are an easier sell for high cultural prestige leading to inclusion in the syllabus of postwar literature" (59). It is no surprise that schools—and public schools in particular—are a site of political contestations fought over race and sex. Public education in the United States is often seen as "the crucible of democratic citizenship and the conduit to capitalist opportunity" (Bergner 323). Since John Dewey and Horace Mann, education has been promoted as the place where democratic values and conscientious citizenship are instilled in children. It is seen as an equalizer, a vehicle for upward mobility, and a ward against oligarchy. Brennan's statement in the Abington decision—about school prayer—suggests this is partly because schools are tasked with securing the future of democracy. The Warren Court ruling in *Brown v. Board of Education*, which is one crucial context for Morrison's novel, also testifies to the role public education had in promoting racial, as well as economic, equality.[70] It can be said that *The Bluest Eye* became a source of controversy because it is often taught in the contested space of the public school. After all, Pynchon's work takes on many of these same themes and is arguably more transgressive and more ambivalent in its morality. That Morrison's novel has a place in the public schools should not, therefore, be overlooked as a cause of the controversy surrounding the novel.

Following other Warren Court rulings that liberalized obscenity standards, it was nearly impossible for any locality in the United States to limit adult access to any literary text of even passing—or even specious—social value. Consequently, debates over limiting access to such material for children took over most of the cultural work of negotiating the value of difficult content, the impacts of sexual representations, and the effects on readers of literary texts in general. *The Bluest Eye*, then, becomes a nexus for several intersecting public epistemologies: the innocence of children, racial justice and stereotypes, neoconservative pushback against the 1960s counterculture and the civil rights movement, and the shifting terrain of free speech debates. It is in this context that the narratives of obscene genius are furthered and altered.

However, there is something else under the surface here as well. There is a set of old antinomies shaping the narrative possibilities surrounding these texts. I refer to the division between international and domestic, paralleled by the division between the public and the private, paralleled by the division between the economy and the household. These old dichotomies help determine what spheres are open to certain writers and certain subjects. In this case, the juxtaposition of Pynchon's and Morrison's texts further reveals that this ideological division—thoroughly policed by cultural critics and the educational structures I described a moment ago—also underwrites some dimensions of the narratives of obscene genius and obscene pathology.

The spheres of global politics, technology, and economics are symbolically policed to be white male spaces (often classed as universal or historical), and they are also the privileged terrain on which genius is won. Conversely, writers such as Morrison are presumed to have particular, local, and personal appeal that tends to foreclose their works from being classed works of genius. Conversely, while largely excluded from those international stages, they have privileged access to the narratives of pathology. This is because explorations of race and gender are often assumed to be particular in their application to certain people or groups while excluding the notion of universality marked as white and male. Similarly, the home—the space of devalued affective relations and devalued feminine labor—is also the primary site of a pathology that is always in itself classed as deviation from the universal norm. In fact, pathology is itself nothing more than deviation marked as undesirable and constrained by the particular, embroidered with metaphors of contamination and surveillance, while genius is deviation marked as desirable and pointing toward the universal. *Gravity's Rainbow* and *The Bluest Eye*, then, demonstrate a new wrinkle in the counter-narratives of obscenity that links them to older divisions that have served to police racialized and gendered boundaries through centuries.

3 / Porn Wars and Pornotroping: Counter-Narratives of Obscenity amid Transitions in Feminist Activism

Kathy Acker, the author of over a dozen novels from the 1970s to the 1990s, sits topless on a motorcycle looking over her shoulder (see Figure 2). The photo, taken in 1991 outside the San Francisco Art Institute by Kathy Brew, has become iconic, appearing in a review of Acker's work in *The Village Voice* that year and in promotional material for the documentary *Who's Afraid of Kathy Acker* (2007). It is, essentially, about Acker's body—not the archetype of an author at work in thoughtful seclusion, but the bare body of a woman in the world. While we might resist sexualizing a female author out of a desire to treat her as an intellectual subject rather than an embodied one, in this case, Acker puts her own body into play, suggesting we reconsider the presumption that an embodied subject is not also an intellectual one.[1]

While the viewer might be drawn to Acker's defiant gaze, the photo is dominated by the elaborate tattoos on her back. Beneath the design ripple the strong contours of muscles and bones.[2] Because she is shirtless, a portion of a breast that will be removed six years later during a double mastectomy is visible.[3] Her nudity foregrounds her sexuality and the shock value of the naked form, while her short hair, muscular body, and aggressive pose highlight her transgression of feminine norms. Acker's pose reveals her willingness to champion the body as a site of power and contestation of gender and sexual norms, while the brazenness of this public spectacle demonstrates the high value the author places on this ideological site, even as society demands the body be hidden from view. Though often a site of oppression, the body emerges in this image and

FIGURE 2. Photo of Kathy Acker by Kathy Brew, 1991 © Kathy Brew. Used by permission.

in Acker's work as an important locus of resistance. This photograph, then, inaugurates a discussion of how the body, in its non-normative manifestations and through its visibility, can reveal the contours of a complex politics of sex and culture at the end of the 1970s and beginning of the 1980s that illuminate the twinned narratives of obscenity I have been charting.

The so-called "sex wars" were characterized by debates among feminists and in culture broadly about the role of sex, desire, and particularly pornography in gender power imbalances. Simultaneously, women advocated for greater freedom in sexual, marital, and reproductive economies, seeking to liberalize sexual norms and reduce stigmas associated with sexual expression. At the same time, however, mainstream feminism was coming under fire from lesbians and women of color for heterosexist and racist practices and assumptions. Women of color were responding to specific histories of embodiment that included tropes of hyper-sexualization, dehumanization, and exoticism. Thus, sex, which had been a site of oppression and objectification, did not offer easy or equal avenues of resistance to all women. This aspect of the struggle over the place of women's bodies is powerfully evoked by many of the writers in Cherríe Moraga and Gloria Anzaldúa's *This Bridge Called My Back* (1981). The collection of essays presents an impassioned call for a voice for women of color and others excluded from second-wave feminism and marks a major turning point in the development of third-wave feminism.

In order to illuminate certain cross-currents in this conflict of ideologies and to show how the afterlives of obscene literary works diverge along racial lines, I will turn to two novels from this moment that are deeply embedded in its sexual politics. First, I consider Acker's *Blood and Guts in High School* (1984), an important novel that dramatizes the twisted demands patriarchy places on women's subjectivity.[4] I juxtapose this novel with Alice Walker's roughly contemporaneous novel *The Color Purple* (1982), which is much more widely read and studied, and which provides an important alternative perspective that avoids what could be described as the abstracting postmodernism of Acker's novel, while also counterbalancing it with a consideration of how sexual and racial politics intersect.

A comparative reading is initially suggested by superficial overlaps between the novels. For example, both begin with incestuous rapes that cause the protagonists difficulty in understanding their subjectivity and forming attachments to others.[5] On a deeper level, both novels engage primarily with the possibilities (and limitations) of women's identity in a world governed by a social order that not only privileges men, but silences women's voices through sexual violence and predicates social participation on adherence to family norms that elevate the father's prerogatives over all others. Both novels also sparked controversy for their sexual content, as I will describe. The novels have their distinct differences, too, such as their form, their engagement with race and sexuality, and the trends in their reception. It is this combination of stark differences with notable similarities that makes them a productive juxtaposition because, like the texts in Chapter 2, they reveal how similar content can be received in dramatically different ways as a result of ongoing structures of racism that shape the literary landscape.

"Speaking Desire Out Loud": Resistive Sexualities in Second-Wave Feminism

> War, if not the begetter of all things, certainly the hope of all begetting and pleasures. For the rich and especially for the poor. War, you mirror of our sexuality.
>
> KATHY ACKER, *Empire of the Senseless*, 26

In the preceding quote, one of the central figures in Acker's 1988 novel *Empire of the Senseless* ruminates on the birth of piracy as a flowing into the workforce of the de-mobbed soldiers of nationalist wars in the sixteenth century.[6] The erotic allure of violence is coupled with the unrestrained pursuit of pleasure as a metaphor of sex in patriarchy. I turn to this passage because it highlights the connections between violence, pleasure, and capital that underpin Acker's unorthodox intervention in second-wave feminism. Understanding sex as an economy and patriarchy as a labor hierarchy allows Acker to create fictional worlds that critique what she sees as the underlying principles of status quo power structures in the late twentieth century through grotesque hyperbole. Because it is conveyed through explicit depictions of abusive, often criminal, sexual acts, the feminist critique running through Acker's body of work frequently teases the border of obscenity, and *Blood and Guts in High School* was banned in Germany and Australia as a possible threat to minors. These novels and her essays appear in the context of disagreement within the feminist movement about the status of bondage, sadomasochism, pornography, and other sex acts and representations. Acker was unabashedly partisan in these disagreements; she understood the dangers of exploitative sexual economies and cultural systems, but she also saw in the body and in sexual pleasure opportunities for women's liberation. She imagined these possibilities in her novels, and in her essays she responded to those, such as prominent anti-pornography activists Andrea Dworkin and Catharine MacKinnon, whom she saw as infantilizing women or foreclosing avenues of empowerment.

However, using sex and sexuality in this way also enacts a critical ignorance of the very contrary experiences of women of color. Acker's work, though periodically engaging race in her characteristically convoluted way, nonetheless enacts a sexual politics that takes its bearings from a particular cultural and historical perspective that was not available to all women. Because older cultural metanarratives depicted white women as having no autonomous sexuality, expressing one's own sexual desire—especially one that was shocking or taboo—took on political tones by resisting these patriarchal tropes. In sharp distinction, women of color were responding to a cultural history that often construed them as having no subjectivity *except* via sexuality. Thus, in this context, embracing sex and sexuality ran the risk of reaffirming, rather than contesting, dominant representations, especially for African American women in the long shadow of rape and concubinage under slavery.

I turn to Acker, then, in order to foreground only the first step in understanding a complex moment in sexual representations in which the charge of obscenity reveals the multiform operations of sexual politics as it operates to enforce both gender and racial hierarchies. While explicit sexuality serves emancipatory purposes in some cultural contexts, it serves oppressive purposes in others. By considering this moment, we can see not only that obscenity itself is fluid in this regard, but that the underlying sexual oppression under patriarchy is *also* flexible to the point of sustaining profound contradictions. These contradictions converge in the effort to resolve a question of praxis of which Acker represents (but does not exhaust) an important vector.

Like both her political allies and the anti-pornography activists with whom she found herself at odds, Acker's interest in explicitly rendered, dominance-themed sexuality is rooted in a concern over power dynamics. Nonetheless, while her thinking is informed by the same writers and theorists other feminists were responding to, her tactics were often extreme and even those who agreed with her underlying ideals often objected to Acker's methods. Thus, Acker's relationship to feminism is somewhat fraught; Cynthia Carr calls her "a feminist by instinct, at war with feminist orthodoxy."[7] While the reference to instinct belies the deeply theoretical background informing her writings, the point about the seemingly haphazard and often provocative nature of Acker's work is spot on. As is often the case with postmodernist authors, critics have wondered if Acker's work has, or *can* have, a political valence. For her part, Acker has always been cognizant of the contradictory nature of her stylistic and political projects and attempted to grapple with—if not resolve—them.[8] Acker's pursuit of this perhaps-impossible goal has led her outside the conventions of literary fiction, and Nicola Pitchford argues that the resulting postmodern play with language is actually fundamentally, rather than accidentally, political. She explains, "The question that runs throughout Kathy Acker's work is how people outside the mainstream of power—primarily women, but also men of color, gay men, and the poor—can claim agency when in fact ... their identities [are] defined within existing systems of language and power."[9] Owing to the poststructuralist linguistic thinking Pitchford alludes to, Acker's novels examine the interpellation of women (and others) in language and the negotiation of subjectivity that is at the root of sexual interactions, and they do so through the sometimes-problematic techniques of postmodernism.

Acker's method is heavily informed by the work of prominent poststructuralist and post-Freudian feminists of the 1970s and 1980s. The writing of Hélène Cixous is especially resonant with Acker's work and reveals what her fictions aim to dramatize.[10] No single document demonstrates these resonances as clearly as Cixous's "Castration or Decapitation," which appeared in French in 1976 and in English in 1981—a few short years before *Blood and Guts*. The essay lays out the fundamental difficulties of feminist praxis in a phallogocentric culture. Cixous ventriloquizes "Old Lacan takes up the slogan 'What does she want?' when he says, 'A woman cannot speak of her pleasure,'" before she continues, "It's all there, a woman cannot, is unable, hasn't the power. Not to mention 'speaking': it's exactly this that she's forever deprived of. Unable to speak of pleasure = no pleasure, no desire: power, desire, speaking, pleasure, none of these is for woman" (45). In this passage, Cixous identifies the psychoanalytic construction wherein a lack of access to language and desire constitutes a lack of subjectivity and power for women. Dramatizing the effects of this foreclosure, Acker's female protagonists are tormented by their lack of access to sexual and subjective agency. They compulsively seek to speak, to overcome the barriers Cixous identifies, and they will very specifically seek to speak their pleasure, to name it and call it into being.

Countering the notion that sexual desire is too insignificant for serious analysis, Cixous reassures us that there is a lot at stake. She writes that the underlying principle in the logic of the couple is difference, and the logic of difference structures the most rampant and insidious inequalities. She contends that women

> have it in them to affirm the difference, *their* difference, such that nothing can destroy that difference, rather that it might be affirmed, affirmed to the point of strangeness. So much so that . . . when the preservation or dissolution of sexual difference, is touched on, the whole problem of destroying the strange, destroying all the forms of racism, all the exclusions, all those instances of outlaw [*rapports de mise hors-la-loi*] and genocide that recur through History, is also touched on. (Cixous 50)

Here she speaks to the stakes of an analysis of sexual politics in conjunction with other fields of oppression and to the value of an artistic project such as Acker's. Through Acker's efforts to undermine the binary that privileges male desire while making women only objects of that desire, we are able to explore alternatives to the most significant inequalities of the twentieth century. In this way, we might turn an examination of pornography and the transgressive exhibition of the body and desire toward the subversion of hierarchies and subjection in culture at large.

Anti-Porn Feminism and Sex-Positive Pushback

Despite her stated desire to use sexual expression in service of a more equal and open society, Acker inspired negative reactions for her style and tone, as well as for her explicit content and its potentially regressive effects. In 1984, for example, Roy Hoffman condemned Acker's *Blood and Guts* as "abusive to women." Though he acknowledged the parodic elements of Acker's depiction of a girl made a slave by patriarchy, he deemed it a failed parody, a book that recapitulates, rather than challenges, what it aims to undermine.[11] Hoffman's review is representative of criticism that acknowledges Acker's feminist politics, while remaining skeptical that her novels accord with a feminist praxis. Friedman reminds us: "Some mainstream feminists . . . take her work seriously enough to condemn it as pornography. Since her language is crude . . . and she graphically depicts sadomasochistic sexual acts, they view her work as misogynistic; the pornographic sequences typical in it, they argue (quite correctly) would never be tolerated in the work of men."[12] These critiques rightly suggest that a work can have a life independent of its author's politics and that Acker's professions to liberatory politics don't necessarily mean that the works have that effect. However, they also ring hollow in the face of Acker's actual depictions of sex, which tend toward the grotesque or comic rather than erotic, with exposition in stilted psychoanalytic or philosophical language. Scenes, then, that might belong in a pornographic movie are accompanied by their own absurd theoretical commentary that diffuses erotic potential and redirects the reader to the political issues being examined.

The critiques of Acker's work represent a strain of thought and activism rejecting depictions of sexuality that dramatize the play of dominance. Figures like Dworkin and MacKinnon argued that porn, no matter the narrative or coupling or specific content, was inherently demeaning to women because it engaged in male power fantasies and dramatized heterosexuality's subjugation of women.

For example, in 1981, Dworkin argued, "The major theme of pornography as a genre is male power, its nature, its magnitude, its use, its meaning" and that, moreover, this theme is evident not only in the actual media in question, but in the process of creating and distributing it: "These strains of male power are intrinsic to both the substance and production of pornography; and the ways and means of pornography are the ways and means of male power."[13] Using this rubric, where pornography constitutively reifies male privilege, normalizes patriarchy, and demeans women, Dworkin agitated for strict controls on its production. This approach became known both as the civil rights approach to antipornography activism and, more pejoratively, as sex-negative feminism. Using this logic, Dworkin and MacKinnon convinced local governments to pass anti-pornography statutes in Minneapolis, Indianapolis, and other municipalities on the grounds that the creation, distribution, and viewing of pornography violated women's civil rights.[14]

Though sharing the same goals, Dworkin's unequivocal rhetoric and methods put her at odds with feminists like Acker as she indicted both pornography and sexuality *as such* (a potential site of empowerment for Acker) as complicit in the oppression of women by men. Dworkin found success in the public sphere, but contemporary theorists found the underlying arguments unconvincing. Judith Butler intervened, contending that if we reduce pornography to a direct instantiation of male privilege at every level, then it would be impossible for it to give rise to an awareness of this very fact; it would simply enact its violence in every instance and never be the ground of reflection.[15] Dworkin and Butler, then, demonstrate through their own analysis that pornography can, in fact, give rise to thoughtful reflection. Butler further contends that such criticisms of pornography misunderstand the relationship between fantasy and reality and rely on a "set of untheorized presumptions" (105) that creates a theoretical impossibility in which "the real is positioned both before and after its representation; and representation becomes a moment of the reproduction and consolidation of the real" (106).

While it is important to acknowledge the real power imbalances that result from and are widespread in the pornography industry, to condemn the body of pornographic material as well as the genre itself neglects the affirmative potential of, for example, queer and feminist porn.[16] In addition, broad attacks on porn often presume sex workers lack agency, which sex workers themselves reject. In a 1987 polemic against those she considers "sex-negative" feminists, including Dworkin, porn performer Nina Hartley contends that, rather than genre, "*What really matters is time, place, degree, mutuality and consent. I believe that a woman is capable of consent. If we aren't granted that one prerogative then we are not being granted full adult status.* **Either women are capable of managing their sexual lives or they are not**" (emphasis in the original).[17] Thus, for Hartley, a woman's freedom to engage in sex work and to control her body, her pleasure, and her labor is a necessary part of full subjecthood.[18] Pitchford echoes the sentiment, contending that she "finds in the rhetoric of antipornography critiques" of Acker's work (and that of Angela Carter) "that the tendency to treat all representations as necessarily reproducing oppressive consciousness results in a static, oppositional model of difference that leaves women without agency and threatens to erase the differences among them" (155). Thus Pitchford and Hartley sound consonant notes, arguing that restrictions placed on women's sexual practices infantilize women, even in situations where objectification is a very real danger. In this debate, we see the contours of a broader schism about what constitutes a responsible politics of sex and the body that impacted how Acker's transgressive works were received. Dworkin sees sex work and pornography as inherently demeaning, while Hartley sees sexuality and explicit depictions of sex as only one part of a broad spectrum of representations and actions in which "*time, place, degree, mutuality and consent*" are more important than genre.

I have catalogued somewhat extensively the work of Dworkin and the rhetoric of the porn wars because Acker was deeply suspicious of Dworkin's activism and took issue with her politics in both fiction and non-fiction—directly naming Dworkin in interviews and even passingly casting her as a villain in the novel *Don Quixote: Which Was a Dream* (1986).[19] Acker also critiques what she calls Dworkin's "dualistic argument that men are responsible for all the evil in the world" and says that "Her views go beyond sexism. She blames the act of penetration in sexual intercourse. I find that view not only mad but dangerous. With all the problems in the world, such a view doesn't do feminism any good" (qtd. in Friedman, "Conversation").[20] The reason Acker might find this view dangerous is explained by Pitchford, who notes, "Not only does the concept of sexual pleasure become severely limited if one eliminates all sexual practices found in male representation; more importantly, the concept of 'women' grows equally exclusive if defined solely through its opposition to a monolithic notion of hegemonic (i.e., white, straight) masculinity" (153–54). A too-restrictive conception of sexuality, then, limits the forms of subjectivity feminism can speak for; as such, Dworkin's efforts can alienate segments of the feminist coalition and limit its effectiveness on practical and theoretical levels.

These tensions over the status of the representations of sexuality and the body—especially pornography and other sexually explicit works—reveal the complexity of obscenity politics. Rather than focus on simplistic narratives of permissiveness or prudishness, we have to appreciate the dense web of intersecting and sometimes conflicting campaigns that can grow out of shared ideologies, as well as the strange bedfellows that sometimes result when groups with contrary beliefs (such as Dworkin and Christian conservatives) share near-term goals while disagreeing about fundamental principles.[21] Somewhat counterintuitively, then, the use of obscenity as an optic actually helps us avoid construing the roots of the problem as only a contestation over the status of sexual representations.

The important racial histories at stake in these debates ought not to be ignored because they demonstrate a certain privilege on the part of those who would condemn pornography and sex work so readily. Arguing that construing all heterosexual sexuality as equivalent in patriarchy—thus condemning both prostitution and marriage—stems from a limited and privileged worldview, Audre Lorde writes, "Poor and third world women know there is a difference between the daily manifestations and dehumanizations of marital slavery and prostitution, because it is our daughters who line 42nd Street."[22] Moraga echoes this sentiment, saying:

> unlike battered women's, anti-rape, and reproductive rights workers, the anti-porn "activist" never has to deal with any live women outside of her own race and class. The tactics of the anti-pornography movement are largely symbolic and theoretical in nature. . . .
> It is not that pornography is not a concern to many women of color. But the anti-materialist approach of this movement makes little sense in the lives of poor and Third World women. Plainly put, it is our sisters working in the sex industry.[23]

Thus, the abstracting position that conflates sex work, marriage, and other sexual interactions and relations erases the lived experiences of women, disproportionately privileging the viewpoint of women of higher economic classes and white women, while also removing the ground for material change in other sites. By looking at Acker's and Walker's novels together, we can trace their different and shared trajectories. Both were stridently feminist, both were challenged for their sexual content, both were concerned with the body's power. Their different trajectories, publication histories, and scholarly treatment reveal how racialized historical realities can profoundly shape literary afterlives.

Kathy Acker's Political Aesthetics and Aesthetic Politics

> The Law is not patriarchal because it denies the existence, even the power, of women. . . . The Law is patriarchal because it denies the bodies, the sexualities of women.
>
> KATHY ACKER, "Reading the Lack of the Body," 78–79

I begin tracking Acker's route to inclusion in the canon (such as it is) by looking more closely at how her efforts to explore subjectivity and its implication in power dynamics often foregrounded bodies. In fact, Acker called the body "the only place where any basis for real values exists anymore."[24] Acker's approach to embodiment grows out of a complex theoretical politics that resonates with her unconventional biography.[25] Acker studied at Brandeis and the CUNY Graduate Center, received a

B.A. from the University of California, San Diego, and was conversant in various schools of literary theory and philosophy, something her writing reflects in its esoteric allusions and complex engagement with language and subjectivity.[26] Importantly for my consideration of her political work, Acker was a student of Herbert Marcuse, an influence that can be seen in her attempts to dismantle political structures through a reconsideration of the subjective experience of sexuality. In a seeming contrast to this intellectual pedigree, Acker worked as a performer in a Times Square sex show early in her writing career.[27]

These widely divergent experiences result in work that combines both extreme cerebral and very visceral aspects. Friedman notes that Acker's texts are, paradoxically, "filled with sets of disrupted movements over which not even discontinuity rules" ("Now Eat," 37). The discontinuity Friedman describes nonetheless offers coherence in the circulation of certain concerns among vignettes within novels and across multiple texts. Carr describes recurrent situations, forming the basis for an understanding of the Acker corpus and its aesthetic project:

> Her female characters always struggle with dependence on two things they can't trust: language and love. Acker is part of a century-long tradition of writers, from Dadaists to deconstructionists, who rail at the limitations of the word. Her heroines seem interchangeable from book to book, different names tagged to the sound of one voice raging—obscene, cynical, bewildered, and demanding to fuck. They find their only truth in the body, in sexuality.

Carr's characterization is useful because it points to the revelations Acker's novels enable regarding the limitations of language, the resistive potential of the body, and the position of women in a masculine sexual economy, while inserting her into a long tradition that justifies her aesthetic style.

Though Acker's work has been described as "almost anti-literary" and "deliberately assaultive and overt" (Friedman, "Now Eat," 39), Carr's characterization reiterates the sophisticated (if not always serious) intellectual project of her novels, dissuading us from rejecting Acker's work as simply opaque or obscurantist—or perhaps crude. In fact, this aspect of Acker's style may speak to intersections with other feminist practices. In her evocation of the style of revolt particular to third-world women, Gloria Anzaldúa asserts, "*We revoke, we erase your white male imprint. When you come knocking on our doors with your rubber stamps to brand our faces with dumb, hysterical, passive puta, pervert, when you come with your branding irons to burn my property on our buttocks, we will vomit the guilt, self-denial and race-hatred you have force-fed into us right back into your mouth.*"²⁸

The labels "DUMB," "HYSTERICAL," and "PERVERT" easily attach to Acker's work with its simple vulgar language, its manic cadences, and its rampant explicit sexuality. Read in the context of Anzaldúa's embrace of the labels of transgression, Acker's work allows us to see some similarities among outsider work of this period, where what resists the status quo co-opts the system's attempt to denigrate its others. Nonetheless, patriarchal systems of language continue to attempt to refute the power of these outsider positions and taboo representations, discourage their circulation, and stamp their creators with the mark of abjection.

The role of obscenity in this is explicit. Because the limits of legal speech are functions of power, resisting them must sometimes transgress norms of modesty. Anzaldúa writes that her sense of revolt and of political responsibility compels her "to write about the unmentionables, never mind the outraged gasp of the censor and the audience" (169). Anzaldúa's commitment to the bodily in pursuit of a revolutionary feminist world is further evoked when she implores Third World Women, "*Don't let the censor snuff out the spark, nor the gags muffle your voice. Put your shit on the paper*" (173). The ground of political action must be this ground of "shit"—metaphorical but also literal; Anzaldúa expands: "To touch more people, the personal realities and the social must be evoked—not through rhetoric but through blood and pus and sweat" (173). Moraga's theory in the flesh and Anzaldúa's call to touch "personal realities"—written in a way calibrated to demonstrate that hegemony conditions us to interpret the body as repulsive—illuminates the political vector of Acker's vulgarity. We see her work, then, as an indictment of the system that would put such representations out of bounds.²⁹ The deep similarity in ideology and methodology among these figures makes it all the more compelling when the texts face such different afterlives.

The "Colorful, Exciting and Yet Banal and Trivial Gutter Language" of *Blood and Guts in High School*

Blood and Guts in High School is considered Acker's breakout work and introduces themes related to the exhibition of the body and of explicit sexuality that will take on deeper political significance in later works. *Blood and Guts* narrates the experiences of Janey, a young girl involved in an incestuous, coercive relationship with her father, who ends the relationship and sends her to New York for school. There she gets involved in a gang before being captured by a slave trader who attempts to train her to be a prostitute and teaches her to write poetry in Persian. Finally, she travels across northern Africa with the author Jean Genet. Its transgressive themes made it somewhat controversial upon publication. It was placed on a list of books harmful to minors by the German government. It was, moreover, censored for its offensive depictions of sex (including incest), the inclusion of explicit hand-drawn images of genitals and nude bodies, and, pointedly, its lack of artistic value.

According to the official 1986 finding of the German Federal Inspection Office for Publications Harmful to Minors, the book is "confusing in terms of sexual ethics and is therefore equal to 'immoral texts.'"[30] From our own perspective, this confusion cannot be uncritically equated with immorality. The complexity of the novel's representations are in service of resolving a social issue that is similarly complex; this is the kind of engagement with ideas that circulates in the *Miller* ruling and which protects cultural artifacts of this kind in the United States. Nonetheless, the German government claimed that the book "renders a positive picture of deviant pathological sexual acts. Sexual excitement is increased by sadomasochistic acts," and that "this kind of description gives reason to worry that the still unformed juvenile readers will be hampered from becoming fully responsible personalities and sexual partners" (Acker, *Hannibal*, 146). Though it would be difficult to outright ban the book in the United States on these grounds, nonetheless, the condemnation is useful for evoking some of the novel's themes and depictions, and it crystallizes opinions stateside that circulated about the novel but which could not have the force of law.

In the U.S. context, the presence of sexuality—even offensive representations of sexuality—cannot justify a ban; the text must also lack artistic merit. It turns out the German government did find the book to lack such merit. The decision declares flatly that the book "is neither art nor does it serve any artistic purpose" (Acker, *Hannibal*, 147). The judgment reflects ingrained attitudes about art, including disdain for the pastiche style and coarse language of the novel: "The chosen elements of style do not enhance the novel to the level of art. A colorful, exciting and yet banal and trivial gutter language in itself cannot relay any artistic qualities within a novel" (148). The findings of the committee seem important to grapple with, but it should be clear that this is not definitive. The book might, in fact, with the benefit of retrospect, be found to have been innovative in its style and disdain for this confrontational style might be muted with time as the cultural innovations of the punk movement of which Acker was a fixture gained wider recognition.

Though the German declaration focuses on specific instances of explicit descriptions, the book more often only gestures toward sex and sexuality, eliding specific descriptions in favor of exploring the psychology of the characters through stream-of-consciousness exposition, cut-up techniques borrowing from William S. Burroughs, and detailed narration of mundane events. The focus of the novel, then, is not titillation or the eroticization of violent acts, but the mental states of those driven to these behaviors and the epistemological conundrums they face.[31]

Acker's novel begins with Janey's abuse by her father. Their interactions are described via first-person narration as a breakup between an adult couple, and we infer that Janey is psychologically traumatized. The two talk openly of sex in explicit terms, and the relationship between them is so shockingly abnormal that we can only read Janey's sexual desire, jealousy toward older women's claims on her father, and failure to question the terms of the relationship as the result of her degraded state and corrupted childhood.[32] This sets the stage for an allegory of sexual victimization that dramatizes the internalization of patriarchal values about the role of the female body, which leads to the complete breakdown of Janey's psyche that will be reflected in the nearly incoherent nature of the text. In this way, the novel meditates—in grotesque terms—on the effect of a patriarchal sexual economy that impacts women even in childhood.

Janey spends the rest of the novel on a convoluted journey seeking fulfillment or simply to make her way in the world. She often palliates a sense of alienation with sex, violence, and delusion, alternating between a horrific reality and an idyllic, if chaotic, fantasy. The fantasy of fulfillment and self-determination for women constrained by a society that values them primarily as objects is one of the novel's main themes and prefigures the utopic vision of Acker's larger corpus, especially *Empire of the Senseless*. While sexuality is sometimes empowering in this world, it is also potentially empty, a sign of the commodification of female bodies that devalues the historical and cultural contributions of women—that, in fact, deforms those contributions until they resemble *Blood and Guts in High School*. Imagination and the dreamscape become sites of working through a general trauma of disempowered subjecthood, and these are inscribed on the page in both experimental prose and elaborate line drawings. In this context, the book's graphic description of sex and the inclusion of drawings of genitalia simply make explicit the bare facts of life: It's all about sex anyway.

This nihilistic attitude is linked to larger social transgression early on in the novel. After her father abandons her, Janey briefly holds down a job but then joins a gang, unable to resist the allure of crime and sex—both portrayed as substitutes for affection. After briefly giving up on the gang and returning to work, Janey is again lured away. Describing her motivations, she says: "Love turned me back to crime. Tommy and I . . . [d]id everything we could to dull our judgment and acted outrightly as violent as possibly. . . . I could hardly stand being so happy. The sex made me crazier than the crime" (Acker, *Blood and Guts*, 41–42). In scenes like this, criminality (as a form of social transgression) and sex are the fruits of twisted affective relationships. By tying the foreclosure of affirmative emotional relationships to violence and sex, Acker's novel dramatizes the psychological effects of a masculist sexual economy on the women who must participate in it under the threat, as Cixous argues, of decapitation.

For *Blood and Guts*, the purpose of this kind of transgression—where explicit, violent, and meaningless sex is routinely depicted—is to reveal the consequences of the commodification of female bodies. The grotesque text is a representation of the psychologically damaging effects on patriarchy's victims and thus functions as an indictment of the structures of power that produced it. Though the prose is erratic, it is worth noting some of the narrator's frenetic and chaotic pronouncements:

> Once upon a time there was a materialistic society one of the results of this materialism was a "sexual revolution." Since the materialistic society had succeeded in separating sex from every possible feeling, all you girls can now go spread your legs as much as you want 'cause it's sooo easy to fuck it's sooo easy to be a robot it's sooo easy not to feel. Sex in America is S&M. This is the glorification of S&M and slavery and prison. (Acker, *Blood and Guts*, 99)

We initially read Janey's pathological behavior—accepting sexual slavery and seeking out demeaning sexual encounters and violent crime—as a result of her corrupted childhood, but it is also a consequence of a greater cultural structure wherein the body and the mind become only nodes in a network of exchange where the gains of the sexual revolution accrue primarily to men. Moreover, Janey's ironic pronouncement implicates consumer culture in what Acker construes as an oppressive sexual economy that unites the eroticization of suffering (in sadomasochism) with a history of economic exploitation through violence (slavery). Here, Acker's political project erupts in her attempt to explain what might have seemed like crude delight in explicit depictions of violence and degradation. In this moment, Acker seems to argue against a nihilistic commodity-oriented economy of sexual representations rather than for it.

The message that sexuality and economic exploitation are interimplicated is expanded in successive passages where Janey describes her situation as twin kinds of slavery. On the one hand is "Body slavery: I have to eat and get shelter so need money. Also my body likes sex and rich food and I'll do anything for these." On the other hand is "Mind slavery: I want more than just money. I live in a partially human world and I want people to think and feel certain ways about me. So I try to set up certain networks . . . These networks become history and culture . . . They tell me what to do" (Acker, *Blood and Guts*, 111). Janey is aware of the extent to which deep structures of power guide her thoughts and actions, even to the point of determining her desires, but her complex self-awareness doesn't provide obvious answers and thus fails to explain her behavior clearly, either. While this system creates abject positions for Janey and all women, it allows men to persist in the status of victimizer and users—subjects with power and self-determination. In the novel, Jean Genet explains the hierarchy of civilization to Janey in stark, brutal terms: "Rich men / Poor men / Mothers / Beautiful women / Whores / Poor female and neo-female slut-scum / Janey" (130–31).[33] This hierarchy, reified in the novel and meant to mirror reality beyond the covers, not only denigrates Janey specifically, but lays bare the logic of patriarchy where men are more powerful than women, but women who serve patriarchal functions (reproduction, for example) are also more valued than those who refuse the system. Janey, then, exists in a state of total abjection which Acker aims to construe as a hyperbolic form of the general abjection of women.

In its brutality, the novel pushes social conditions to the point of grotesqueness. But this grotesqueness of expression is meant to reveal the grotesqueness of the discursive situation: Janey's abjection is an indictment of the system that produced her condition. Acker's novel reflects a reality in which the sexual economy that determines women's role in the world is no longer glossed, but laid bare. Acker's use of obscene modes then enables a critique of a sexual economy that begins with and ends with the father and the authority of the patriarch, following a pattern established by Henry Miller, though applied here against the misogyny Miller's transgressions seem to buttress.[34]

The novel's incomplete politics and confused ideology seem to acknowledge the difficulty of creating sexual representations that legitimately celebrate female sexuality within linguistic and cultural structures that are so thoroughly patriarchal. However, what does obtain here is a momentary vision of Acker's utopic dream: a world where a more equal expression of love is possible between fully realized subjects and where desire is open and public, relying on the liberatory power of concrete expressions of it.[35] This affirmation of desire finds its roots in the body and in the complementary de-institutionalization of the mind. Acker's mode of accessing this de-institutionalized condition veers through

Deconstruction and Post-Structuralism. Acker elaborates on this idea in an important passage from *Empire of the Senseless*, which is worth quoting at length:

> That part of our being (mentality, feeling, physicality) which is free of all control let's call our "unconscious." Since it's free of control, it's our only defence [sic] against institutionalized meaning, institutionalized language, control, fixation, judgement [sic], prison.
>
> Ten years ago it seemed possible to destroy language through language: to destroy language which normalizes and controls by cutting that language. Nonsense would attack the empire-making (empirical) empire of language, the prisons of meaning.
>
> But this nonsense, since it depended on sense, simply pointed back to the normalizing institutions.
>
> What is the language of the "unconscious"? . . . Its primary language must be taboo, all that is forbidden. Thus, an attack on the institutions of prison via language would demand the use of a language or languages which aren't acceptable, which are forbidden. Language, on one level, constitutes a set of codes and social and historical agreements. Nonsense doesn't per se break down the codes; speaking precisely that which the codes forbid breaks the codes. (134)[36]

In this passage, Acker's narrative voice (which is largely continuous with that in *Blood and Guts*) invokes Post-Structural experimentation as a way of resisting the hegemony of normative language by flouting the imperative to make sense. Acker contends that this produces a recursive binary where non-sense relies on sense and therefore "simply point[s] back to the normalizing institutions." However, Acker also confirms the necessity of essaying such a project. She claims that "speaking precisely that which the codes forbid breaks the codes," suggesting that it is explicit, transgressive representations that present the strongest threat to the old exclusions.

Turning the abject into a symbol of power by embracing taboo behaviors represents the major tactic of Acker's explicit feminist politics and explains her method as largely the same as figures like Bruce and Miller. In these cases, bold expressions that transgress modesty are seen as absolutely pivotal to rejecting oppressive structures. In this case, however, Acker appears to intend this as an explicitly feminist project, breaking with the earlier precedent. As Houen notes, "Acker's pirate myth," nascent here and realized more fully in later works, especially *Pussy, King of the Pirates* (1996), "opens new linguistic potentials while using a language of abjection to ensure that those potentials become affective corporeal powers" (190). If we connect the imperative here to compose in taboo forms, we see a political project that valorizes transgressive sexual expression as a means of realizing alternate spaces of being. This project makes plain the potential of pornography and explicit representations—of a body politics based in revelation of desire—that challenges those who would ban pornography as constitutively degrading.

I have examined Acker's early work here primarily to draw together the threads of her complex weave of poststructuralist theory, feminist politics, and a concern for sexuality and its representations. Acker was an important figure and her work, though complex and difficult—and often shocking or offensive—demonstrates some of modes of resistance to patriarchy that grew out of feminist activism that was deeply engaged with post-structuralism and psychoanalytic theory. Nonetheless, this is only one vector of resistance, so I position it here in relation to the work of Alice Walker and the very different histories of racialization her work engages. The consonance between Acker's projects and those of earlier figures who represent the narrative of obscene genius is curious. Like those authors and artists, Acker's politics seem explicitly designed to use the breaking of taboo as the grounds for resistance to an oppressive system. Her continuing cult celebrity and glowing reviews seem to support the idea that she fits into this narrative, though her attack on misogyny makes the picture somewhat more complex and signals an important departure from her predecessors.

Third-Wave Feminism and Obscenity

Acker's novel gives us a picture of what a deliberately political, transgressive sexual representation looks like when it grows out of the post-structuralist and postmodern traditions. It is chaotic and assaultive because of its narrative incoherence and shocking descriptions. Often critiqued for simple vulgarity—and banned as a threat to children—this work, however, is not purposeless, even if its purpose is imperfect and partial. It has its limitations in part because it is bound up in precisely this binary that limits debate on the status of sexual representations to sex-negative and sex-positive, because its deep investment in theories of language privilege a Eurocentric episteme, and because identifying sexual pleasure as a means to liberation is itself a complex—and sometimes complicit—notion.

As noted previously, the writings of Moraga and Anzaldúa offer a useful companion to Acker's fiction because they similarly explore the potential of non-mainstream and non-patriarchal desire to promote women's liberation while revealing the workings of patriarchy in literature and culture more broadly. However, they begin to open up alternative valences because, valorizing the perspective of non-white women, they remind us of the different concerns that arise when we consider racialization along with sexual subjectivity rather than considering either in isolation. Moraga wrote in 1982, for example, that "I have come to realize that the boundaries white feminists confine themselves to in describing sexuality are based in white-rooted interpretations of dominance, submission, power-exchange, etc." Moraga puts an even finer point on it by insisting that feminists who see gender as the sole vector of oppression are neglecting the importance of intersectionality and producing a counterproductive sexual politics: "In failing to approach feminism from any kind of materialist base, failing to take race, ethnicity, class into account in determining where women are at sexually, many feminists have created an analysis of sexual oppression (often confused with sexuality itself) which is a political dead end" ("Long Line," 126). Moraga, like Lorde, emphasizes the need to engage directly with race and ethnicity, as well as economic issues, and to avoid the abstraction that both grows out of and produces racial disparities in economic opportunity and stability and political power and representation, even within the feminist movement. Acker's novels, though politically engaged, largely elide race or treat it in oblique, ironic ways. Not simplistically racist, but not anti-racist in an organized fashion either, to some extent they represent just the kind of high-theoretical, detached approach that Moraga and Lorde decry as enabling an abstract citizenship implicitly coded as white.[37]

Lorde elaborated on some of these concepts in her contributions to *This Bridge Called My Back*, especially her influential essay "The Master's Tools Will Never Dismantle the Master's House." In it, Lorde emphasizes the historical occlusion of the voices of women of color in feminist debates, noting, "It is a particular academic arrogance to assume any discussion of feminist theory in this time and in this place without examining our many differences, and without a significant input from poor women, third-world women, and lesbians."[38] She is in part attacking the use of poststructuralist theory to guide feminist praxis at the time. Not only does this recapitulate a masculist intellectual history, she contends, but it limits change. Lorde explains that the methods of academic analysis, particularly when rooted in European high theory, entail the supposition of male supremacy. She asks, "What does it mean when the tools of a racist patriarchy are used to examine the fruits of that same patriarchy? It means that only the most narrow perimeters of change are possible and allowable" (98). In this context, she coins the notion that *"the master's tools will never dismantle the master's house,"* adding, "They may allow us to temporarily beat him at his own game, but they will never enable us to bring about genuine change" (99, emphasis in original).

Lorde's essay is remembered as a powerful call for the development of new modes of knowledge that grow organically out of the experiences of women of all races and sexualities, but it is worth also remembering her practical concern for the viability of concrete advancement in the lives of women. She is interested in the reality that the use of methods borrowed from a patriarchal system will only produce superficial change. In so doing, she suggests that a project like Acker's of disassembling norms of language while relying on structures of knowledge imported from the logocentric philosophical tradition has limited political potential. Perhaps offering a way to exceed this limitation, Hortense J. Spillers engages with the psychoanalytic tradition that Cixous and Acker extend but is primarily concerned with carefully attending to the historical experience of African American women in slavery. Like Lorde and Moraga, Spillers addresses the failures of academic theory and second-wave feminism to attend to the different histories and tropes of embodiment applied to and imposed on African American women. Spillers is important not only for extending the indictment of second-wave feminism, but in raising issues that must be confronted in seeking a more productive alternative. In particular, in her essay "Mama's Baby, Papa's Maybe," she introduces the notion of "pornotroping," which I want to use as a node of connection between anti-pornography activism, sex-positive resistance to that activism, and a necessary understanding of the different histories of embodiment that characterize the representations of non-white women in a U.S. cultural and historical context.

The word "pornotroping" shares a root with "pornography," but the similar etymologies belie distinct semantic vectors. Pornotroping is not the enactment of metaphors and symbols related to erotic or sexual material; rather, it represents the complex of historical fields, representations, discourses, and actions that attempted to figuratively reduce African American women to mute flesh incapable of signifying or being recognized as fully human.[39] In order to elaborate on the concept and disassociate it from simpler and more historically laden terms such as "objectification," Spillers returns to the Middle Passage to reconnect her discussion to the history of slavery that produced the distinct manner of dehumanization she wants to voice.

Writing in reference to the "socio-political order of the New World," she highlights how "That order, with its human sequence written in blood, represents for its African and indigenous peoples a scene of actual mutilation, dismemberment, and exile. First of all, their New World, diasporic plight marked a theft of the body—a willful and violent (and unimaginable from this distance) severing of the captive body from its motive will, its active desire." Continuing, she argues that cultural norms related to the body that the captive individuals brought with them are broken down, but that "this body, at least from the point of view of the captive community, focuses a private and particular space, at which point of convergence biological, sexual, social, cultural, linguistic, ritualistic, and psychological fortunes join." The re-creation of spaces of intimacy and new cultural and social processes and relationships would be a means of defending against the violence of enslavement. However, as Spillers describes, four social and representational procedures intervene to further disrupt this defense:

> This profound intimacy of interlocking detail is disrupted, however, by externally imposed meanings and uses: 1) the captive body becomes the source of an irresistible, destructive sensuality; 2) at the same time—in stunning contradiction—the captive body reduces to a thing, becoming *being for* the captor; 3) in this absence *from* a subject position, the captured sexualities provide a physical and biological expression of "otherness"; 4) as a category of "otherness," the captive body translates into a potential for pornotroping and embodies sheer physical powerlessness that slides into a more general "powerlessness," resonating through various centers of human and social meaning. (Spillers 67, emphasis in original)

In the narrative Spillers constructs, the violence of slavery simply obliterates existing configurations of gender and sexuality for captive and enslaved people because it totally removes the social conditions under which those configurations arose and were maintained. The enslaved people do, however, retain their experiences and create new ad hoc structures of gender and affiliation, but these, too, are wiped away by the oppressors' rhetorical structures and modes of categorizing or "knowing" the gender of the oppressed. The dominant power simply fills in new gender roles and imposes them. Spillers describes these roles as including some contradictory binaries of total sexual threat versus total disempowerment. Otherness also becomes inscribed in this sexuality.

Spillers articulates the concept of pornotroping in the relationship between the body and "sheer physical powerlessness." Importantly, this notion is a form of meaning making; it is a system of troping. It is *also* a system of sexual tropes. But in the knowledge system these tropes participate in, the structures of power are even more imbalanced than the concepts of dominance and submission that Acker engages in her writing about BDSM. The concept of submission, notably, is not appropriate to a context of total coercion, in which even the possibility of willful submission is violated. In this structure, moreover, there is no escaping racialization, and any discussion of sexual politics absent an explicit indictment of white supremacy is meaningless.[40]

Having thus at hand a term that articulates a sense of objectification, but attends to race-specific histories and the problematics of offering sexual desire as a means of escape from a system of patriarchy, we can begin to understand the limitations of a false binary between objectification and subjectivity. "Objectification" is a word that embodies a critique of discourses that reduce the body from a site of empowerment to something metaphysically impoverished and lacking in agency. But in its orientation, it is a rejection of the body's reduction to a site of pleasure (for men). Growing from a similar premise, "pornotroping" encapsulates the evacuation of subjectivity, but emphasizes less the body's function as a site of pleasure, and more its function as a site of pain, rupture, and violation. As a counterpoint to the feminisms of Cixous and Acker, then, we must add the insights of third-wave feminism to more fully unravel the structures of oppression that are revealed to be more than patriarchal, but also white supremacist.

In this vein, Walker's *The Color Purple* offers an important counterpoint to Acker's novel. Both books explore and dramatize aspects of roughly contemporaneous feminisms, providing a more complex picture of how dominant voice policing of sexual representations works, while the differences in their literary afterlives illuminate new contours of how obscenity can differently impact a work's reception based on racist assumptions inherent in the marketplace. Walker's novel also begins with the rape of its main character by a man she understands to be her father. Like Janey, the development of Celie's subjectivity is overwhelmed by this act of violation. Unlike Janey, however, Celie's story is one of overcoming. The novel traces the dark times she experiences after her supposed father trades her to another man, to whom she is no more than a servant and sexual object. The one person who loves Celie and whom she loves is her sister Nettie, who also faces the threatening sexual advances of their father and of Celie's husband, Albert/Mr. _____. Nettie escapes their father by coming to live with Celie and Albert, only to leave after he responds violently to her rejection of his advances. She then flees to Africa as a servant of a black missionary and his wife.

While Nettie learns about the Olinka tribe and European colonialism in Africa, Celie continues to struggle against a brutal male supremacy in her own community. Her husband is in love with the blues and jazz singer Shug Avery, with whom Celie eventually falls in love, too. Through an introduction to sexual pleasure, Shug helps Celie see that she might live for herself and that doing so might be a way of accessing a divine spirit analogous to the God to whom she addresses her early letters in this epistolary novel. In this way, Celie journeys from a state of total degradation under a baldly exploitative and dehumanizing patriarchy to one of independence in a more woman-identified community. Through this dramatization, Walker seems to be operating under a parallel artistic strategy to Acker. Both authors portray patriarchy stripped of its euphemisms and obfuscations and then imagine a more equal world influenced by the author's feminist theories.

The novel was widely praised, and received numerous awards. Published in 1982, it won both the Pulitzer Prize for fiction and the National Book Award in 1983. It was made into a film of the same name in 1985, directed by Steven Spielberg and with an all-star cast that included Danny Glover, Oprah Winfrey, and Whoopi Goldberg. It was similarly adapted into a Broadway musical in 2005. The film and musical were subsequently nominated for numerous Academy and Tony Awards. The novel was also widely hailed by critics and the public. In his 1982 review in the *New York Times Book Review*, for example, Mel Watkins calls the book Walker's "most impressive" book, one that "easily satisfies [the claim]" that Walker is "a lavishly gifted writer."[41]

The reception of the novel was not overwhelmingly positive, however, and some of the strongest critiques came from those who were concerned about its depiction of negative images and tropes that recall the cultural history Spillers details. Trudier Harris wrote a scathing critique of the novel in which she describes her long process of agonizing over its representations of African American life. She evokes the position of some that the novel is wrongly valorized because it threatens to instantiate more than challenge the structures it depicts, even though it ostensibly does so in order to overthrow them.[42] Harris argues that in addition to monopolizing attention that might be directed at other deserving texts and authors,

> Response to its unequaled popularity, first of all, has created a cadre of spectator readers. These readers, who do not identify with the characters and who do not feel the intensity of their pain, stand back and view the events of the novel as a circus of black human interactions that rivals anything Daniel Patrick Moynihan concocted. The spectator readers show what damage the novel can have; for

them, the book reinforces racist stereotypes they may have been heir to and others of which they may have only dreamed.[43]

In this passage, Harris links the film to the infamous 1965 Moynihan Report that blamed a "tangle of pathologies" in the African American community for the economic and social ills faced by African Americans. Though intended to justify social programs, the report was criticized on the right for not emphasizing individual responsibility, but it has also come under a more withering critique on the left for lending a veneer of legitimacy to stereotypes about the pathology of African American families.[44] Harris is concerned that *The Color Purple* does something of the same work by giving viewers—especially white viewers—an image of black culture that seems to reinforce these very presumptions, especially the cruelty of African American fathers. In this way, she calls up the narrative of obscene pathology, as well as the situation of Morrison and Carby's argument that black women writers must always grapple with negative stereotypes about their womanhood as the cost of entering public discourse.[45]

Exacerbating this possibility for Harris is the fact that, as she put it, "a large number of readers, usually vocal and white, have decided that *The Color Purple* is the quintessential statement on Afro-American women and a certain kind of black lifestyle in these United States" (155). Harris emphasizes the effect the novel might have on the circulation of certain negative stereotypes of African American life, especially in this moment. In this sense, it is not only that the negative attitudes or stereotypes of "spectator readers" are confirmed, but that they might supplant other available images or representations, and thus limit the possibility of a more varied and nuanced understanding of African American culture. Harris has articulated other criticisms of the novel, but this one merits some elaboration because it calls attention to the way in which a sexually transgressive work by a writer of color will often be called to account for existing white supremacist stereotypes about racial sexuality as the cost of its publication, circulation, and participation in discussions of literary canonization.

Harris's objections center on Celie's passiveness in early passages, which she finds a caricature of stereotypes, notoriously calling the protagonist "a bale of cotton with a vagina" (155). Celie seems, at the outset of the novel, almost impossibly ignorant of her body and her identity. Part of the issue is likely that Walker's novel, though interpreted and read in the realist genre, often takes on an exaggerated or allegorical style not unlike Acker's. Though decidedly human and evoking sympathy in a realist mode, the book also seems self-consciously to be a representation or metaphorization of the workings of patriarchy. Harris is aware of this element of the book, but contends that the novel presents itself not as an allegory or fantasy, but as a realist novel and that it can and should be critiqued on those grounds. Harris avers that "Since it professed to be a novel, I would treat it as such. And since it professed to be realistic fiction, I would respond to that as much as I could" (159). For Harris, because of the likelihood that other readers will interpret it as depicting actual conditions, she must respond to the effects of such an interpretation, concerned more for how the book will be received by the culture at large than its internal aesthetics.

This is due in part to how the representations will *seem* real because they accord with stereotypes and misrepresentations with a long history; thus, for Harris, *The Color Purple* runs the risk of cementing and strengthening the negative images it intends to overturn. Harris expresses her concern in part as the worry that Celie's story might be "used to create a new archetype or to resurrect old myths about black women" (156). If the novel instantiates the figures it means to overthrow because of its massive popularity among an ignorant or uncritical public, then it might spread and shore up those very figures of pornotroping.

Sounding notes in echo of Spillers, Jacqueline Bobo defends the film and novel not so much on aesthetic or political merits, but on the work they do in regards to pornotroping (though she does not use this term). She writes, "During enslavement black women were worked as hard as men, used as breeders, then constructed in mythology as wanton and sexually lascivious. After slavery black women were usefully constructed as mean and evil castrating wenches, emasculating their male partners and further impeding the progress of the race. Contemporary works by black women writers, of which *The Color Purple* is part, are a corrective to prior notions of black women."[46] Though not everyone shared Harris's concerns about how Walker's novel would be received, such concerns do remind us of the complex bind of the systems of pornotroping that the novel engages and brings to the fore the political stakes of any representation of transgressive sexuality for women of color because these works must intersect with existing systems of knowledge that have typically reinforced a white supremacist, misogynist order. Harris reminds us that in the public at large motivated misinterpretations happen even with respect to work that is self-consciously emancipatory and conceived to counter negative representations. The novel is not exhausted by these concerns, and instead exceeds and resists them while also imagining alternative ways of being. However, such artificially imposed discourses of pathology still become nodal points in discussions of the novel, just as they do for others by writers of color and other marginalized people.

Obscenity challenges to *The Color Purple* were common. The book's sexual content and celebration of lesbian desire were rejected by some social activists, and this led to a complicated publication history. Walker faced simultaneous celebration and censorship. Patricia Holt noted that Walker has been "one of the most censored writers in American literature" and recalls her mixed celebrity in 1994 when the State of California sought to honor her as a "State Treasure" at the same time that the California Board of Education removed two of her short stories from the high school reading list.[47] Her most famous novel has a somewhat tangled history of censorship, as well. It appears as number five on the American Library Association's list of frequently challenged works of classic literature ("Banned & Challenged Classics").[48] The ALA records over a dozen instances of the book's place on school readings lists being challenged because of its explicit sexual content, depictions of violence, and use of profanity. These challenges occurred despite the book's critical acclaim and reflect negotiations about appropriate content for children and parents' rights to oversee what their children are exposed to. In many ways, then, they reflect earlier challenges to Morrison's *The Bluest Eye*, while they also prefigure later efforts by the Parents' Music Resource Center to restrict music. Still, the specific history of the book is worth noting, as it demonstrates that the book was simultaneously perceived as a valuable work of art and a potential threat to readers who might be scandalized or corrupted, a classic convergence in twentieth-century obscenity controversies.

Walker's novel occasioned not only popular reviews but a wealth of critical interpretations, something that is part and parcel of the novel's all but certain canonization and has led to its frequently being taught in secondary schools and universities. Because the novel is so rich and multifarious, criticism has been understandably varied, too. Authors such as Wendy Wall and M. Teresa Tavormina have considered the role of quilt-making and cloth work in the novel, which can be seen as contributing to a long tradition of African American quilting as a counter-hegemonic practice. The novel's use of language has also come under close study. Because the epistolary novel is narrated in Celie's voice as it evolves with her consciousness, it provides several models of speech meant to evoke different mental states; Keith Byerman and King-Kok Cheung have examined this aspect of the novel. Similarly, African American vernacular and blues-influenced rhythms are prominent elements in these analyses. Other elements of the novel, including its function within the African

American literary tradition, the genre of the epistolary novel, and as a form of feminist theorizing are revealed by scholars, including Henry Louis Gates Jr., Lauren Berlant, Molly Hite, Martha J. Cutter, and Linda Abbandonato.

In her article "Philomela Speaks," Cutter places *The Color Purple* in a long tradition of rape narratives and uses the Greek mythological figure Philomela to explain how Celie's growing command of her own voice in the latter part of the novel overturns existing tropes of rape that end with the victim's silence. Cutter writes that:

> Like the novels of Morrison and Naylor, Alice Walker's *The Color Purple* invokes this archetypal rape narrative, but Walker is most interested in re-envisioning this myth through an alternative methodology of language. . . . Unlike the original mythic text, as well as the novels of Morrison and Naylor, Walker's text gives Philomela a voice that successfully resists the violent patriarchal inscription of male will onto a silent female body.[49]

Works like Cutter's help us understand the long tropological and mythological tradition within which Walker's work makes its meaning. It does so by invoking some tropes in order to overturn them, a model for the novel's treatment of patriarchy that encourages us to see any one part of the novel as constituting only a partial evocation of Walker's vision. Moreover, it gives us a means for making sense of its scenes of violation.

Cutter also joins other critics who elaborate on Walker's creation of a feminist utopia that mirrors her concept of the woman-identified community. For Cutter, Celie's linguistic development contributes to this: "The novel . . . indicates that alternative methodologies of language (whether spoken by men or women) need not perpetuate the mythic cycle of feminine destruction encapsulated within patriarchal discourse and patriarchal narrative" (175). In her growth into a more expressive language, Celie demonstrates one important step toward an alternative world that avoids the injustices of patriarchy, and Cutter suggests this can be rooted in new linguistic modes. I suggest this should guide our interpretation of Walker's use of difficult and explicit sexual elements, since it reinforces the notion that Walker is engaging with the stereotypes Harris identifies as a central feature of her effort to overcome them, an overcoming that cannot happen without candid reckoning but which is not limited by this engagement.

Abbandonato brings into focus some of the feminist aspects of the novel. As others will also do, she elaborates on how *The Color Purple* enacts part of its important resistive project by simply dramatizing nonconforming sexualities and women refusing the roles assigned to them in patriarchy. She writes that patriarchy and compulsory heterosexuality "can only operate smoothly so long as sexual nonconformity is kept invisible. An important project of feminism, then, is to make the invisible visible: to topple the dominant ideology by placing the unorthodox and the marginalized at the center of the discursive and cultural stage."[50] This is pivotal in directing my examination of *The Color Purple* through the lens of obscenity because I am interested in what representations are made off-limits and how the obscene functions to keep "sexual nonconformity" invisible. Whitney Strub has argued convincingly that legal obscenity discourses function particularly to limit visibility of non-mainstream sexualities and desires, which often reflects anxiety about the normalization of such behaviors.[51]

This normalization is precisely what those who would seek to represent such desire hope will happen. Abbandonato, for example, writes that "Celie's lesbianism is politically significant, subverting masculine cultural narratives of femininity and desire and rewriting them from a feminist point of view" (1109). However, the specific move from abuse to healing in this representation is important because it reveals the function of the narrative structure. Celie's shattered and abused identity is healed through the affirmative support of a same-sex partner, a move that not only brings lesbian desire into view, but celebrates its ameliorative potential: "It is her love for Shug that enables Celie to bury her sad double narrative of paternal origins and construct a new identity within a feminine domain" (1111). The construction of a new identity that Abbandonato is describing saves Celie from the hell of her narrative origins: "Implicit here is an escape from patriarchal law. In breaking the taboo against homosexuality, Celie symbolically exits the master narrative of female sexuality and abandons the position ascribed to her within the symbolic order" (1111–12). This new possibility, however, is open to others, too, including men. Albert learns over the course of the novel to mend his ways, and at the end of the novel, the world that exists in Celie's orbit gives a glimpse of a future that suffers less from unequal gender binaries.

Berlant also offers useful insights; they are particularly concerned that the novel's indictment of racism is obscured by certain genre shifts. For example, instances of white supremacist violence—though present in, for example, the lynching of Celie and Nettie's true father—are told in a fairy-tale mode and through rhetorical elisions that diminish their racism while emphasizing class-based discrimination and violence. Berlant argues that the racial violence in the novel is thus displaced into the economic sphere—Berlant says it functions "to racialize the scene of class struggle" (843)—and so sees the novel leaving the structure of racism in place, even as it suggests that race is often a subterfuge for economic inequalities and violence rooted in them. Berlant also points out a facet of the text that is important in a reading focused around pornotroping. While discussing the narrative structure that elevates Celie by the novel's end, Berlant writes, "*The Color Purple*'s strategy of inversion, represented in its elevation of female experience over great patriarchal events, had indeed aimed to critique the unjust practices of racism and sexism that violate the subject's complexity, reducing her to a generic biological sign" (857). The passage here neatly transitions from the discussion of the plot structure to the important facet of pornotroping: the reduction to "a biological sign." Though Berlant is concerned this comes through embracing capitalism and the consumer fetish, Celie does throw off the symbolic structures and real violence that had reduced her to this biological sign, a sexual object or source of domestic labor. If you consider the novel as a whole, the perhaps ambivalent re-inscription of capitalism exists alongside a symbolic reversal in which *The Color Purple* exorcises negative cultural images through a direct engagement with them.

I hope here to augment this reading of the novel's critical life by looking closely at a few key scenes in the hopes of clarifying the novel's specific contributions to overcoming the pornotroping that contributes to narratives of pathology, which tend to haunt obscene works by marginalized people. In particular, there are scenes that are strikingly reminiscent of *Blood and Guts* and demonstrate that certain tropes and figures—especially the sexual domination of the father in patriarchy—are shared concerns for both authors. In *The Color Purple*, Celie's story, like Janey's, begins with her rape by her father. In Walker's novel, it will later be revealed that Alfonso is not her true father, but her stepfather, which erases some of the stain of incest for her, allowing for partial recovery from the trauma she experiences in this first scene of the book. Nonetheless at the time of the rape, when she is fourteen, she thinks he is her father, and as readers we do, too. Celie's mother has fallen ill, and rebuffs Alfonso's advances, upon which he tells Celie, "You gonna do what your mammy wouldn't" (Walker 1). The scene represents Alfonso's desire as free-floating, attaching to any female object. This casts him as monstrous, of course, but it also clarifies that for him the women in the novel—at least within the family—are interchangeable objects of gratification to an extent that supersedes social norms and taboos.

I would argue that to some extent Alfonso is represented not as an aberration, but as the clearest example of a patriarchal system that the other men in the novel also participate in. His monstrosity is not a matter of kind but of degree, and I read him as an eruption or unveiling of the system of patriarchy, not an outlier from it. In this way, the incestuous violation in the novel is an excessive representation that makes explicit the underlying logic of the bourgeois family. This contention is supported by the mobility of Albert's desire as well. He is relatively easily convinced to shift his initial interest in Nettie onto Celie when Alfonso refuses to allow Nettie to marry. The two women are not entirely indistinguishable to him; he sees Nettie as prettier and more desirable, but he is swayed from pursuing her by Alfonso's arguments about Celie's capacity for work. Albert is also swayed in part by Celie's infertility, a result of complications during her second pregnancy. Alfonso offers Celie as an object of care-free gratification: "God done fixed her. You can do everything just like you want to and she ain't gonna make you feed it or clothe it" (Walker 10). The concept of Celie's consent or pleasure does not occur to either man. We can see from this that the women are expected to participate in an economy not only of sexual pleasure but of labor and care in a broadly oppressive system of exploitative and coercive domestic service.

Celie discovers her independence from this system through lesbian sexual exploration with Shug Avery. It is Shug who first introduces Celie to her clitoris and describes the sensation of orgasm. Prior to Shug's instruction, Celie had never felt or even conceived of sexual pleasure. In fact, her experience of sex is characterized by the lack of feeling that she has cultivated to survive her multiple sexual traumas. When describing intercourse with Albert, she tells Shug, "Most times I pretend I ain't there. He never know the difference. Never ast me how I feel, nothing. Just do his business, get off, go to sleep." Shug is incredulous and says "Why, Miss Celie. You make it sound like he going to the toilet on you," to which Celie responds, "That what it feel like" (Walker 77). Through this exchange we can see the extent to which Celie has numbed herself to all feeling and the effects of Albert's treatment. Shug undoes this numbness over time by introducing Celie to her own body and its pleasures. This discovery is life-changing for Celie because of how she has been forcibly entered into an embodied economy of care in which she has no autonomy and in which seeking her own pleasure is violently disciplined. This economy is the system of exploitation for which pornotroping is the logic.

One additional scene—the one from which the novel's title is taken—can give us a sense of the specific character of sexual liberation that

Walker envisions, and it indicates one reason for the negative reactions of potential censors because of its violation of taboos regarding not only sexuality but also the treatment of religion. In this scene, Shug tells Celie about her amorphous notions of spirituality, which are grounded in the physical world and in pleasure, rather than in a patriarchal god or hierarchical religious organization. Shug describes her liberation from religion as beginning with an appreciation of nature, saying, "My first step from the old white man was trees. Then air. Then birds." From there, it progresses to a sense of unity with the world: "It come to me: that feeling of being part of everything, not separate at all." The ideas expressed by Shug challenge organized religion and white Christianity in particular, and thus seem taboo not only for Celie but for the book's audiences. It is key in the context of obscenity that this feeling of beatitude is understood as very nearly sexual. Shug says, "When it happen, you can't miss it. It sort of like you know what, she say, grinning and rubbing high up on my thigh" (Walker 191). Here, the suggestion is that spiritual enlightenment and sexual pleasure are not antithetical (Celie asks, "God don't think it dirty?" to which Shug replies, "Naw . . . God love everything you love" [191]). Moreover, feeling pleasure is a way of serving God and of engaging in religious celebration. This is a major deviation from puritanical notions of the sinfulness of pleasure, just as it is a radical revision of Celie's understanding of her role in the world.

In many ways, this refiguring of the relationship between sex and spirituality is the most significant ideological offering of the novel and a deliberate blending of antithetical elements that is shared by many other obscene works. The book is explicitly sexual in parts, but more frequently it depicts frank conversations like those between Shug and Celie, and thus offers not erotic content but metaphysical contemplations of the erotic. The difference matters because it suggests that at least one reason for concern over the novel was not only its prurient material, patently offensive or not, but its ideas. I invoke the language of the *Miller* test here to recall that these are precisely the concerns that define the border between obscene and non-obscene material. The Puritan ethic underlying obscenity case law presumes pleasure to be purposeless and anathema to religious devotion. Walker's vision is very much counter to this, but it does so in large part through its contemplation of ideas—which are expressly protected in the *Miller* ruling. The controversy around Walker's novel, then, is illuminating, but it did not manage to restrict access to the book, which carves out a space for sincere consideration of the possible purposes of pleasure by exploring metaphysical issues—issues of social value—directly through sexuality.

"A Society That Wasn't Just Disgust": Utopias of Desire and Counter-Narratives of Obscenity

In many ways, the novels espouse similar political projects, as can be seen in their overlapping yet distinct critical genealogies and the similarity in approaches to explicit content shared among Acker, Walker, Moraga, and Anzaldúa. And in fact, both novels fit the initially parallel narratives of market and canonical success. Acker's novel remained a cult favorite, and while she was never a fully mainstream figure, her novel is still read, studied, and taught, and she enjoyed continuing fame as the subject of a later documentary, a popular model for famous photographers including Robert Mapplethorpe, and as a noted influence on figures as diverse as the punk band Bikini Kill and photographer Cindy Sherman. Her innovative aesthetic and provocative theoretical politics, then, are seen as an outsider engagement with issues of deep metaphysical significance, and thus the work's reception fits into the narrative of obscene genius. Conversely, Walker's novel and its innovations were haunted by the narrative of obscene pathology, in which a successful work by an author of color does succeed, but that success is often earned at the cost of worries that its primary audience might be a white one that responds enthusiastically to seeing familiar stereotypes on display and its sense of liberal white saviorship confirmed. Walker achieved success, and her novel remains hugely influential and has become a major cultural phenomenon—the film was, in fact, nominated for ten Oscars, including Best Picture. But the cloud of negative criticism remained, and the history of stereotyped and twisted representations of African American sexuality continued to influence what was possible. For all their similarities, attending to the obscenity controversies around these works helps reveal that racial disparities play a significant role in how those novels' ideas are received and carried on.

The results of carrying out projects like Acker's and Walker's can vary substantially. Acker pursues her transgressive work under difficult conditions, but they are not the same conditions under which a writer like Walker pursues similar efforts. While Acker envisions a horizon in which pleasure is freed from patriarchy and is experienced as an important element of subjective development, Walker must contend with a welter of cultural tropes that reduce African Americans to sexuality as a means of justifying and furthering their subjection. Thus, Acker can advocate for porn, while Walker must contend with pornotroping. Acker can benefit from what Foucault calls "the speaker's benefit"[52] and gain cultural cachet by challenging the taboos of sexual modesty. Walker, instead, faces greater risks by breaking these taboos. In particular, she faces the risk that the reception of her work will center the stereotypes of deviance that she seeks to undermine through the narrative.

Exploring the possibilities of feminine desire within a patriarchal sexual economy along differing lines of race and sexuality has taken these two artists into spaces that are not always pretty—and that seems to be part of the point. For instance, in *Blood and Guts*, the protagonist must experience intense degradation at the hands of men in part to critique the extent to which she struggles to truly free her desires from the conditioning of patriarchy. She is made a sex slave and the victim of incest. Though Janey struggles to see a way out of her traumas and their psychological echoes, Acker's protagonist in the later novel *Empire of the Senseless* does begin to imagine it. While she cannot yet inhabit a world free of the oppression she has seen, she can begin to envision it; her final words sound a note of optimism: "I stood there in the sunlight, and thought that I didn't as yet know what I wanted. I now fully knew what I didn't want and what and whom I hated. That was something. And then I thought that, one day, maybe, there'ld [*sic*] be a human society in a world which is beautiful, a society which wasn't just disgust" (Acker, *Empire*, 227). This note of tempered hopefulness about a world not overdetermined by disgust is predicated on negative knowledge (what not to want and whom to hate), but suggests the possibility of positive knowledge in the future.

In considering how Acker and Walker envision these kinds of tentative utopias and seek to untangle the body and pleasure from very different strands of historical constraint, we can see that sexuality is a highly charged field in which the choice of partners, choice of acts, and the imbrication of sexuality with histories of racialization require careful responses. Pornography and non-pornographic-but-taboo representations of desire belong to any serious intersectional politics and can play an important role in overturning the structures of patriarchy, but the work that must be done on them is not simple. Acker and Walker, like Moraga and Anzaldúa, propose sexuality and desire as modes of self-exploration and self-knowledge, though ones that often produce negative or disconcerting epiphanies or inaugurate journeys whose end points seem eternally to recede.

Nonetheless, undeterred, protagonists in both texts see on that receding horizon the possibility of "a world which is beautiful, a society which [i]sn't just disgust." Ironically, however, it is the possibility of their fantasies bumping into inconvenient realities that gives these works their opportunity to alter the way we conceive of the world. That is, the very distance between the world they envision and the world we inhabit is the space of action. Butler, for example, argues that it is when the phantasmatic pushes up against the real and is taken seriously as something with real-world implications—by those who protest against taboo works or who take them as serious threats to the established order—that it is most productive: "It is precisely the moment in which the phantasmatic assumes the status of the real, that is, when the two become compellingly conflated, that the phantasmatic exercises its power most effectively" (107). This clarifies the anxiety with which representations of non-hegemonic desire of various kinds are resisted by the patriarchy: In imagining a world in which the structures break down, their utopias posit such a world as not-yet-real rather than unreal and thus challenge the foreclosure of equality that attends patriarchy, turning the impossible into the imminent.

4 / AIDS Politics Is Local: Narratives of Plague and Place in the Culture Wars

"My Scare Value Is High. My Area Is Controversy": Facing Off with Roy Cohn

The disembodied head stares at you, slightly off-kilter with a half-sagging frown that seems somehow unintentionally menacing.[1] The look conveys blunt pragmatism, total clarity of purpose and willingness to play the villain to achieve it. Taken in 1981, the portrait later appeared in Robert Mapplethorpe's *Certain People* (1985) alongside other notable people, including Debbie Harry, Arnold Schwarzenegger, and Annie Leibovitz. It is the face of Roy Cohn, hovering in mid-air against a dense black background (see Figure 3). Still five years away from his death and only 55, Cohn looks tired, perhaps with good reason. By this point, he had already helped elect Ronald Reagan with the help of Roger Stone. He had already mentored Donald Trump and defended him in court against housing discrimination charges. He had already been feared and reviled as Joseph McCarthy's lead counsel during the 1950s red scare, demonizing political opponents and LGBTQ+ people under the pretext of ferreting out Soviet influence. He had already helped falsify evidence and improperly communicate ex parte with a federal judge to ensure the conviction and execution of Julius and Ethel Rosenberg. He had a long and notorious career. None of this is obvious from the face itself, which shows only the one scar on his nose, the result of a childhood surgery. Instead, the expression is almost shockingly dull, though the gaze is intense, a result of the heavy-lidded aspect of Cohn's face and perhaps the hyper-focused photographic technique, which renders it gravelly and finely textured.

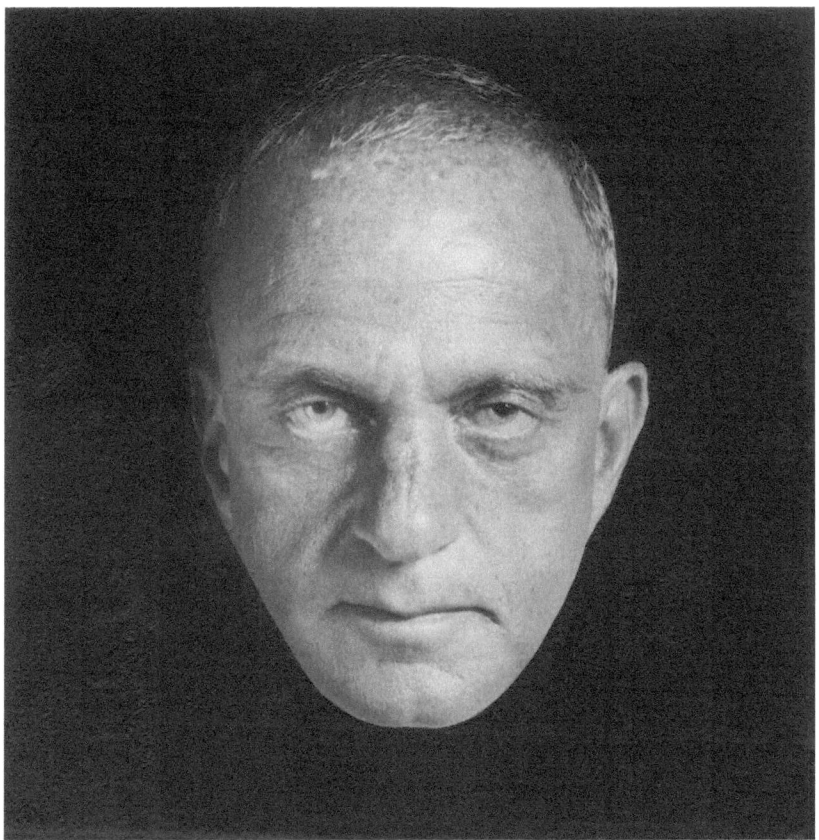

FIGURE 3. Roy Cohn, 1981 © Robert Mapplethorpe Foundation. Used by permission.

Cohn's career is one of bold ambition, intensely adversarial—even vicious—relationships with his enemies, lavish parties with powerful friends, and numerous contradictions. Though he participated in McCarthy's lavender scare and persecuted gay men and women in the U.S. government, it was rumored that he slept with men, and he died of AIDS in 1986 while pretending to suffer from terminal liver cancer. Though the *National Review* cited his enduring loyalty to his friends and benefactors (such as Senator McCarthy) to say that his key feature was "his total lack of ambiguity,"[2] he nonetheless seems to be a riddle to those who viewed the world differently than he did. The contradiction between his complete moral self-assurance and often-villainous behavior make him fascinating to many, and such contradictions inspired both Mapplethorpe and Tony Award–winning playwright Tony Kushner to use him in their art. In fact,

Cohn is a striking node of connection between the two artists, serving as a model for Mapplethorpe (who would himself die from AIDS only a few years after Cohn in 1989) and the source for one of the most engrossing characters in Kushner's monumental play, *Angels in America*.[3]

Cohn remains an important historical figure because we are still living in the wake of so many historical events in which he played a role. Perhaps the answer to the riddle of Cohn's contradictions will shed light on an important, if still vexing, period of American history during which American exceptionalist sentiment and perceptions of American greatness ran high, but concrete realities of inequality, racism, and homophobia seemed ascendant, too. As a man and as a symbol—and as a subject for some of the most iconic artists of his era—the figure of Cohn invites us to investigate further the interweaving of disparate threads: AIDS, anti-communist hysteria, neoconservative politics, photography, and drama.

In order to understand how the narratives of obscene genius and obscene pathology I am grappling with operated—and even fell apart—at the close of the twentieth century, this chapter begins with an examination of Mapplethorpe's final exhibition, *The Perfect Moment*, which traveled the country in 1988 and 1989, and then considers Kushner's *Angels in America*, which debuted in full on Broadway in 1992 and toured nationally beginning in 1994. The fortunes of these two texts reveal the trials and triumphs of representing same-sex desire during the height of the AIDS crisis and so crystallize a major facet of how obscenity discourses are used to police non-mainstream identities as one front in the culture wars.

In some senses, the analysis in this chapter takes a departure from the previous ones since sexuality will come to the foreground in ways that have not been as prominent in previous chapters. However, sexuality is an increasingly significant factor in obscenity discourses as the twentieth century wears on, and the racial concerns of the previous chapters still resonate powerfully with the cultural dynamics of the late 1980s and 1990s. Attending to these intersecting concerns is necessary to reflect the overlapping and mutually constituting nature of different matrices of oppression, but beyond this necessity there are direct historical phenomena that underly turning to sexual politics in this moment as a complement to discussions more centered on race.

To begin, the constitution of racial and sexual stereotypes of pathology among dominant national mythologies is simultaneous not separate. As I described in the introduction, racism is frequently expressed through differential strands of sexual normativity. That is, racism posits racially coded gender and sexual norms, or, as Ferguson puts it, "gender and sexual differences variegate racial formations."[4] This variegation of sexual difference accounts for why, for example, Kathy Acker's and Alice Walker's work face such divergent receptions and have different politics imputed to them. In this chapter, then, I hope to understand how such formations arise together and slip past one another.

In many cases, racial-sexual stereotypes emerge from material circumstances. In the context of Asian American studies, for example, David L. Eng describes how racialization is constituted simultaneously with gendering and sexualization: "The nation state's sustained economic exploitation, coupled with its political disenfranchisement, of the Asian American male immigrant is modulated precisely through a technology of gendering not adjunct but centrally linked to processes of Asian American racial formation."[5] In this case, specific histories of economic exploitation, such as the Chinese Exclusion Acts and the restriction of Asian immigrants to certain professions and geographic areas, created the social conditions of what Judy Tzu-Chun Wu calls "the compulsory condition of 'deviance' among the early generation of Asian Americans."[6] Analogous processes with their own specificity occur in different racial contexts, informing how false narratives of racial pathology arise, merge, and transform in response to new economic imperatives. Ferguson echoes Eng in noting, "Nonwhite populations were racialized such that gender and sexual transgressions were not incidental to the production of nonwhite labor, but constitutive of it" (13). In effect, all of these authors detail how historical contingencies were transmuted into racial stereotypes that were then taken for truth and used as justification for further inequalities. Capital is the driving force behind this process for Eng, Wu, and Ferguson because it demands that inequalities driven by profit be naturalized as biological or cultural inevitabilities.

All of this has left its fingerprints on political history, too. Didi Herman describes how activism on the political right morphed gradually into anti-LGBTQ+ activism, especially by demonizing those living with AIDS. Herman argues that in the late '70s, discourses of anti-communism came to be consistently applied to LGBTQ+ people and movements by the Christian Right.[7] Strub sees the transition as thematically consistent, finding a natural sympathy between Cold War hawks and Christian fundamentalists, because "Cold War ideology had posited healthy American families as a critical bulwark against communism, and with America's global position declining ... shoring up the American family, a once-venerable institution left shaken by the sexual revolution, took on newfound social and political importance for religious conservatives invested in the national character."[8] Strub also notes that this is more or less acknowledged as an extension of earlier appeals to racism. He argues regarding certain moralist campaigns, for example, that "antiporn sentiments . . . quickly replace the standard and increasingly irrelevant conservative tropes of racism and anticommunism in New Right rhetoric. Pornography helped set the stage for the broader 'family values' platform of opposition to feminism, gay rights, and abortion access to come" (*Perversion* 7). Essentially, what Herman and Strub describe is a shift from anti-communism and anti–Civil Rights rhetorics to anti-LGBTQ+ rhetoric and moralism, a shift that maintained manifold exclusions, especially heteronormative discourses. In short, this shift drew the racial stereotypes of the Jim Crow era into the culture wars of the century's end.

These thinkers help us make the leap from pathologizing discourses that were explicitly racialized (such as those encapsulated in the Moynihan Report) to those that focus on sexual behavior and family structures. We see that they are simply transformed or sublimated one into the other as a means of maintaining broad structures of belonging and privilege. As Ferguson pointedly states, "Heteronormativity is racialized," and "It is not only gender and sexual integrity that are at stake for heteronormative formations, like the state, but racial integrity and purity as well" (17). This means that there is an intersectional imperative to consider sexuality as a component of the larger debate about obscenity's inequalities I have been embarked upon, but also that the political reality suggests that the social forces themselves overlap considerably.

The neoliberal and neoconservative policies that shaped the historical context for this chapter found traction in part because they were couched in terms of national identity and international mission. Complementary to the well-known exceptionalist rhetoric of the Reagan administration were efforts to police the narratives of American identity and purpose in a way that might support economic shifts toward capital investment, justify foreign interventions in strategic regions globally, and appeal to electoral coalitions developed in the 1960s and '70s. As the U.S. economy gradually recovered from recession through the 1980s and the tensions of the Cold War subsided in the days before the fall of the Berlin Wall, a new rhetoric was also needed to retain the loyalty of the Christian Right who had shifted the Republican Party's anti-communist platform toward increasing social conservatism. This confluence of forces animates resistance to the gains of ethnic, racial, and sexual minorities, groups that had already been (speciously) linked with communism and the threat of Soviet infiltration during the 1950s (by Cohn, McCarthy, and others).[9] As the New Right took over, its politics changed; Strub describes the new coalition this way: "This shift from an externally focused siege mentality predicated on fears of communist conquest to an internal siege mentality based on reactionary cultural and sexual politics constituted much of the 'new' component of the New Right" (116). This resulted in the public clashes over art and media during the late 1980s and 1990s that became known as the culture wars, a battle fought along lines of race, class, gender, and sexuality, all filtered through questions of national identity and federal funding. These cultural battles stretched on through the beginning years of the AIDS epidemic in the 1980s, extended well into the 1990s, and continue in many forms today.

The culture wars were often fought over government funding for the arts, which resulted in highly polarized debates in public and in Congress over the content of controversial works. For example, controversies over Andres Serrano's photograph *Piss Christ* and Mapplethorpe's *The Perfect Moment* led to severe funding restrictions for the National Endowment for the Arts in 1989. Serrano's work was provocative in part for using bodily fluids as a medium at a time when, as bell hooks reminds us, "the mass media had begun to warn us that our vital substances could be lethal," while Mapplethorpe's photos frankly represented homoerotic themes and subjects that were still largely taboo. The debate in Congress about the use of federal funds to support art that might be controversial made it harder for agencies to encourage innovation in art and shifted the center of gravity of future conversations to focus more on the possibility of mass appeal rather than challenges to the status quo.

This charged atmosphere shaped how the narrative of obscene pathology would play out for Mapplethorpe and Kushner, particularly because their works flouted or resisted narratives of infection and pathology that were already being used to stigmatize people living with AIDS and LGBTQ+ people. Not only did Mapplethorpe's exhibition generate controversy for the National Endowment for the Arts, but conservative politicians who were opposed to the exhibition succeeded in pressuring D.C.'s Corcoran Gallery to cancel the exhibition's showing there. This was not the end of the controversy; the Cincinnati Contemporary Arts Center was prosecuted when they presented the collection, becoming the first museum ever to be prosecuted in this way. The museum prevailed in court, but the prosecution reveals the continuing currency of socially conservative opposition to sexually explicit art—especially non-heteronormative art—even a quarter-century after the Supreme Court ruled that such work could not be banned. *Angels in America* encountered a parallel but distinct fate just a few years later. Though also widely celebrated in major cities and winning both the Tony Award and Pulitzer Prize, opposition in Charlotte, North Carolina, caused headaches for the local repertory theater and arts council. While somewhat more muted, the protests nonetheless show the continuing hurdles for LGBTQ+ artists, even in a period of rapid change in LGBTQ+ visibility and equality around this time. The controversies surrounding *The Perfect Moment* and *Angels* crystallize this rhetorical shift.

In addition, the two histories highlight the importance of local politics in determining the fate of transgressive sexual representations. Lauded in Philadelphia, Mapplethorpe was nonetheless shut down (temporarily) in Washington and prosecuted in Cincinnati. Similarly, *Angels* was a smash hit in New York, but a lightning rod in Charlotte. Because the Supreme Court rulings on obscenity include provisions that works can be banned if they violate "community standards," obscenity prosecutions often take on such localized characters and require attention to shifting demographic trends and historical context.[10] Thus, the legacies of obscene literature are often too complex to reduce to single vectors or easy racial, gender, class, or sexual binaries (including the binary operating between the narratives of obscene genius and obscene pathology), nor do they represent straight-line progress toward a more open society or greater equality. Instead, these cases remind us to attend to the particular, remember that theoretical lenses can obscure as well as reveal, and that rigor demands we contend with the specificity of material conditions as well as the broader trends of cultural movement.

"AIDS Words ... Are Never Simply 'Facts'": The Rhetoric of the AIDS Epidemic

The narrative of obscene pathology that I lay out in the Introduction seems to take part in the symbolical and rhetorical tropes of the AIDS epidemic in the moment I am describing, and so its unique character at this time and for these artists deserves examination.[11] What would eventually become known as HIV/AIDS was first described among small groups of gay men in New York and California in 1981. The syndrome was defined by the presence of opportunistic infections that seemed unusually aggressive and that were otherwise exceedingly rare, suggesting underlying immunosuppression. By the following year, organizations and clinics such as Gay Men's Health Crisis in New York arose to help provide care and support, as well as resources designed to prevent transmission, despite the fact little was known about how it spread. At the same time, Congress acted to fund research into the new epidemic, and the Centers for Disease Control first used the term *AIDS*.[12] Despite this rapid initial progress in the early years of the 1980s, the epidemic remained largely outside public consciousness and scientific knowledge was limited, in part because of the perception that the disease was specific to the gay men and intravenous drug users who were its first known victims. It was not until 1984 that the virus that causes AIDS was identified and not until 1985 that the first test to screen for the presence of the virus was developed.[13]

In subsequent years, growing awareness and increased research would eventually lead to better treatments, but even after the development of new drugs, access to information and treatment was uneven because of homophobia and racial and class barriers and because funding for research and prevention became one of many fronts in culture wars' attacks on marginalized groups. Cultural rhetoric that invoked the specter of AIDS and relied on metaphors of contamination and disease activated unacknowledged fears about a more diverse and inclusive society. This was a way of buttressing exclusionary narratives of national identity based in notions of the family as under threat from sexual practices other than heterosexual monogamy, the nation as besieged by foreign invaders, and the body politic as menaced by debilitating corruption. In this way, anti-gay AIDS rhetoric bridged anti-communist discourses that were waning and culture wars discourses that were ascendant.

Senator Jesse Helms of North Carolina demonstrated that this culture wars' approach to AIDS was motivated by homophobia when he succeeded in attaching what became known as the Helms Amendment to a 1987 appropriations bill. The amendment denied funding for AIDS education programs with gay-positive and sex-positive themes.[14] Further, in a letter to the editor in the *New York Times* that year entitled "Morality Will Effectively Prevent AIDS from Spreading," Helms shows his willingness to speciously promote a particular Christian morality as the only defense against AIDS, writing, "Americans who don't want to risk being killed by AIDS have a clear choice and a safe bet available: Reject sodomy and practice morality. If they are unwilling to do that, they should understand the consequences."[15] Also in 1987, he introduced but failed to advance the draconian AIDS Control Act, which would have criminalized the donation of blood or organs by gay men and Haitians, among others. It also ordered the armed services to release seropositive individuals and the CDC to keep records of them. In sinister conjunction with the latter, it also would have required that broad swaths of the population be tested during routine contact with health officials. The extreme surveillance Helms proposed and its targeting of non-white immigrants and gay men indicates that more than public health concerns animated the amendment, but rather the culturally exclusive motives Helms evinces.[16]

Efforts to limit sexual health information based on restrictive notions of proper sexual conduct were devastating to existing institutions of AIDS education and activism, which had largely arisen in urban gay communities before mainstream awareness of AIDS took hold. The amendment states, "None of the funds made available under this Act to the Centers for Disease Control shall be used to provide AIDS education, information, or prevention materials and activities that promote or encourage, directly, homosexual sexual activities,"[17] language that significantly complicated efforts to limit transmission because suggesting safer sexual practices might still be construed as "condoning" sexual contact between same-sex partners. One example of the kind of activism that would be ineligible for funding but was central to early efforts to prevent the spread of the disease was the manual *How to Have Sex in an Epidemic*, written and distributed by members of the gay community in New York. The authors encourage the use of condoms, various non-penetrative acts, and alternative affective arrangements—such as closed circles of sexual partners not limited to monogamous pairs—as ways to continue to pursue sexual pleasure and affirm the validity of same-sex desire. While helpful in limiting the spread of the disease and emerging directly from the affected community, this work would be off-limits.

The pathologizing of LGBTQ+ people through negative AIDS rhetoric concealed a broader ideological desire among some members of the government to regulate the intimate lives of all citizens. To wit, the bill also requires that "Education, information, and prevention activities and materials paid for with funds appropriated under this Act shall emphasize . . . abstinence from sexual activity outside a sexually monogamous marriage" (United States, *AIDS*). Of course, this notion is consonant with other efforts to police the practice of marginalized groups; they are always also an effort to restrict all sexual practice in the population according to specific regimes of reproduction. Such efforts attempt to direct sexual desire into channels that promote organizations of society favoring white middle-class structures and ontologies of futurity. Moreover, looking at such efforts in conjunction with the proposed AIDS Control Act, we can see the outlines of a broad politics that places sexual politics—and dynamics of pathologization—at the center of efforts to shape national identity and citizenship.

This instrumentalization of AIDS discourse toward exclusive notions of identity worked symbiotically with already-existing stereotypes. Cindy Patton reminds us that because actual encounters with the disease were rare in the early 1980s, "The epidemic gained its social meaning in relation to deep prejudices about race, class, gender, sexuality, and 'addiction'" (25). Patton suggests that AIDS became a site of projection for existing cultural tropes, which highlights the metonymic relationships between the terms of homophobia, classism, racism, ability, and misogyny (though they remain meaningfully distinct). Patton points out that, consonant with long-standing biases, discourse around AIDS construed non-heterosexual sex as a terminal practice for LGBTQ+ individuals and drugs as a terminal practice for people of color. AIDS also provided opportunities for savior-style volunteerism (Patton 25–26) in what Patton calls the "white middle-class AIDS industry" (44). Even further, sex workers were inordinately blamed for transmitting HIV to the heterosexual community, a practice that reinforced stereotypes about the illegitimacy of sex work (39). These dynamics reify deep-seated notions of race and sexuality in which white, hetero, middle-class society is pure and righteous (even excessive in its generosity) while outsiders and others reap the consequences of their indulgence while threatening to contaminate the community.[18]

Susan Sontag clarifies what's behind the rhetoric of pathology at work here in *AIDS and Its Metaphors* (1988), focusing on belonging and national identity. Patton described the inherent divisions between the "general public" and those in "risk groups"—usually people marginalized according to sexuality, race, class, or ability—and Sontag relates this in/out dynamic to the metaphors that typically attend Western ways of talking about epidemics:

> Every feared epidemic disease, but especially those associated with sexual license, generates a preoccupying distinction between the disease's putative carriers (which usually means just the poor and, in this part of the world, people with darker skins) and those defined ... as "the general population." AIDS has revived similar phobias and fears of contamination among *this* disease's version of "the general population": white heterosexuals who do not inject themselves with drugs or have sexual relations with those who do.[19]

Through her placement of AIDS in a longer history of Western epidemiology, Sontag shows that the projection of damaging metaphors onto marginalized groups is hardly unique to AIDS. In doing so, she contests the notion that the conclusions we draw about AIDS are inherent to it. Rather, the alignment of the medical and scientific communities with white middle-class values is revealed to be less a function of the historical specificity of AIDS and more a function of the ongoing project of heteronormativity.

For Sontag, the trope of the plague plays a particularly insidious role in this way of talking about AIDS. She notes, "One feature of the usual script for plague" is that "the disease invariably comes from somewhere else" (*AIDS* 47). In the case of AIDS, the "somewhere else" is Africa (and in early writings Haiti, and even New York, Los Angeles, and San Francisco, as those are construed as outside the mainstream of America), and we can see how narratives of foreign-ness intersect with military metaphors of alien invasion that are also used to characterize illness. These metaphors suggest a kind of nativism: mistrust of the outsider and belief that those who contract HIV must somehow be marked as not belonging. This notion finds expression in limitations on immigration and military service for seropositive individuals at this time, while the military metaphors often used in such circumstances resonate with the rhetoric of ethnic homogeneity (fighting invaders), and prescriptions for cleansing and purity take on a sinister tone.[20]

The rhetoric of plague also works in concert with culture war tactics. Because plagues are often interpreted as being inflicted on morally errant societies, they inspire calls to return to traditional ways. Such calls find dubious proof in the apparent judgment of plague, and in fact, plague rhetoric had already been circulating on the Christian Right with respect to increasing sexual permissiveness, and AIDS fit that narrative neatly.[21] Further, as Sontag points out, as with older uses of the term "plague" when "Responses to illnesses associated with sinners and the poor invariably recommended the adoption of middle-class values" (*AIDS* 54–55), so moralizing around AIDS suggests that the habits of a white middle class—monogamy, heterosexuality, abstinence from drugs and pre-marital sex, and so on, as well as submission to the regime of testing and surveillance—are the proper remedies for an infected society, even if hope for individual sufferers is not offered by a disease characterized at the time as leading inexorably to death.

As Lee Edelman has attested, the association of LGBTQ+ people with death serves to cover over a larger social compulsion to reproductive futurity. Linking any sexual practice other than penile-vaginal intercourse to waste, narcissism, and a host of other pathologies, heteronormativity aligns itself not with an arbitrary preference for a particular kind of sex, but with the reproduction of the social order. Civil society and capitalist production, then, rely on pathologizing non-reproductive sex and its representations, including Mapplethorpe's photos and Kushner's play. The pre-existence of this rhetoric, suffusing disciplines as different as medicine and economics, reveals as false the idea that AIDS proves the morbidity of same-sex desire. Rather, AIDS became a vehicle for an epistemology that already assigned morbidity to same-sex desire in order to stigmatize it.[22]

Thus, AIDS pathology discourses served as a coalescing point for various forms of exclusion circulating since mid-century, not all of which were limited to sexuality. Explicitly indicting cultural and social pushback against perceived excesses of the 1960s—the kind of resistance that brought Nixon to power and underwrote the Reagan administration's social politics—Sontag describes the often-obscured historical throughlines in a manner that merits quoting at length:

> Denunciations of "the gay plague" are part of a much larger complaint, common among antiliberals in the West and many exiles from the Russian bloc, about contemporary permissiveness of all kinds: a now-familiar diatribe against the "soft" West, with its hedonism, its vulgar sexy music, its indulgence in drugs, its disabled family life, which have sapped the will to stand up to communism. . . . Although these specialists in ugly feelings insist that AIDS is a punishment for deviant sex, what moves them is not just, or even principally, homophobia. Even more important is the utility of AIDS in pursuing one of the main activities of the so-called neo-conservatives, the Kulturekampf against all that is called, for short (and inaccurately), the 1960s. A whole politics of "the will"—of intolerance, of paranoia, of fear of political weakness—has fastened onto this disease. (*AIDS* 63)

Sontag's efforts to highlight the ideological continuity among various facets of neoconservative ideology demonstrate that, just as discourses about sex are ultimately about belonging, so discourses about belonging in turn serve a larger disciplinary belief system, one based on will, opposing laxity and permissiveness and predominantly authoritarian, rather than based on policy preferences or even an electoral coalition's vested interests. While we should retain our awareness of the disproportionate effects of these negative discourses on LGBTQ+ folks, it is also helpful to identify the connection between the oversight of individual sexual practices and a broader movement of power and capital.

In many ways, then, AIDS marks an important transition in national discourses. AIDS proved a convenient impetus for an ascendant culture of seriousness and restraint that was in marked contrast to the ethics of fun that characterized earlier counterculture movements. Acknowledging the somber fact that "in the age of AIDS, all life involves some risk" (Berkowitz and Callen 9), the authors of *How to Have Sex in an Epidemic* soberly advised that "The party that was the '70s is over."[23] With AIDS came a growing sense that the utopic spirit of the '60s and '70s had reached an inflection point. What kind of transition would occur begins to crystallize when we read the authors' reassurances that "What's over isn't sex—just sex without responsibility" (40). The impulse to responsibility sounds like a call to grow up, to construe the experiments of the '60s and '70s as a childhood to be left behind, and to settle down to the serious business of adult life. But it is also a call to monogamy and bourgeois values, to assimilation and respectability; the subsuming of these under the heading of maturity is itself part of a history of construing pleasure seeking, as well as same-sex desire, as regressive.

AIDS, at first a mysterious epidemic affecting primarily already-stigmatized communities, produced a discourse that allowed for the open circulation of prejudiced notions in the guise of self-evident truths and commonsense measures. That's why the authors of *How to Have Sex in an Epidemic* lament, "The AIDS crisis has . . . produced a lot of recommendations which are really misplaced morality masquerading as medical advice" (35). Moreover, the nature of AIDS as a sexually transmitted disease means that philanthropic, medical, and penal intervention literally became an effort to alter sexual mores, pushing toward models of desire and behavior that map onto the same notions of ideal sexuality espoused by the Helms amendments: monogamy, reproductivity, and heterosexuality.[24] This moment, therefore, is significant for an understanding of a broader politics of obscenity, in which policing sexual practices and representations is a method of controlling social organizations, subject formation, and civil participation. But more important here, they reveal the altered contours of the constantly transforming narratives of pathology that were circulating at the time and which would be applied to Mapplethorpe and Kushner.

Hardly a Perfect Moment: The Afterlife of Mapplethorpe's *X Portfolio* and Final Exhibition

Though the Republican presidential nominating convention in August of 1992 (just months before the New York premier of *Angels*) represented a high-water mark in the culture wars, and Pat Buchanan's notorious floor speech crystallized the political strategy of polarizing discourse around questions of national identity and exclusion, the political fight over culture began to take shape years earlier, with Mapplethorpe's exhibition playing a prominent role.[25] The National Endowment for the Arts had been fighting for its life in Congress after funding controversial projects such as Andres Serrano's 1987 photograph *Piss Christ*. Torn up on the floor of the Senate by Al D'Amato and routinely vandalized when exhibited, the photograph stoked religious disagreements by presenting a figure of Christ submerged in the artist's urine. Though Serrano's photo sparked the controversy, Mapplethorpe was the artist most centrally embroiled in the NEA controversy.

Mapplethorpe worked with themes of sexual transgression and homoeroticism from the early days of his career, but large-scale controversy over his photographs only emerged on the occasion of the 1988 retrospective exhibition of his work titled *The Perfect Moment*, which was partly funded by the NEA. Following D'Amato's denunciation of *Piss Christ*, Helms brought the controversy to the Mapplethorpe retrospective. Though the photos that offended Helms had been in circulation since the 1970s and were featured in prominent New York shows without incident, Helms took issue with them when they were shown with federal grant support. This made Mapplethorpe's work a battleground for the exclusive ideologies animating AIDS pathology discourse and the culture wars. As Brian Herrera notes, "Queer people and people of color became poster children for what conservative America doesn't represent, like Robert Mapplethorpe and *Piss Christ*. It was a way of using particular artists to mark a line in the sand and say we therefore do not support the arts. And using the shock of the artists and their work and their identities as proof that they were corrupt and thus unworthy of funding and, by extension, not good Americans."[26] Here, Herrera connects AIDS rhetoric that enforced heteronormativity and racism, the culture wars' language of belonging and futurity, and the national debates over queer art that erupted in the late 1980s.

Herrera's reference to "the shock of the artists" is apt. Mapplethorpe's work was often dismissed as provocative while lacking substance. Echoing hooks's reflection on Serrano's "in-your-face display of very obvious improprieties," David Joselit notes, "The enormous popularity of Robert Mapplethorpe's photographs is often explained (or explained away) as a form of sophisticated naughtiness."[27] And just as hooks argued that there was substance beyond the shock, Joselit finds that Mapplethorpe's photographs address important issues that fixation on their taboo content obscures: "Mapplethorpe's broader relevance . . . is typically denied to him—typically obscured by labeling him a subcultural fetishist" (19). In this case, the association of Mapplethorpe's work with "naughtiness" robs it of seriousness and cements the notion that the erotic does not have political value. Moreover, as with *The Terror of War*, which I discuss in Chapter 2, the sexual content allows viewers to miss or mistake the meaning of the work.

Missed or mistaken, Mapplethorpe's work in S&M themes as well as gay erotica performs a specific political project related to abjected subjectivities and disavowed desires. In particular, Joselit, citing Craig Owen, explains how attempts to exclude LGBTQ+ themes from public sites (of representation or education) governs the behavior of both gay and straight individuals. Joselit indicates that Mapplethorpe uses the position of "subcultural fetishist" to speak back to the underlying sexual tropes in broader culture, describing the tendency in his work as a "complex, compound dramatization of the interplay between sexual aggression and submission—in men and women, heterosexual and homosexual" (19). Though obscured by the controversy surrounding Mapplethorpe's photos, the sexual politics they advance are important for challenging old binaries of being. Therefore, going beyond the *presence* of sex to attend to the *meaning* of sex becomes critical to understanding just what obscenity charges attempt to conceal.

The *Perfect Moment* included over 185 pieces, and curator Janet Kardon recalls that the exhibition "centered on the classical themes—still lifes, portraits, and figure studies—and place[d] special emphasis upon the unique objects," such as diptychs and triptychs combining photographs with other materials.[28] The collection thus traces recurrent themes through multiple works while presenting photographs and select multimedia pieces in unique situations that cannot easily be reproduced. The exhibition, Kardon avers, is a unit, a work unto itself. Though this may reflect a curator's insistence on the power of the museum experience in an age of mechanical reproduction, it also insists that the individual photographs cannot be interpreted individually but, rather, must be considered a cohesive ensemble, a crucial point given that obscenity judgments often hinge on the severability of offensive portions from the works they exist within.

The exhibition's troubles began in 1989, when the Corcoran Gallery in D.C. canceled a scheduled showing after objections by Helms and others. According to the gallery's director at the time, the large Federal presence in D.C. contributed to the controversy-shy stance they took.[29] Though the Corcoran canceled without taking a definitive position on the exhibition's content, that content did take center stage when the Cincinnati Contemporary Arts Center and its director, Dennis Barrie, were charged with obscenity the following year—the first ever prosecution of a museum for the art it displayed.[30] Despite taking precautions like displaying the most explicit works on a high table to prevent children from seeing them, Barrie and the CAC were charged on two counts of "pandering to obscenity" for two photos of children with visible genitals from the portraits collection and for sadomasochistic and urophagic images taken from a collection of photos from 1978 called the *X Portfolio*. Unlike the Corcoran, the CAC chose to forego federal support, obviating the funding issue and forcing obscenity to be the grounds on which the material was challenged. In addition, before the exhibition opened, they petitioned for but were denied a preliminary ruling that the show was not obscene on the grounds of artistic value. Nonetheless, aware that they would likely face legal action, they went forward with the show and, within hours, were shut down by the Hamilton County Prosecutor's office. The defendants faced a difficult trial, but were acquitted of all charges in October 1990.[31]

A year after his acquittal, Barrie reflected on his experience, contending that *The Perfect Moment* "appeared in a time of hysteria over the arts" and that the museum was merely caught up in the larger culture wars.[32] Though the museum had its own reasons for moving forward with the show and proved they were just as willing to make sexual representations the means to pursue a political goal related to freedom of speech, the furor created by the exhibition and the involvement of state forces indicate that something about Mapplethorpe's work struck a nerve in larger debates about national identity.

To discern why his work was so controversial, we must consider it closely. The most often-noted effect of viewing Mapplethorpe's work is genre bleed between erotic images and classical forms. Kardon notes, "Mapplethorpe makes a point of *not* distinguishing between his flower studies and his pornographic imagery" (12–13). Patti Smith, who collaborated with Mapplethorpe extensively, explained his artistic sentiment from an earlier show similarly: "His bold, elegant show mixed classic motifs with sex, flowers, and portraits, all equivalent in their presentation: unapologetic images of cock rings beside an arrangement of flowers. To him one was the other."[33] Thus, the exhibition's aesthetic argument, as it were, entails a celebration of same-sex desire as classically elegant and also suggests that the world around us is suffused with unacknowledged eroticism. This is particularly significant because they argue for the beauty, rather than abjection, of gay desire in particular and thus advocate for less restrictive notions of identity.[34]

Examples of genre-bleed abound in the collection. For example, in the tetraptych *Manfred* (1974), Mapplethorpe highlights the use of classical forms while playing with masculine and feminine visual tropes. The three images of the eponymous subject present him either shirtless or fully nude, posed in an arched doorway (the fourth frame is blank). The sexuality of the images is explicit (the male subject is aroused), but the three photos deploy different tropes of sexual passivity and activity. While the second portrait shows Manfred wearing pants and standing in an assertive, head-on pose with his upper-body muscles highlighted by contrast lighting, the other two photos show him nude and leaning with softer lines, suggesting receptivity rather than aggression. Similarly, Mapplethorpe explored the complexities of femininity in his photographs of the bodybuilder Lisa Lyon. Eight photos of Lyon were included in the exhibition, two in the catalogue. In one from 1982, Lyon appears alone in Mapplethorpe's studio, holding a bodybuilding pose that evokes Greek or Roman sculptural forms (an interest of Mapplethorpe's). While her firm musculature is visible, her long hair and earrings and the bikini she wears invoke contrary visual scripts, bending representational conventions through presentation of a non-normative female form.[35] These images demonstrate Mapplethorpe's deployment of contrasting visual tropes to test and trouble the boundaries of representational forms.

The effect of juxtaposing very different genres in the context of the exhibition can create in the spectator a feeling of dissonance and even discomfort that is directly related to their status as obscene works. Kardon described the show in terms that highlight the troubling effect of the images—and their power—noting in relation to the highly formal nature of Mapplethorpe's photos that

> The scenes appear to be distilled from real life; when elevated to an unnatural innocence, they create a frisson between the licentious subject of the photograph and its formal qualities that purifies, even cancels, the prurient elements. . . . Depicting blatant sexuality in a pristine photographic language infuses these works with enormous impact and energy; the contrast between the subject and its manner of presentation allows the viewer the option of being either voyeur or connoisseur. In either instance, the images remain potent entrapments. (10)

In this passage, Kardon seems preemptively to respond to censors as the show's curator by invoking the language of the *Miller* ruling, emphasizing that the disconnect between the "licentious subject" and the "formal qualities" "purifies, even cancels, the prurient elements." Thus, she goes even farther than *Miller* requires, claiming not that the sexual elements of the work are protected by the artistic merit of the work as a whole, but that the artistic qualities simply erase their sexuality.[36] Of course, she then acknowledges that the sexuality remains, making the images "potent entrapments" that suspend us between the spaces of reflection and arousal.

The use of the word "frisson" to describe the rupture between different responses is important, too. Roland Barthes assigns a similar dynamic to Mapplethorpe's work to make a distinction between the pornographic and the erotic: "the erotic is a pornographic that has been disturbed, fissured."[37] The idea applies to Mapplethorpe's deployment of pornographic elements in service of a more complex aesthetic vision. Barthes describes pornography as "unary," characterized by a "unity of composition" that renders it "banal" (41). However, he calls Mapplethorpe's work "proof *a contrario*," pointing to the presence of something arresting in excess of the image's incitement to arousal: "Mapplethorpe shifts his close-ups of genitalia from the pornographic to the erotic by photographing the fabric of the underwear at very close range: the photograph is no longer unary, since I am interested in the material" (41–42). In this sense, the multivalent signification of the image—and its entrapment of the viewer in movement along divergent axes of arousal and detachment, engagement and reflection—is what enters them in the realm of art.

One of the most commonly mentioned images from the retrospective is *Man in Polyester Suit* (1981). The work was included in the "Figure Studies" section of the exhibition, which consisted of photos from the *X Portfolio* and the *Z Portfolio*. *Man in Polyester Suit* was originally published in the *Z Portfolio*. A focus so fine you can count the stitches allows for a consideration of the suit's layered material, recalling Barthes's contention about the nature of art and porn. The subtle grading of light, shadow, and texture across the folds of the garment also contrast with the frankness of the exposed genitalia, creating a dissonance that complements the mild shock of seeing the penis in the otherwise highly formal composition. *Man in Polyester Suit* thus demonstrates Mapplethorpe's decontextualization of the sexual to both make it innocuous and highlight the difficult simultaneity of arousal and reflection in his work. According to Kardon: "The photograph catches the viewer in a binary pull: The action cannot be perceived unless the eye constantly darts in opposite directions as in a tennis match, or, in this instance, between the mundane polyester suit and what outrageously protrudes from its trousers" (11). Kardon's description of the viewer's eye movements from one area of the photograph to another parallels the affective shuttling the viewer experiences between aesthetic contemplation and a more visceral reaction—perhaps shock, perhaps arousal, perhaps curiosity, or embarrassment.

The reason for the photo's ubiquity in reviews may be that its content—a man's torso in a three-piece suit, with his penis exposed through the trousers' open fly—conveniently suggests many of the themes of Mapplethorpe's work while avoiding some of its darker elements. That is, the presence of the penis also allows writers to discuss the sexual themes of Mapplethorpe's work, yet the image is tame in comparison to some others. Along these lines, despite the extent to which the image militates against coyness, Kardon demonstrates a common desire to euphemize by referencing "what outrageously protrudes from its trousers" instead of simply naming the penis. This delicacy might also be why the *X Portfolio* gets only passing mention in the exhibition catalogue's introduction,[38] but the reticence is not only verbal: The catalogue also elides the images. Possibly seeking to avoid the legal difficulties faced by the exhibition (an assumption supported by the anxiety over the *Miller* test evident in her phrasing), the book contains only one image from the *X Portfolio*, a photo called *Joe, N.Y.C.* from 1978: a photo of a single person in a leather fetish suit with studded collar. There is no nudity and no person-to-person contact. The interpretation of the image, then, depends partly on context, and for an uninitiated viewer (or who is unfamiliar with Mapplethorpe's other work) the image becomes merely perplexing. Thus the image is largely stripped of its power to shock and most of its meaning through this decontextualization and merely stands in for the unmentioned/unmentionable content of the other photos in the *X Portfolio*. It is only the sign of BDSM elsewhere.

Perhaps the most important image from the *X Portfolio* is a self-portrait of the artist from 1978. In it, Mapplethorpe wears leather chaps and a vest, as well as leather boots, and he looks back seriously at the camera while holding a leather whip, the handle of which protrudes from his anus. In its depiction of the visual codes of sexual domination (the leather clothing and the whip), the photo suggests an interplay of pain and pleasure that would be quite visceral if it were not defused by the stiff formalism of the image. As with many of Mapplethorpe's photos, there is minute focus on relatively mundane details: the braided strands of leather in the whip stand out, as do the paths of veins and shadows across Mapplethorpe's forearm, and the almost brittle look of his fingers as they hold the whip also demand our attention. The floor's polish reflects the intense studio lights, and the grain of the polished wood stands out, calling our attention to the image's artificial staging. By contrast, the central element of the photo—the penetration that was grounds for obscenity claims and is the literal center of the image—is lost in partial shadow. Though highly explicit, the image is not exactly gratuitous, and the presentation of highly taboo material via artistic modes that border on stilted means that the content is stripped of eroticism and made aggressively neutral. The photograph seems therefore to induce the shuttling of vision from the act of penetration to the peripheral details of space, form, and lighting, while the viewer shuttles from visceral to abstract responses.

The inclusion of a self-portrait in the series, particularly one that implicates the author in the non-mainstream acts depicted throughout the portfolio, breaks down the boundaries of formal art. Because of this photo, the tendency to disembody the artist is disallowed, and the work gains a new element of difficulty and immediacy—posing the aesthetic alongside the bodily instead of playing them against each other. Moreover, it is no longer his photographs, but his own body, his actions and his sexuality that become the center of the obscenity prosecution. To engage the portfolio, we must engage the body of its author, not (only) his aesthetic or his objects, and the portrayal of his sexuality brings into the open—into the museum space—the sexual realm that segments of the population preferred remains private or invisible. In this way, the self-portrait enacts the same kind of confrontation that the portrait of Kathy Acker I discussed in Chapter 3 performed and which occasions a reconsideration of the experiences of viewership.

According to Smith, Mapplethorpe may not have meant to make a statement about LGBTQ+ visibility through his work. She writes, "He was not looking to make a political statement or an announcement of his evolving sexual persuasion" (Smith 199). Still, his photos allow for a more confident visibility, and as for the *X Portfolio* in particular, she says they encourage living unapologetically: "His subjects are not saying, Sorry I have my cock hanging out. He's not sorry and doesn't want anybody else to be" (236). In this way, Mapplethorpe seems to shy away from any explicit politics of LGBTQ+ visibility, preferring tropes of artistic boundary-testing, fidelity to personal vision, and innovation; and yet underlying these things is clearly the desire to document the beauty in people and acts that are typically denigrated and expand the limits of what—and whom—can be afforded dignity and place.

The broader cultural work performed by the *X Portfolio*—undermining conventional notions of power, gender, sexuality, and body normativity while challenging various modes of abjection and silencing—is potentially radical, both for the moment of their first release and the moment of the exhibition more than a decade later. However, the content of the photos was so shocking to certain sensibilities in 1990 that the reflection and engagement necessary to draw out these highly charged themes was effectively foreclosed, and indeed this is part of their aesthetic, making them convenient targets for reassuring simplistic narratives, such as those coming out of the culture wars.

The tendency to confine any interpretation of this complex exhibition to narratives of obscene pathology in order to justify wide-ranging discriminatory policies is demonstrated by Helms's response to them. Helms brought his usual bluster to his condemnations of Mapplethorpe's photography when he introduced amendments to Senate appropriations bills to limit government funding for projects that depicted homoerotic acts. In an echo of his efforts a couple of years earlier, Helms again worked to amend an appropriations bill to achieve cultural ends in 1989, offering three different amendments seeking to limit what the NEA could fund.[39]

The final language of the bill, which passed in October 1989, is interesting in its own right for resonances with obscenity case law:

> None of the funds authorized to be appropriated for the National Endowment for the Arts or the National Endowment for the Humanities may be used to promote, disseminate, or produce materials which in the judgment of the National Endowment for the Arts or the National Endowment for the Humanities may be considered obscene, including but not limited to, depictions of sadomasochism, homoeroticism, the sexual exploitation of children, or individuals engaged in sex acts and which, when taken as a whole, do not have serious literary, artistic, political, or scientific value. (*An Act* sec. 304a, 41)

Essentially, the law requires the NEA and NEH to include an obscenity review in its funding decisions, creating a de facto obscenity statute at the federal level for this particular agency. It is pointed that the Senate chose to specifically address the NEA and NEH in terms recalling the content of Mapplethorpe's work. It speaks, then, not only as a restriction on future actions, but also a rebuke of past actions.[40]

It is notable that Congress, following Helms's lead, chose to delineate those specific representations that were prohibited. Such moments of clarity are as rare as they are instructive.[41] The list includes, among more conventionally excluded content, homoeroticism and sadomasochism, terms that indict Mapplethorpe indirectly and that *also* constitute acts that are not inherently exploitative. Rather, something about the content itself must be at issue. For some, the reason was merely practical or even democratic; they argued that the federal government should restrict itself to funding work that would be perceived as beneficial or beautiful by a majority of Americans, rather than pushing the boundaries of what was possible or acceptable. However, those like Helms were more overt in their desire to inhibit the normalization of LGBTQ+ identities. They sensed that the representation of non-mainstream sexual acts represented a serious challenge to the system of marginalization necessary to construe the LGBTQ+ community as a threat to an imagined moral majority. Silence, on the other hand, maintains the status quo of exclusion.

"Or if You Have to Talk, Talk Dirty": The Terms of Contamination in *Angels in America*

"AIDS activists know that silence equals death, but we also know that this cannot be *said*, it must be *performed*."[42] With these words, Cindy Patton highlights the necessity of embodying a critique of enforced invisibility not only through speaking out, but by acting out.[43] Her words also call to mind the central role that performance played during the AIDS epidemic because theater foregrounds the role of the body in aesthetic meaning-making. Kushner's *Angels in America* intervenes in the historical moment I've been discussing by dramatizing narratives of bodies, families, and the nation through the experiences of the gay community coming to terms with the epidemic and of a larger American community grappling with the possibility of a more inclusive future. Michael Cadden remarks on this duality of purpose, writing, "For Kushner, AIDS, while retaining a gay-specific identity, is about the fate of the country."[44] The play, then, is often read as both an effort to humanize people living with HIV/AIDS and to explore the questions of belonging and identity that were contested during the culture wars.

Though celebrated when it debuted in New York, there was some concern that the national tour would be challenged in more conservative locations over its open portrayals of same-sex love. Michael Krass, costume designer for the touring production, remarked, "We were very aware that we were bringing a story and a set of political thinking to people who had not heard it. Who had not seen it represented, had not seen two boys kissing onstage or off—" (qtd. in Butler and Kois, 253). Fortunately, the resistance didn't materialize to the extent feared. Peter Birkenhead, who played the character Louis, notes, "In so many cities we were surprised at the incredibly warm reaction we got, which says a lot about our own prejudices as sophisticated New York artists" (qtd. in Butler and Kois, 254). Essentially Birkenhead noticed that their fears of widespread conservative backlash were exaggerated and that instead they were welcomed by a non-coastal community that largely shared their experience or their political views.

That doesn't mean the play was without controversy, though, and the tour faced a handful of challenges. For example, the crew recounts threats in Clearwater, Florida and a wintry protest in Lawrence, Kansas led by Fred Phelps of the Westboro Baptist Church. The play also ruffled feathers when the theater department at Catholic University attempted to stage the play in D.C. in 1996, partly because of the presence of conservative officials such as Helms, and in this way, the controversy echoed the situation of the Corcoran when it sought to stage *The Perfect Moment*. The theater department was forbidden from staging the production by the university administration, though eventually a compromise was reached and the play was staged off campus. The administration's objections, and those of the Church, don't necessarily indicate a widespread cultural phenomenon so much as a theological debate within Catholicism. However, as Gitta

Honegger (who chaired the theater department) notes, something about the cultural climate of the era was at work, too: "Obviously we knew from the start that it could be problematic, given the whole university, the religious ethics, and so on.... It was a time when fundamentalist religion was becoming stronger in this country. I'm not sure in an earlier decade it would've been a problem" (qtd. in Butler and Kois, 276).

Moralist resistance to the play was most pronounced when it was staged in Helms's home state of North Carolina in 1996. At their request, Charlotte Repertory Theatre staged the played, rather than the national touring group. Charlotte Rep was optimistic and excited, but local sentiment was divided over the frank and sympathetic depictions of gay relationships, and a brief nude scene was also the subject of some controversy. Charlotte Rep faced opposition both within their organization—two members of the Board of Directors resigned—and from without—external funding sources dried up (Houchin 251). A fairly aggressive protest campaign was also spearheaded by Joseph R. Chambers, already a public figure because of similar crusades against other works, notably *Barney and Friends* (1992–2009) and Disney's *The Lion King* (1994).

Part of the tension stemmed from the specific historical moment and geographic place. Charlotte's rapid growth in the preceding decades had altered the cultural climate but not created a unified culture. A mishmash of different groups, including more affluent, educated employees of new banking centers, led to overly optimistic projections about what was possible in 1996. Kevin F. Free, who played Belize in the Charlotte production, noted that "Charlotte was supposed to be the New South. The New South was supposedly progressive, more inclusive of gay inhabitants, people of color" (qtd. in Butler and Kois, 284). However, these assumptions proved to be not entirely true. At root, Charlotte director Steve Umberger contends, there is a "strange tension between an aspiration to be a 'world-class place,' ... and a very small-town way of thinking that's always been at the core: a Southern, conservative, church-going sensibility" (qtd. in Butler and Kois, 284–85).

Though representatives of this "Southern, conservative, church-going sensibility" considered challenging the play on the grounds of obscenity, the accolades heaped on *Angels* would make any finding that the work lacked serious social value unlikely.[45] They therefore sought to stop the performance based on the assertion that a nude scene where a character is examined by his nurse would violate local indecent exposure laws (Houchin 250–52). Ultimately, Charlotte Rep was able to secure an advance ruling protecting them from any interference by prosecutors and police,[46] and while the opening was protested by a small contingent organized by

Chambers, they were reportedly outnumbered by those who protested in support of the performance.⁴⁷

In fact, anecdotally it appears that the protests against the play may have galvanized the arts community and turned out audiences interested in promoting free speech, the arts, and LGBTQ+ equality. By all accounts, the play was a hit and its run was extended because media publicity made Charlotteans curious to see the play responsible for the furor. The following year, Charlotte Rep even saw a significant increase in subscriptions as a direct result of their having staged *Angels*.⁴⁸ This is no surprise given the obscenity narratives I am tracing here. As with other controversial artworks, *Angels* succeeded in Charlotte not in spite of the controversy, but because of it. Modest, even kooky, resistance ended up convincing larger numbers of the play's defenders and those who support free artistic expression to show that support with their feet and their dollars, as well as generating local and national media coverage.

Nonetheless, there were long-lasting negative effects on the arts community in Charlotte. This was, after all, a place experiencing cultural tensions resulting from a somewhat uneven cultural renaissance. As *The Economist* noted when the county's Board of Commissioners, with a new contingent of conservative members, voted the following year to cut funding to the local arts council, "Where art is concerned, the natives and the newcomers sometimes [found] their tastes colliding" ("No Gays").⁴⁹ The debate over funding was quite explicitly a reaction to the production of *Angels* the previous year, and the rationale given by the Board was that the measure was intended to "protect children from exposure to perverted forms of sexuality" (qtd. in "No Gays"). This makes clear that those who opposed integration of sexual minorities into the mainstream were willing to use their control of public finances to further their goal of exclusion and heteronormativity. This reaction was, further, part of a larger piece of legislation that was specifically targeted at prohibiting county funds from being used for gay-positive programs—a gesture essentially identical to Helms's on the national level.⁵⁰ In these ways, the national debate about arts funding played out in miniature in Charlotte, even echoing the terms of pathology and anti-gay-positivity, while being animated largely by local demographic shifts.

The play that caused the uproar is long and multifaceted. Invoking Henry James, Jonathan Freedman describes it as "a loose baggy monster of a play, housing in its capacious representational tent (inter alia) Brechtian alienation devices, American mythologies, Broadway schtick, kabbalistic folktales, sitcom wisecracks, [and] vaudeville blackout sketches."⁵¹ The play is so monstrous, in fact, that its two parts are seldom performed together because they run roughly seven hours beginning to end. Similarly, its production history reflects the complexity of writing, developing, and staging such an ambitious play. Though its first half, *Millennium Approaches*, was workshopped in 1990 and premiered in May 1991 in San Francisco, its second half was still in development at the time. *Perestroika* was then workshopped in Los Angeles through 1992, where it ultimately premiered. The first performance of the work in its entirety was in November 1992—the very moment of the Bush-Clinton election. Thus, the play makes its entrance onto the public stage at a moment of particular pique in the culture wars.[52]

The plot centers on Prior Walter, a man recently diagnosed with AIDS who is subsequently chosen as a prophet by a band of abandoned angels. God has left mankind and the angels to fend for themselves. Lacking guidance and in fear of the terrible wreckage humanity is visiting on each other and the world, the angels decide that they must force God to return by halting the progress of humanity. To this end, the angels endow Prior with prophetic vision and an epic mission. Their language suggests that AIDS is the mark of stasis that he is supposed to bear to the world, the sign to turn back and resist a changing society: a rhetoric of plague. They tell him, "Oh Exemplum Paralyticum: On you in you in your blood we have written: STASIS! The END."[53] The marks on him (Kaposi's Sarcoma lesions) and in his blood (HIV) are meant to indicate to the world that the movement—*intercourse*—of humanity must end. Prior eventually concludes that the angels are misguided, rejecting their call to halt the progress of humanity and demanding instead "more life." Prior himself rejects this apocalyptic plague narrative about AIDS, but it nonetheless serves as the narrative foil he wrestles with throughout the play. The weight of this metanarrative of a compulsory end to sex and affirmation takes place in a larger social allegory and allows the play to introduce some of the moralist and reactionary discourses Kushner refutes, particularly as they make use of narratives of pathology to stigmatize LGBTQ+ identity as a danger to the nation.

As Prior grapples with the abstract complexities of what AIDS portends for society, other characters deal with its concrete details. Belize, a black drag queen and nurse, ministers not only to the physical suffering of Prior and the fictional Roy Cohn, but to the emotional suffering of Louis Ironson, who struggles to come to terms with his responsibilities as Prior's partner. Neither Joe Pitt nor Harper Pitt has HIV, but they are drawn into the web of narratives around the disease because their devout Mormon, heterosexual marriage conceals Joe's struggle to accept his own same-sex desire. Joe owes his career in politics to Cohn and finds himself caught up in an affair with Louis. The resulting turmoil brings Joe's mother, Hannah, and Prior together in a surrogate mother-son relationship. Along the way, the realities of life break down conventional relationships, and new ones take their place, a gesture that affirms the importance of affective ties while questioning the value of received forms for them, such as the nuclear family.

The complicated nature of the play's effort to move into new affective territory offers both ambivalence and promise. Freedman describes a particularly hopeful aspect of the utopic vision:

> [Kushner] offers the image of redeemed community in the guise of a utopian Americanness where the nation is reconstituted as a postnuclear family made up of quarreling outsiders.... That Kushner is echoing a problematic nationalist discourse is ultimately less important than his appropriation of it for a frankly queer political project—and of the family-as-nation metaphor for a nonprocreative notion of both family and nation that includes all forms of family in a new national narrative. (57)

In other words, Kushner's play does re-enact problematic American metanarratives—including those about family that had been used to demonize LGBTQ+ folks—but adapts them to more inclusive forms, thereby hoping to redeem the nation and possibly to move forward with new forms of community that are more open. Kushner's use of gay and seropositive characters represents the potency of LGBTQ+ politics and AIDS discourse for understanding and negotiating the contours of American identity, resisting their characterization as totally outside the nation.

Freedman's use of the phrase "postnuclear" is doubly significant. We can understand it on the one hand as referring to the incipient end of détente with the Soviet Union and the Cold War moment directly invoked by the title of the second half of the play: *Perestroika*. The Soviet period of "reorganization" roughly coincides with the action of the play, so the pervasive anxiety of a nuclear strategy based on "mutually assured destruction" also inflects the concept of a "postnuclear family," offering hope beyond nuclear annihilation.[54] On the other hand, we must also read the use of "postnuclear" in terms of the replacement of the nuclear family and its concomitant insistence on procreation, genealogies, heterosexuality, and binary ideologies gender. The only heterosexual relationship in the play, in fact, turns out to be a sham. Instead, ad hoc families formed in response to crisis will supplant the nuclear family. In this sense, the imagined culture is "postnuclear" because it succeeds both the nuclear aggression of the Cold War and the nuclear family, while the entendre demonstrates the overlap between these concepts that glossed divisions within the New Right to allow anti-communism to slip into family-values rhetoric.

One of the models of affective relationships that Kushner responds to in detail is the father-son bond and, specifically, the way that patriarchal relationships serve as the template for many of the circuits of political power in the United States. Skewering the first family as the putative model for the nation, Louis contends that it cannot be authentic: "It's not really a *family*, the Reagans, I read *People*, there aren't any connections there, no love, they don't ever even speak to each other except through their agents" (77). If the shining example of the American nuclear family is the Reagans, then families are a sham. All show and no substance, the Reagans are adept at playing a family on TV, but fail where it counts: "connections." "Connections" refers to affection and filial bonds here; when these same emotions cement the political relationships established by Roy Cohn, though, they take on the additional meanings that the word connotes in the business and political worlds.

For Cohn, the people to whom one is connected are networks of loyalty to be exploited. Nonetheless, the relationships this model relies on are also intimate. In one early scene, Roy explains the operation of political influence to Joe, who has been his protégé. Through the terms of Roy's excurses, Kushner inverts the family-values rhetoric of the culture wars. Roy tells Joe:

> The most precious asset in life, I think, is the ability to be a good son. You have that, Joe. Somebody who can be a good son to a father who pushes them farther than they would otherwise go. I've had many fathers, I owe my life to them, powerful, powerful men. Walter Winchell, Edgar Hoover. Joe McCarthy most of all. He valued me because I am a good lawyer, but he loved me because I was and am a good son. He was a very difficult man, very guarded and cagey; I brought out something tender in him. (58)

In these passages, Roy's words describe the father-son relationship as centered on the transfer of power, highlighting the role of family metaphors in the structure of the state. But Kushner's choice of words also suggests a sexual component to the mentorship. The emphasis on tenderness and transgression of boundaries creates romantic and sexual undertones. Other aspects of the scene speak in innuendo, too, but perhaps more to the point, the scene is linked through jump cuts with a simultaneous scene of Louis cruising for anonymous sex in Central Park's

Rambles. The juxtaposition causes the themes of sex and power to blend into one another.

The breakdown in Louis and Prior's relationship preceding the scene mentioned previously demonstrates the play's manner of engaging with the rhetoric of contamination that AIDS occasioned. On less alarmist terms, Kushner tries to find a more human approach to the unfolding realities of a deadly sexually transmitted disease than was being circulated at the time. Louis struggles to cope with his responsibilities to care for Prior. In an early scene, Prior wakes Louis up in the middle of the night in distress. The two argue over whether to call an ambulance, and Louis goes off-stage to call when Prior loses control of his bowels. The scene ends with Louis, who is deathly afraid of contagion, crying, "I can't I can't I can't" (54). The presence of feces and blood has made unavoidable the danger and responsibility of living in close contact with someone whose body is being ravaged. The fastidious, self-centered Louis decides he is unable to handle it and moves out while Prior is in the hospital.

Soon, Joe and Louis become involved, and for Joe, this is a moment of previously forbidden authentic life. He embraces the desire he has long denied and is electrified. The two men spend a month in bed exploring each other sexually. During their first tryst, Louis grapples with the discourses of contamination, gradually growing in his acceptance of the realities of illness and pointing toward less pathologizing ways of seeing AIDS. As the two men enter Louis's new apartment, Louis apologizes for the mess, to which Joe responds, "It's a little dirty," attempting to minimize Louis's self-consciousness. Louis, though, responds defensively that it's "*Messy*, not dirty." The difference matters, he explains: "It's dust, not dirt, chemical-slash-mineral, not organic, not like microbes, more like—" before cutting himself off (Kushner 139). So what *is* the important difference? The things that are out of place in Louis's apartment are "not organic" and "not like microbes." They are not replicating, living things and not disease carriers or pathogens. Unprompted, Louis bubbles over with his anxiety about contamination. It is this anxiety that keeps him from being able to care for Prior, and he still clings to it. He even suggests—ostensibly to assuage Joe's fear of contracting HIV—that they "can cap everything that leaks in latex, smear our bodies with nonoxynol-9" and have "safe, chemical sex. Messy, but not dirty." Louis's suggestion emphasizes chemical-slash-mineral aspects of sex that might make it messy (smeared with spermicide) but not dirty, that is, not contaminating and definitely not organic.

This kind of messy, chemical approach to sex is something that people may have to embrace if they intend to have sex in an epidemic, according to the authors of the booklet by that name. They argue, for example, that "Discussing precautions before you have sex might seem like a turn off, but if you enjoy staying healthy, you may eventually come to eroticize whatever precautions you require prior to the sexual encounter" (*How to*, 16) and "Demonstrating a concern for healthy sex may even make you more appealing!" (17). However, the play doesn't necessarily share this enthusiasm for safer sex methods. After all, the valorized characters are not those like Louis who erect barriers between themselves and the bodies touched by HIV, but those who minister to them like Belize. Louis is castigated in the play for his insistence on messiness when real life is dirty.

This, however, is a moment when he begins the change that will redeem him by the end of *Perestroika*. The scene shifts; Louis begins talking about how smell is a sense that breaks the boundaries between people as the molecules of one person become airborne and travel into another person's nose, a form of sexual contact. This arouses Joe, but it also shows Louis moving from an insistence on strict bodily boundaries to acceptance of breaking those boundaries in an erotic encounter. In the final moment of the scene, Joe talks inanely and the typically verbose Louis interrupts him to say, "Sssssh. Words are the worst things. Breathe. Smell" and then, "Or if you have to talk, talk dirty" (Kushner 142). In Louis's newfound embrace of the "dirty"—even if it is only talk—he is not only embracing the sexual and the transgressive, but the potentially infectious, the bodily. This signals a warming toward the realities of life that must be the foundation for a new America, the "more life" that Prior seeks in place of the antiseptic cleanliness of stasis. Louis must accept that true contact between people—erotic or affective—entails breaking down the boundaries between us fearlessly.

Freedman's analysis of the epilogue illuminates the play's vision for the future. Most of the characters are gathered at the Bethesda fountain in Central Park, but the exclusions are notable. Roy's importance as the play's bugbear makes his absence particularly significant. Roy's greed for power and his unrepentant willingness to harm others have no place in the new polity. His unmitigated self-interest and delusional vindictiveness are more dangerous than Louis's failure of responsibility. For these reasons, Roy must be sacrificed—and as Freedman points out, this happens in the play quite literally. Roy is in possession of an illicit stash of the anti-retroviral medication AZT at the time of his death, and Belize, who has access to his hospital room as his nurse, steals the drug to give to Prior and others. Thus, "Cohn dies, it seems, so that Prior might live to preside over the new queer postnuclear family" (Freedman 55). Roy represents the old world of self-hatred, persecution, and corruption that Kushner envisions passing away as a result of the AIDS crisis, not the new world of affirmation and acceptance.⁵⁵ This gesture reverses the culture wars imperative that the person with AIDS die in order to preserve society's purity, and it denies the idea that the morbidity of AIDS is divine retribution for the corruption of homosexuality. This latter is the dominant-discourse insistence that Patton paraphrases as, "People with AIDS must in the end always be silenced, their words given over to an expiating hermeneutic" (131). Ironically, it is the words of self-hate and of oppressive state policies that are silenced. Conversely, Prior, the out gay man with AIDS, survives the play to take part in a more affirmative America.

In *Angels*, Kushner grapples with the divisive rhetoric of the culture wars while also resisting decades of oppression of LGBTQ people. Through a revision of American metanarratives of redemption, Kushner tries to heal a fractured America through its own promise. However, Freedman points out the contradiction in this laudable goal: "Kushner desires to create . . . an understanding of transcendence that allow a space for queer citizenship in a culture, obsessed with the mythography of rebirth and the inevitability of miracle, that privileges the ideal of family and reactivates the mythos of national coherence and destiny" (41). The two strains clash because American mythologies of rebirth and apocalyptic futurity emphasize a reproductive ideology that casts queerness as its other.⁵⁶ Further, renewal of this kind is a hallmark of the American narrative that ironically incorporates elements of Christian eschatology. As Sontag puts it, relating the predictable metaphorization of AIDS as apocalypse, "There is . . . the need for an apocalyptic scenario that is specific to 'Western' society, and perhaps even more so to the United States. (America, as someone has said, is a nation with the soul of a church—an evangelical church prone to announcing radical endings and brand-new beginnings)" (*AIDS and Its Metaphors* 87). In this sense, the apocalyptic sentiment for which AIDS becomes a sign is simply the re-emergence of a persistent millennialism that marks American national identity and that Kushner registers in the title of the first half of the play, *Millennium Approaches*. Nonetheless, the play's argument that a queerer nation is consonant with the larger American mythos is significant and certainly a rebuke to those who mobilized against gay visibility driven by the same millennialism. It is likely this underlying challenge to exclusive discourses of nationhood that stoked the anxieties underpinning many protests of the play.

Embracing pathology as a site of critique and opportunity for utopic vision was part of Kushner's genius. In *Angels*, the character of Prior Walter eventually partially accepts that his abject position empowers him to confront the hypocritical moralism of those who condemn him or wish he would disappear. Once he cannot reject his identity, he learns to turn his pathologization into power, and there might be something in this that illuminates a shift in political possibility in this moment. Kushner's play was celebrated for daring to depict same-sex desire and the bodily realities of living with AIDS. Instead of accepting the social taboo that bodily suffering and sexual desire should be silenced, Kushner brings them into the play to dramatically critique the effects of such silencing and the base motives behind it. In so doing, he re-appropriated the pathologizing discourses aimed at LGBTQ+ folks and those living with AIDS and turned them into a lasting aesthetic achievement and a kind of cultural capital—a form of genius—thereby inverting the binary of obscene genius and pathology.

A Cure for What Is Wrong with America: Place and the Pace of Change

The inclusive tone of Bill Clinton's 1993 inaugural address offers a sharp contrast with Buchanan's speech at the GOP convention the preceding August, in which he cast America as starkly divided along ideological lines. And yet, Clinton's speech also offers proof that the narrative of pathology continued to provide the governing metaphors of the moment. "There is nothing wrong with America," Clinton opined, "that cannot be cured by what is right with America." Clinton's use of the word *cure* reflects the potency of plague metaphors and the underlying rhetoric of pathology, imagining social struggles in ways that suggest surveillance, restriction, and purity. To be sure, the speech was meant to convey hope and optimism for an end to inequality and discrimination, and Clinton attempts to unify the divided country by affirming the current strife as a temporary part of the progress of American history and mission. At the same time, Clinton admonishes those who are dissatisfied and angry: Do not seek to overturn society, seek to reform it. This is consonant with the message of *Angels* that America's destiny is an inclusive one that recuperates its past failures and struggles and makes them meaningful as steps on the road toward perfection. Kushner's play offers an end to discrimination as well as the hope of sympathy between groups and empathy between individuals, yet it also furthers overarching myths of American exceptionalism in tension with its queer potential to reveal deep-seated problems with the structures of American mythology.

Angels and *The Perfect Moment* have yet another valence. After all AIDS was not only a crisis and a disease; it was also a rallying cry for the cause of visibility in a time when silence and invisibility meant death. Cultural production that made present, sympathetic, and complex the figure of the LGBTQ+ individual countered the violent dehumanization of cultural rhetorics of AIDS pathology. Contrary to this increasing visibility, and pursuing a nationalism that relied on heteronormative and patriarchal models of subjectivity and submission, figures such as Helms were able to mobilize a rhetorical slippage linking the AIDS epidemic to non-normative sexualities, treating them as a kind of moral plague of which AIDS was only a symptom. Through their works, Mapplethorpe and Kushner resist the rhetoric of Helms and others who capitalized on AIDS to push conventional notions of the family and sexuality while invoking tropes of cultural contamination to further racial and sexual prejudices.

Pathology was the ur-discourse of AIDS, and so its presence as a shaping force for the reception of both Mapplethorpe's exhibition and Kushner's play needs little teasing out. However, it does demonstrate powerfully the resonance of the narrative of obscene pathology as it played out here. In both cases, the controversies that arose centered on the exposure and representation of gay men and same-sex desire, but both cases are inextricably linked with AIDS as well. Most superficially, Mapplethorpe died of AIDS just before *The Perfect Moment* caused the funding crisis for the NEA, and *Angels* is centrally about AIDS. More deeply, however, it is the underlying rhetoric of contamination and cultural warfare that underwrote the controversies. Conservative moralists didn't just construe AIDS as a gay disease, but as a divine plague, and the metaphors of corruption and morbidity slide back and forth from the medical to the sexual to the scriptural.

These works rose to prominence in part because they confronted these very rhetorics by humanizing and aestheticizing the experience of same-sex love and desire and resisting the dehumanizing terms of the culture wars. In so doing, they transform the narrative of obscene pathology. And while this can be seen as a triumph, it also ratifies the conclusion that transgressive works by writers from marginalized communities must often chart their course to success through the narrative of pathology, rather than along other paths. Both works became cultural touchstones and iconic works. Kushner's play is still regularly performed and Mapplethorpe's photos continue to be shown. In many cases, they also galvanized supporters as a result of controversy rather than in spite of it. Still, the path by which this could be accomplished causes the narratives of pathology to still haunt us. Discourses of obscene pathology may not win the day, but they remain a powerful vector for political engagement and a center of gravity for representational possibilities.

In closing, I want to briefly consider the politics of place that influenced the obscenity controversies attending *Angels in America* and *The Perfect Moment*. A number of instructive similarities emerge between events in Charlotte and Cincinnati. Just as Barrie would note that his museum was largely a target of opportunity in a battle happening mostly at the national level, so director of Charlotte Rep Keith Martin noted that his organization was merely convenient tinder in a long-smoldering conflagration over cultural difference, stating, "The conditions were ripe for a fire.... Where lightning struck to kindle that conflagration was anybody's guess." Also, just as Barrie considered the CAC a mainstream organization, so Martin notes, "Prior to *Angels*, we were known as a mainstream company."[57] In both cases, organizations that had previously avoided controversy were singled out. The culture warriors were already spoiling for a fight; all that was needed was a suitable location.

Whereas in the first part of the twentieth century, New York was the most common site of obscenity prosecutions because of its association with the publishing industry and the importation of European works that challenged American puritanism, an increasingly mobile society and one in which more transgressive works were being produced domestically saw obscenity prosecutions move away from traditional urban bastions of liberality and into locations where the politics were more divided. It was not staunchly conservative sites where *The Perfect Moment* and *Angels in America* provoked the most prominent obscenity battles. Rather they were a border city, Cincinnati, and a bastion of the New South, Charlotte. These are not spaces with obvious ideological leanings, but rather places where shifting demographics bring together groups with polarized views. Washington, D.C., played a similar role for both texts with the Corcoran and Catholic University incidents, because the federal government brings together political figures from ideologically and regionally diverse constituencies. These cases therefore demonstrate that obscenity prosecutions and controversies are not a matter of *patently* offensive material—as SCOTUS jurisprudence requires—but of *debatably* offensive material; in fact, they stage the debate about what *is* offensive, and through it, mediate questions of what we value as a society, marking out the contested cultural borders of the nation.

Other notable obscenity controversies also took curious geographic turns due to the nationalization of media and the resulting possibility of prosecutorial forum-shopping. Though Dead Kennedys and their label, Alternative Tentacles, were headquartered in San Francisco, they were prosecuted for *Frankenchrist* in 1985 in Los Angeles, and George Carlin delivered the recorded version of his "7 Words You Can't Say on Television" monologue in California, but it resulted in the prosecution of a radio station in New York.[58] In truth, the question has never been of a unitary culture deliberatively changing its own mores, but of a varied culture in turmoil both regionally and chronologically.

This emphasis on place reflects the profound significance of minor phrases in the jurisprudence. The *Miller* test says that offensiveness should be determined according to "contemporary community standards," while being somewhat vague on what that community is. The Warren Court noted in the earlier *Jacobellis v. Ohio* that the presence of this phrase in the evolving tests has often misled prosecutors and jurors to believe that the standards of obscenity (and thus of First Amendment protections) vary from locality to locality. Nico Jacobellis, in fact, was being prosecuted in a suburb of Cleveland for a French film that had not been prosecuted when it was shown in Columbus and Toledo. The justices strenuously disagree with the notion that local standards should reign, arguing that this would allow the most conservative communities to set the moral standard for the nation and serve generally to chill expression (192–95). Nonetheless, this very danger persists in part because local communities do differ in what they consider offensive. Thus local interpretations by prosecutors can still result in costly trials, even if those trials are overturned at higher levels. Regional variations in moral standards can still result in boycotts and protests, too, which have complex ramifications for sales. These battles over representation emerge precisely when the nature of the community is in doubt and when differences within communities are perceived as significant. What is considered offensive in these cases becomes, as it was for many culture warriors, a discussion not of what we will do, but who we are.

Place, then—and demographic shifts within those places—are crucial to understanding how obscenity functions. It is never only a battle among national political forces or between distilled principles of sexual morality and freedom of expression. It is, rather, a series of localized tactical skirmishes. This should remind us that overly abstracting methodologies can obscure rather than reveal. If we were to focus exclusively on the clash of opposing forces at the national level or only on the progress of jurisprudence or aggregate public opinions concerning challenging art, we would fail to understand that it is the unevenness of this progress which causes such controversies to arise.

The narratives of obscene genius and pathology outline recurrent themes, but in cases like the ones in this chapter, they can also point out their own limits. Genius continues to signal the virtues of belonging in the in group, and transgression is often a path to success. Pathology exists as a through-line but shifts according to targeted groups and historical contingencies, while also offering sites of critique. Each group is confronted with different stereotypes of pathology, and these are often manufactured according to the particular exigencies of the moment, whether that is criminal pathology (Chapter 1), familial pathologies (Chapter 2), gendered pathologies (Chapter 3), or sexual pathologies (Chapter 4). Nonetheless, local tensions make use of pre-existing scripts and so take predictable paths. When writers representing mainstream identities break the rules, their work is assessed according to their perceived literary antecedents and their aesthetic talent. When writers representing marginalized identities break the rules, their work is assessed according to stereotypes of deviance and danger. This dichotomy reflects a deep-seated racism and heteronormativity in the reception of these works that may, indeed, be multifaceted but which is, nonetheless, obdurate and unyielding.

Epilogue

For disciplinary and practical reasons, *Obscene Gestures* ends with the close of the twentieth century, but the advent of the internet around that time altered the landscape of obscenity in a number of ways that would be extremely generative for future study. First, the diffusion of content producers across the globe made them subject to different, international legal standards, while the growth in user-created content made it hard to isolate and make an example of individual actors. Second, the internet bypassed the postal system and ports, which had been a significant component of federal obscenity laws since the Comstock Acts. Third, it amplified pre-existing gig-economy dynamics, making it harder to demonize producers, many of whom are working under conditions of precarity. These changes likely spur the emergence of new contexts and discourses that can shape how obscenity controversies arise, take hold, and are resolved, and that are deeply influenced by pre-existing racial, gender, and sexual dynamics.

In addition to such changes, there are also signs that the old culture wars are starting to be viewed as, well, old. Those people who clutch their pearls about the same things their parents clutched pearls about seem increasingly uninteresting, even as they continue to try to make enough hay over such controversies to gain or maintain political power (and still succeed frustratingly often). Cardi B. and Megan Thee Stallion's "WAP" is a good example of this positive change.

"WAP" was released in mid-2020, and it immediately became a hit, debuting at #1 on the Billboard charts due in part to a record-setting

93 million U.S. streams in the first week.[1] Not only was the song popular, but it was also critically acclaimed as fun, important, and liberating. *Pitchfork*'s Lakin Starling, for example, contends that "the detailed play-by-play in the verses doesn't aim to impress guys—and that, the song suggests, is why Cardi and Meg's expertise is credible. They center themselves as women in order to freely celebrate their coveted power, sex appeal, and A1 WAP."[2] Even the typically conservative *Wall Street Journal* touted the rappers' success in articles such as "The Results Are In: 'WAP' Is a Bop," noting the record-setting debut and female-empowerment politics of the song.[3]

The exuberance of "WAP" stems from the charisma of the singers, the skillful raps, and the clever lines, but also in part from its unabashed revelry in taboo. We have come to expect paeans to the singers' sexual prowess from male rappers, but it's still a little unusual for female rappers. While this can reinforce misogynist tropes for male performers, the history of patriarchy has made such self-celebration taboo for women in general and Black women in particular. Breaking those taboos is often seen as empowering for the women and their fans. And while those tropes and histories of sexual oppression remain, precursors such as Missy Elliot and Lil' Kim worked hard paving the way for "WAP," and in the twenty-first century, a song like this can feel almost like harmless fun.

And yet clearly not everyone thought it was harmless. As Charles Holmes recaps in *Rolling Stone*, "'WAP' wasn't 24 hours old yet before Republicans tried to steal the spotlight and stoke a meaningless backlash."[4] A California congressional candidate claimed to have been scandalized when he heard the song accidentally, while Twitter trolls attempted to deride the song as crass or demeaning. One commentator attempted to cast a "wet-ass pussy" as cause for medical concern, explicitly invoking the pathologization of Black women's sexuality in cartoonish fashion. One thing that stands out about the controversy, though, is that while it traded on the same tropes of past eras that continue to have real negative impacts, it felt contrived almost immediately. Few people had the energy to be truly outraged, and what outrage was generated was ridiculed. By the time the year-end reflections rolled around just a few months later, the ode to female sexual power was included by nearly all mainstream pop culture outlets among their "best of" lists, including *USA Today*, *Time*, and *Rolling Stone*, and the controversy seemed to be left behind.

However, the controversy wasn't left behind at all. In keeping with the dynamic I attempt to describe in the book, its main effect was to give lasting energy to the song as a phenomenon and to frame it as more overtly political. *Pitchfork* specifically poses the artists' skills as a refutation of the backward politics of their critics, declaring that "Cardi and Megan ... are unruffled by respectability politics and slut-shaming, choosing instead to use these outdated tropes for fuel" (Starling), while *Time* reported that Cardi B. and Megan Thee Stallion's "raunchy bars soaked in sexual innuendos ... had conservative pundits and male hip-hop artists laughably clutching their pearls."[5] The outrage, then, never gained steam and will be primarily remembered as reminding everyone that what Cardi B. and Megan Thee Stallion did was actually meaningful politically, behind its goofy fun.

Also not surprising, the outrage ended up benefiting the artists. As Holmes reminds us, "[O]utrage is by far the most powerful currency in the modern music market" (Holmes). While in the late twentieth century, the production of clean versions of songs was controversial and efforts to restrict content led to Congressional debate and public boycotts, now most record companies produce clean versions of songs as a matter of routine, and while "Decades ago, that may have been done in part to avoid political controversy. Now business is the driving force, as labels chase down every click and playlist placement to maximize songs' streaming income."[6] Though controversy has always driven sales, now self-censorship is a market opportunity, not an ideological capitulation. This reflects the recording industry adapting to the post-PMRC reality. The music industry has learned to capitalize on the economics of outrage that before cut deeply into record sales, and the internet does appear to have something to do with that.

And yet, despite hopeful signs of progress, structural inequalities that characterized obscenity controversies in the twentieth century stubbornly refuse to be left in the past. Rather than transforming the social landscape, the changes wrought by the internet have exacerbated existing inequalities among sex workers, film producers, advertisers, tech executives, and others. Because corporations monetize rhetorics of transformational change by co-opting democratic platitudes as corporate branding, we would do well to treat claims of rapid social transformation with skepticism, particularly because of the broad American tendency to rewrite social injustices as the work of market or technological forces falsely construed as ideologically neutral. A recent event in the world of online porn demonstrates one way the old forces are still very much at work.

In late 2020, *Pornhub*, the largest of the porn tube sites, faced public scrutiny after a *New York Times* article about content on the site that depicted child exploitation and nonconsensual acts. Subsequently, Mastercard and Visa stopped processing payments through the site.[7] Combined with similar action by PayPal earlier in the year, this represented a major threat to *Pornhub*'s bottom line, and in reaction it pulled down all videos posted by unverified users. The result was a purge of millions of videos, about two-thirds of its total content. The move was presumably designed to make it more difficult for users to post exploitative content and easier for the site to remove it.

Ironically, many sex-industry workers had been lobbying the company to ban content from unverified accounts for years, frustrated that the old policy promoted content piracy. They also shared the concerns of other members of the public that unregulated content tended to enable bad actors, including traffickers. However, sex-industry representatives didn't necessarily welcome the actions of Mastercard, Visa, and PayPal because halting payments left workers without revenue streams they relied upon and threatened to push them to smaller, less-reliable sites and less-profitable distribution methods. So while *Pornhub*'s actions were more or less welcomed, the actions of the credit card companies that led to it were not and may have negative impacts on the sex-work industry.

This result may not upset the groups advocating for this action. One of the more significant groups involved, the National Center on Sexual Exploitation, is explicitly against any form of commercial sex work, including all forms of pornography, which they argue, represents a public health crisis.[8] Echoing the anti-pornography activism of Andrea Dworkin and others who use the language of civil rights, the group's international affiliate asserted in its letter to Mastercard "that pornography itself is a form of sexual exploitation."[9] In fact, NCOSE often uses rhetoric like this that closely parallels language used by the sex-negative anti-porn activism of the 1970s and 1980s.

That's no surprise; after all, it's the current incarnation of Morality in Media, one of the major anti-obscenity players in those earlier debates.[10] Under previous names, the organization was centrally involved in many of the major cases I study in this book, starting with *Memoirs v. Massachusetts* and *FCC v. Pacifica*, where its members orchestrated the inciting "offenses."[11] They also filed numerous *amicus* briefs on major obscenity cases, and its members were part of protests over Robert Mapplethorpe's *The Perfect Moment* in Boston.[12] In that sense, though the organization was restructured in 2015, it provides a compelling link between contemporary anti-pornography efforts and their predecessors. In fact, the same organizations are still fighting those same fights using the same rhetoric. Along the way, concern over legitimate ethical issues (fighting trafficking, for example) becomes entangled in efforts to police the sexual expression of consenting adults.

One salient feature of both controversies is that the most impactful actions were oriented toward capital. Legislative and legal pressure on *Pornhub*, for instance, was completely unsuccessful, as were individual and collective action on the part of content producers and victims of trafficking and revenge porn. The activism that *did* have an effect was aimed at market-shaping corporations processing financial transactions. Similarly, the explicit lyrics of "WAP" were understood from the start to offer financial rewards for the recording company, and whatever public controversy arose played into this rather than against it. It seems that if there has been a shift in obscenity dynamics since the close of the twentieth century, one major facet of it has been a transition away from governments and civic institutions—and even mass action—toward corporate control. None of this is a surprise because capital has always been deeply involved in the discourses of morality that have shaped racial, gender, and sexual politics. Considering obscenity, however, may reveal contours of a relative resurgence in this dynamic, contra an assumption of a more centralized governmental and civic control during the mid-twentieth century, which perhaps always simply occluded the way that the state can serve capital.

Thus, it seems, the internet has left some things unchanged, but the old dynamics of obscenity remain very much with us. Though some progress has been made, many of the same battles are taking place with new dynamics but the same urgency. Now more than two decades into the twenty-first century, we remain haunted by very similar—and very vicious—racisms and heteronormativity, by the mendacious co-optation of free speech discourse, and by a cynical counter-creative economy that rewards creators unequally.

Acknowledgments

Obscene Gestures grew out of a desire to brush transgressive artworks against the grain. The conversations around them are so often mystified by moralist shock and anti-establishment awe that the politics undergirding them—ranging from the sage to sophomoric—are lost or misunderstood. Early mentors of mine, including Peggy Kamuf and Nicole Rizzuto, taught me to turn my interest in these works toward serious critical aims and thereby laid the foundation for this book. Cathy J. Schlund-Vials then built this foundation into a passion and a project. In my scholarly life, I have frequently been fortunate to be guided by brilliant people, but Cathy's expansive knowledge, incisive and unsparing advice, and boundless generosity allowed and forced me to become a better scholar, and the rigor of this project as well as its orientation toward justice are due to her wisdom and her example. Throughout the many years of this project's development, I also benefited from the creative and patient advice of Chris Vials, Kate Capshaw, Martha Cutter, and Kathy Knapp, who found the value in my work and helped me to uncover it. Through formal and informal dialogue, probing questions and poignant challenges, they helped me to recognize my best insights and to appreciate the limits of my perspective. They were also crucial support in the grueling academic process, propping me up as a person as much as a scholar.

Josh Lambert also played an important role as a mentor and friend all along the way but especially in shaping the key moves of the argument and the archive of the book. His insistence that the argument rigorously define its scope, methods, and findings sent me back to the drawing board more than once, but the result is a book that rests on firmer foundations and presents more compelling answers to its many questions. He also served as an invaluable resource on the history of literary obscenity and a model on how to treat the subject with sensitivity, as well as humor. Two colleagues in particular helped this project along, too. Jorge Santos has incorrigible faith in my work and encourages me shamelessly. Beyond this, though, he is profligate with his time and unsparing in his criticism, a combination that helped to sharpen my otherwise bloated prose, frame the most promising material in the best light, and avoid being an ass, mostly. Jarred Wiehe has also given keen insights and had the faith in me to be direct about what worked and didn't in the draft, with the result that its rougher edges have been smoothed somewhat. Additionally, my home institution, the University of South Carolina, Lancaster has afforded me several research and travel grants to complete this project, and it would have been impossible without their support. The book, then, is only possible thanks to the generosity of Dean Walt Collins and the support of my faculty peers. Several among them, including Adam Biggs and Kaetrena Davis Kendrick, also offered feedback on the draft that sharpened the critique and made the argument more responsive to the texts.

I also need to thank Richard Morrison, my editor at Fordham, for the enthusiasm and patience he showed in taking this manuscript from an early draft to the completed book. I have had few interlocutors with as much excitement about the material or as extensive a knowledge of the historical moment. It is a delight, a pleasure, and a balm to have his support, and more than once it energized me to continue pushing through the long weekends and grueling rewrites the process demanded.

Finally, it takes a certain insanity to embark on a work like this: taboo, difficult, and uncertain. Perhaps against her best interests, I have been supported in this insanity by Stephanie Golaski, who is always wiser, bolder, and surer than I am and inspires me to be the same.

Notes

Introduction. Outlaws vs. Outcasts: Defining Narratives of Obscenity

1. This quote is widely attributed to Lenny Bruce, including by his daughter and in publications overseen by his estate. However, I have been unable to locate specific details about when and where he said this and have been unable to unearth it in recordings. It is certainly possible that he said it during one of his many ad-libbed sets or in an informal comment. Though it may be apocryphal in origin, it has become part of the Bruce canon.

2. Lenny Bruce, *Lenny Bruce: Let the Buyer Beware*, produced by Marvin Worth and Hal Wilner, Shout! Factory, 2004, from the accompanying pamphlet, page 12.

3. For more on Barth's life and the play *Sophie, Totie, and Belle* (1996), see Joellyn Wallen, Grace Overbeke, Barbara L. Fredricksen, and Alvin Klein. Barth and her contemporaries are, it should be noted, sometimes cited as influences on famous women comedians such as Joan Rivers and Sarah Silverman; see Debra Aarons and Marc Mierowsky.

4. Alvin Klein, "Three Funny Women, Joking through the Pain," *New York Times*, April 28, 1996.

5. Matthew Love, "50 Best Stand-Up Comics of All Time," *RollingStone.com*, February 14, 2017.

6. Debra Aarons and Marc Mierowsky, "Obscenity, Dirtiness, and License in Jewish Comedy," *Comedy Studies* 5, no. 2 (2014): 165–66.

7. Grace Overbeke, "Subversively Sexy: The Jewish 'Red Hot Mamas' Sophie Tucker, Belle Barth, and Pearl Williams," *Studies in American Humor* 3, no. 25 (2012): 33.

8. See Overbeke 41.

9. Overbeke notes, for example, that Sophie Tucker "defied social norms and left her family and infant son to pursue show business. Yet she is unable to completely escape her social role."

10. Overbeke contends that "The fact that it was unacceptable for pre-1970s female comedians to show subversive behavior outside of the domestic and sexual realm is

perhaps the main factor accounting for their small place in history, compared to their male counterparts" (55).

11. Michel Foucault, *The History of Sexuality: An Introduction*, trans. Robert Hurley, Vol. I (New York: Vintage Books, 1990), 6.

12. Abdul R. JanMohamed rightly points out that while Foucault's theories of sexuality are remarkably generative, one gap—which Mohamed seeks to fill—is the role of sexual power to dynamics in race and racialization. For more on the kind of work necessary to extend his ideas into this sphere—which I seek to partially undertake— see his essay "Sexuality on/of the Racial Border: Foucault, Wright, and the Articulation of 'Racialized Sexuality,'" in *Discourses of Sexuality: From Aristotle to AIDS*, ed. Domna Stanton (Ann Arbor: University of Michigan Press, 1992).

13. Mark McGurl, *The Program Era: Postwar Fiction and the Rise of Creative Writing* (Cambridge: Harvard University Press, 2009), 32.

14. For more on the definition of gestures and the distinction between gestures and sign languages, see David McNeill's introduction to *Language and Gesture* (Cambridge: Cambridge University Press, 2000), 1–10; and "Why Gestures," in *Gesture and Thought* (Chicago: University of Chicago Press, 2005), 3–21.

15. See, for example, Florence Dore's *The Novel and the Obscene*, Charles Rembar's *The End of Obscenity*, and Edward de Grazia's *Girls Lean Back Everywhere*.

16. For more, see Bruce H. Kalk, "The Carswell Affair: The Politics of a Supreme Court Nomination in the Nixon Administration," *American Journal of Legal History* 42, no. 3 (1998): 261–87.

17. This interpretation is credited to Charles Rembar, the lawyer who, in 1959, defended Grove Press in its New York trial concerning the publication of *Lady Chatterley's Lover* (1928). Brennan's language in *Roth* was read by Rembar as allowing the ban only on material that is both prurient *and* without redeeming social value, though this may not have been anticipated in the original ruling. Thus, while *Roth* remains the important Supreme Court precedent, the legal logic involved developed in the New York State Courts in 1959–60. See Fred Kaplan, *Grove Press, Inc. v. Christenberry* (1959), and *Grove Press, Inc. v. Christenberry* (1960).

18. The *Jacobellis* case is also well known as the source of Justice Potter Stewart's declaration about the designation "hard-core pornography" that "I shall not today attempt further to define the kinds of material I understand to be embraced within that shorthand description; and perhaps I could never succeed in intelligibly doing so. But I know it when I see it."

19. *Jacobellis* was decided concurrently with another important case, *Grove Press v. Gerstein*, which concerned the 1961 publication of Henry Miller's *Tropic of Cancer*, which I discuss in Chapter 1. Even after *Roth*, the 1961 publication of *Tropic of Cancer* by Grove led to a number of lawsuits against booksellers. Ultimately, following the Roth test, the Supreme Court ruled that the book was not obscene in 1964 and issued its ruling concurrent with *Jacobellis*.

20. *Memoirs v. Massachusetts*, 383 U.S. 413. Supreme Court of the U.S. 1966.

21. *Miller v. California*, 413 U.S. 15-48. Supreme Court of the U.S. 1973.

22. Despite the Court's stated interest in bringing clarity to the semantic discussion, the fact that terms such as "social importance" and "prurience" take the place of delineating what specific ideas are protected and what representations are forbidden means, as Douglas suggests, that social change can produce very different obscenity findings. For example, George Carlin's "Seven Words You Can't Say on Television" routine

notwithstanding, the FCC does not specifically detail what words, acts, or representations are prohibited on public airwaves (though Carlin's routine *has* been banned and SCOTUS upheld the ban; see *Federal Communications Commission v. Pacifica Foundation*). Instead, what constitutes a violation of the FCC's policy—which cites the *Miller* ruling to define obscenity (FCC)—is ruled on a case-by-case basis, a fact that produces a large number of Fourteenth Amendment challenges, including recent cases concerning "fleeting expletives"; see *FCC v. Fox Television Stations* (2009), and *FCC v. Fox Television Stations* (2012). Broadcasters have repeatedly requested specific terms and acts that cannot be broadcast and repeatedly been rebuffed. *Pacifica*, further, proscribes the FCC's authority to limit only that material that comes over broadcast media, and the status of cable, telephone, and electronic pornography was grappled with in the mid-1980s; see, for example, the Senate Judiciary Subcommittee on Criminal Law hearings from 1985 (United States) and Senator Jesse Helms's unsuccessful efforts to pass the Cable-Porn and Dial-a-Porn Control Act the same year. Josh Lambert has also pointed out to me that the FCC's reluctance to stipulate what content is prohibited may be strategic, in that specific constraints would allow for artists breaking the rules to claim doing so is a form of protected civil disobedience.

23. Of the original six justices of the Warren Court who sided with the majority in the more lax *Memoirs v. Massachusetts*, three (Warren, Black, and Fortas) retired before *Miller* to be replaced by more conservative justices appointed by Nixon and three (Douglas, Brennan, and Stewart) sided with the minority in *Miller*. Thus, no member of the original majority was swayed to vote in favor of the more conservative standard. Attrition on the court entirely accounted for the ideological shift. The stark turn was evident in the alignment of the majority in the *Miller* ruling. All four Nixon appointees (Burger, Blackmun, Powell, and Rehnquist) voted in the majority in *Miller*; the fifth vote in the majority was Justice Byron White, who had dissented in *Memoirs*. The ninth justice at the time was Justice Thurgood Marshall, who was not on the court at the time of the *Memoirs* ruling but was appointed by Lyndon Johnson; Marshall dissented from the *Miller* ruling.

24. See Michel Foucault, *Discipline and Punish: The Birth of the Prison*, trans. Alan Sheridan (New York: Vintage, 1995).

25. Josh Lambert, *Unclean Lips: Obscenity, Jews, and American Culture* (New York: New York University Press, 2013), 9.

26. Loren Glass, *Counterculture Colophon: Grove Press, the "Evergreen Review," and the Incorporation of the Avant-Garde* (Stanford: Stanford University Press, 2013).

27. See Whitney Strub, "Lavender, Menaced: Lesbianism, Obscenity Law, and the Feminist Antipornography Movement," *Journal of Women's History* 22, no. 2 (2010): 83–107.

28. Roderick A. Ferguson, *Aberrations in Black: Toward a Queer of Color Critique* (Minneapolis: University of Minnesota Press, 2004), 3.

29. See Lisa Lowe, *Immigrant Acts* (Durham: Duke University Press, 1996), 25.

30. Toni Morrison, *Playing in the Dark: Whiteness and the Literary Imagination* (Cambridge: Harvard University Press, 1992), xii.

31. Toni Morrison, *Unspeakable Things Unspoken: The Afro-American Presence in American Literature*, Tanner Lecture on Human Values (Ann Arbor: University of Michigan, 1988), 134.

32. Morrison describes herself as spending much of her time grappling with a presumed white audience and seeking to extricate her writing from this presumption.

See *Unspeakable Things Unspoken* (146–63) as well as "Black Matters" in *Playing in the Dark*, where she writes, "My work requires me to think about how free I can be as an African-American woman writer in my genderized, sexualized, wholly racialized world" (*Playing in the Dark*, 5).

33. Hazel V. Carby, *Reconstructing Womanhood: The Emergence of the Afro-American Woman Novelist* (Oxford University Press, 1987), 174.

34. This is true despite the Warren Court's assertions in *Jacobellis* that the phrase "local standards" should not imply varying local definitions of obscenity.

1. Classic Counter-Narratives: Deep Psychology vs. Deep Pathology in Two Early Twentieth-Century Novels

1. Wright talks a bit in "How Bigger Was Born" about his own desire to forge an individual artistic path without regard to the mandates of those around him, writing that "I am inclined to satisfy the claims of my own ideals rather than the expectations of others" (Richard Wright, "How Bigger Was Born," *Native Son* [restored text] [New York: Harper Perennial Modern Classics, 2005], 449). His desire to represent his subject on its own terms echoes the individualist spirit Miller espouses. However, at the horizon of Wright's aesthetic is a sense of shared humanity, not individual greatness. Wright wrote that his "heart is with the collectivist and proletarian ideal" ("How Bigger," 449).

2. The novel was famously described this way by Dorothy Canfield Fisher in the novel's original introduction, and the image is echoed by several critics. For example, Lawrence Hogue uses the lab analogy, noting that Wright "places Bigger in test-tube situations to show how his conditioning affects his behavior" (W. Lawrence Hogue, "Can the Subaltern Speak? A Postcolonial, Existential Reading of Richard Wright's *Native Son*," *Southern Quarterly* 26, no. 2 [2009]: 13). Wright himself suggests that he had the image of a lab in mind, asking, "Why should I not, like a scientist in a laboratory, use my imagination and invent test-tube situations, place Bigger in them, and, following the guidance of my own hopes and fears, what I had learned and remembered, work out in fictional form an emotional statement and resolution of this problem" ("How Bigger," 447–48).

3. Harold T. McCarthy says of the book's autobiographical mode, "The narration is autobiographical, but only if one allows for the possibility that dreams, wishes, and lies are essential parts of the central consciousness." Harold T. McCarthy, "Henry Miller's Democratic Vistas," *American Quarterly* 23, no. 2 (1971): 228–29.

4. Ihab Hassan, *The Literature of Silence: Henry Miller and Samuel Beckett* (New York: Knopf, 1967), 53.

5. See, for example, Dixon Speaker, Chapter 2 of Ihab Hassan's *The Literature of Silence*, and Harold T. McCarthy.

6. See, for example, Frederick W. Turner's *Renegade*, Chapter 1 of Hassan's *Literature of Silence*, Steven Foster, and Paul R. Jackson, as well as McCarthy. Walt Whitman, Ralph Waldo Emerson, and Dostoevsky are often cited as forerunners. Miller himself cites these figures, but also throws Lao-Tzu into the mix (Miller, "From Henry Miller, To Lawrence Durrell," in *Art and Outrage: A Correspondence about Henry Miller*, by Lawrence Durrell, Alfred Perlès, and Henry Miller [New York: E. P. Dutton, 1961], 34).

7. See Michael Hardin.

8. See Glass's *Counterculture Colophon* and E. R. Hutchison's *"Topic of Cancer" on Trial: A Case History of Censorship* (New York: Grove Press, 1968).

9. Miller himself cites these figures, but also throws Lao-Tzu into the mix ("From Henry Miller," 34).

10. Frederick Turner, *Renegade: Henry Miller and the Making of "Tropic of Cancer"* (New Haven: Yale University Press, 2011), 9.

11. McCarthy recounts how even in the early part of the twentieth century, "Miller's indifference to political and social movements won him the hostility of those literary critics in the Thirties who were indignant with any artistic effort that was not harnessed to humanitarian goals" (232–33).

12. Henry Miller, *Tropic of Cancer* (New York: Grove Press, 1961).

13. Along these lines, Karl Shapiro calls Miller "a total revolutionary" whose allegiances are to an inborn individualist morality, not to a state and not especially to the American national state (Karl Shapiro, "The Greatest Living Author," introduction to *Tropic of Cancer* by Henry Miller, Evergreen edition [New York: Grove Press, 1980], xxv).

14. Emphasis in the original. Friedrich Nietzsche, *Thus Spoke Zarathustra: A Book for Everyone and Nobody*, trans., introduction, and notes by Graham Parkes (New York: Oxford University Press, 2005), 45.

15. This passage appears to have influenced Anaïs Nin when she was writing the preface to the 1961 edition, in which she uses the word "paralysis" to describe the state of contemporary culture (xxxi) and refers to the "open wounds" of culture that were left by previous thought regimes (xxxii).

16. See the introduction for an explanation of the three-prong test of obscenity used in the trial, which includes a consideration of a text's social value as a potential offset to its offensive content.

17. Loren Glass, *Counterculture Colophon: Grove Press, the "Evergreen Review," and the Incorporation of the Avant-Garde* (Stanford: Stanford University Press, 2013), 103.

18. Anaïs Nin, Preface, in Henry Miller, *Tropic of Cancer* (New York: Grove Press, 1961), xxxi.

19. Provocatively, this is also the kind of language used by feminists in the 1970s and 1980s to express the desire to break out of patriarchal sexual stereotypes of women, and this includes critiques by women of color. See, for example, Cherríe Moraga's notion of a "theory in the flesh."

20. Durrell is unabashed in using the word as he heaps praise on Miller. He writes, for example, that "now he has broken through, he is canonized! Recognised as the greatest example of American genius since Whitman" (Durrell 8). Durrell is explicitly contrasting Miller with contemporaries he considers lesser lights, including Hemingway and Faulkner, whom he calls "literary journeymen" and opines, "It takes a hundred of us to manufacture the subsoil in which a genius can grow" (8).

21. I refer here to Abdul R. JanMohamed's use of the term "racialized sexuality." JanMohamed suggests that the status quo governing sex along racial borders is attended by a marked silence in contrast to the discourse of revelation that attends dominant sexuality, as catalogued by Foucault in *The History of Sexuality*. Because touching this subject would trouble essentialized distinctions between races, thereby threatening the stability of the racial border, JanMohamed contends that an imperative of silence reigns over such issues, and this obscures the operation of racialized power when it intersects with sexuality.

22. The Club apparently offered readers a second, safer selection that month (Conrad Richter's *The Trees*) as a way to head off objections to Wright's novel; see Hazel Rowley, "The Shadow of the White Woman: Richard Wright and the Book-of-the-Month Club," *Partisan Review* 66, no. 4 (1999): 625–34.

23. See Charles Sumner, "For Profit's Sake! Don't Look at that White Lady!" *Southern Quarterly* 26, no. 2 (2009): 134–40.

24. See Sumner 138 and Rowley 628.

25. See Sumner for an explanation of the relationship among free indirect discourse, Naturalism, and Wright's vision for Bigger Thomas.

26. See Ferguson.

27. Wright's assent to the changes was likely under pressure from his publisher and his lack of power in the publishing industry. As Rowley notes, "It was the white literary establishment that accepted or rejected his manuscripts" (627) and "he almost certainly underestimated [the problem] that his fighting words had to pass muster in what was then the all-white territory of book publishing" (626). In this sense, the fact of Wright's willingness to make these changes at the request of the Club was not entirely voluntary, and so he can't be considered to have collaborated with them. As Rowley notes later in her essay, he pushed back more persistently on such changes with his later book *Black Boy* at a time when he was more empowered within the publishing world.

28. See, for example, John K. Young: "As the Wright example indicates, there is a particular difficulty in representing 'the black experience' in terms which depart too far from the mythologized version most often reinforced by mainstream presses" (John K. Young, *Black Writers, White Publishers: Marketplace Politics in Twentieth-Century African American Literature* [Jackson: University Press of Mississippi, 2006], 17).

29. James Baldwin, "Everybody's Protest Novel," *Notes of a Native Son* (Boston: Beacon, 1955), 13.

30. Ralph Ellison, "Richard Wright's Blues," *The Antioch Review* 50, no. 1–2 (1992): 62. *Black Boy* was subjected to very similar forms of censorship as *Native Son* at the request of the Book-of-the-Month Club; see Rowley.

31. See, for example, Ferguson's *Aberrations in Black* and Muñoz's *Disidentifications*.

32. Florence Dore, *The Novel and the Obscene: Sexual Subjects in American Modernism* (Stanford: Stanford University Press, 2005), 92.

33. Dore writes, for example, that "It is in the context of [his] purposefully ideological project, then, that Wright created overt sexual depictions, and we might conjecture that it is his political critique of American racism that motivated his overt representations of sex" (Dore 95).

34. The fact that Miller's text is so much more taboo than Wright's is provocative, though it is important to note that Miller's novel was unpublishable in the United States at this time. Still, a scene like this one seems tame in comparison to *Tropic of Cancer*, and the controversy over it suggests that *Native Son* was receiving heightened scrutiny.

35. He contends that Bigger and Jack were masturbating while watching the newsreel, which readers know is false. Richard Wright, *Native Son* (restored text), introduction by Arnold Rampersad (New York: Harper Perennial Modern Classics, 2005), 410.

36. The excerpts of the Club's communications about this scene are vague and euphemistic. Stating only that they find the passage "a bit on the raw side" and suggesting that Wright could "revise it in a way to suggest what happens rather than to tell it explicitly," the Club emphasizes delicacy of expression rather than concern over content

(qtd. in Arnold Rampersad, "Note on the Text," *Native Son* [restored text], by Richard Wright, introduction by Rampersad [New York: Harper Perennial Modern Classics, 2005], 486). Wright's subsequent revisions—removing the scene of Mary Dalton from the newsreel, among other changes—suggest that Wright understood their objections to comprise more than merely discomfort over explicit language, but over the narrative association of Mary's and Bigger's sexual expression.

37. Roderick A. Ferguson, *Aberrations in Black: Toward a Queer of Color Critique* (Minneapolis: University of Minnesota Press, 2004), 48.

38. Bigger and Jack both mention women as potential outlets for their aroused sexual energies, but those women are not what stimulates the initial arousal. Rather, they are sites of projection for feelings stirred up in the way I describe here.

39. Foucault argues that the proliferation of discourses aimed at regulating sexuality and its expression have produced something quite different than repression: "Since the end of the sixteenth century, the 'putting into discourse of sex,' far from undergoing a process of restriction, on the contrary has been subjected to a mechanism of increasing incitement," Michel Foucault, *The History of Sexuality: An Introduction*, Vol. I, trans. Robert Hurley (New York: Vintage Books, 1990), 12.

40. Abdul R. JanMohamed, "Sexuality on/of the Racial Border: Foucault, Wright, and the Articulation of 'Racialized Sexuality,'" in *Discourses of Sexuality: From Aristotle to AIDS*, ed. Domna Stanton (Ann Arbor: University of Michigan Press, 1992), 109.

41. Wright echoes this sentiment; see Wright, "How Bigger," 439.

42. And, in fact, they invent other rapes seemingly without reason.

43. My intention in noting the different historical standards of consent is not to justify Bigger's actions or normalize early-century misogyny. Rather, I only want to note that objections about Mary's ability to give consent would not likely have motivated the Book-of-the-Month Club to object to this passage given that the changes made her *less* able to consent, rather than more. Instead, it is likely that the component of cross-racial, mutual desire was the dispositive issue.

44. Similarly, the Coroner asks Mrs. Dalton at the inquest "if someone had possessed your daughter sexually while she lay on that bed, could you in any way have detected it?" (Wright, *Native Son*, 316). Mrs. Dalton's inability to even conceive of this owes as much to the disturbing and hurtful nature of imagining such a thing as to her inability to imagine the transgression of the Jim Crow racial barrier. The Coroner's need to insinuate Bigger's rape of Mary is just as important because it signals the value the rape will serve in the narrative he constructs, which begins with Bigger's rape of an innocent white woman victimized by Communists and African Americans and which ends with Bigger's death.

45. Ian Afflerbach, "Liberalism's Blind Judgment: Richard Wright's *Native Son* and the Politics of Reception," *Modern Fiction Studies* 61, no. 1 (2015): 91.

46. This schema is inspired by Ellen G. Friedman's discussion of the utopic potential of Kathy Acker's novels. See Chapter 3.

47. Hassan often echoes sentiments expressed by Durrell, as he does here. Durrell, for example, called *Cancer* "a destructive book in a fecundating sense," which evokes the sense of productive death and rebirth that apocalypse represents (23).

48. Elsewhere (for example, 7 and 38), Hassan interrogates the nature of apocalypse through its etymological roots in the notion of revelation. However, revelation is discussed as a turning point that alters the course of history. Thus, though Hassan's work muddies my preferred terminology, the underlying argument is not affected.

49. As the book jacket for Turner's *Renegade* puts it, "many critics, teachers, and readers still feel uneasy about [*Tropic of Cancer*]. They may be willing to grant that it changed the national literature, but they are unwilling to admit that it is truly representative of much that is important about American literature and culture."

2. Geniuses Abroad, Deviants at Home: Racial Counter-Narratives of the Global and Domestic

1. See Sylvia Shin Huey Chong on the lasting significance of the "Vietnam Syndrome" with regard to obscenity. Sylvia Shin Huey Chong, *The Oriental Obscene: Violence and Racial Fantasies in the Vietnam Era* (Durham: Duke University Press, 2011), 1–31.

2. Huynh Cong "Nick" Ut, *The Terror of War [Napalm Girl]*, June 8, 1972. Photograph.

3. The lasting impact of the photo is attested to by the many retrospectives it occasioned on its fortieth anniversary. For example, see Tiffany Hagler-Geard and Donald R. Winslow.

4. Joe McNally and Janet Mason, "Caught in Time," *Life* (May 1995), 38–44.

5. Quoted in Guy Westwell, "Accidental Napalm Attack and Hegemonic Visions of America's War in Vietnam," *Critical Studies in Media Communication* 28, no. 5 (2011): 409.

6. Donald R. Winslow, "Napalm Girl 40 Years Later," *New Photographer* (July–August 2012): 20.

7. Anxieties about child pornography impact most representations of child nudity. Maurice Sendak's *In the Night Kitchen* (1970) is an example from this era, in which the main character is nude in several scenes. The controversy preceded the publication of Ut's photo by only a few years and would have influenced any decision to publish. It is notable that such images are often controversial even *before the fact* because the possibility of negative public reaction is anticipated and influences decisions about publishing, a form of soft censorship. For more on the controversy over *In the Night Kitchen*, see Josh Lambert (*Unclean Lips: Obscenity, Jews, and American Culture* [New York: New York University Press, 2013], 92), Perry Nodelman, and Horning.

8. Helena Grice interprets this act as consistent with efforts to control the image of the war according to masculine perspectives. "'The Voice in the Picture': Reversing the Angle in Vietnamese American War Memoirs," *Journal of American Studies* 46, no. 4 (2012): 953–54.

9. Anne Higgonet, *Pictures of Innocence: The History and Crisis of Ideal Childhood* (London: Thames, 1998), 133.

10. Werrlein describes the connection regarding *The Bluest Eye* as follows: "While 1940 marks the eve of both war and economic recovery in American history books, it also marks the year Richard Wright's *Native Son* kicked off an angry protest movement against racism. Morrison captures this underrepresented aspect of American history." Debra T. Werrlein, "Not So Fast, Dick and Jane: Reimagining Childhood and Nation in *The Bluest Eye*," *MELUS* 30, no. 4 (2005): 55–56.

11. Mark McGurl names both Pynchon and Morrison specifically in describing these traditions. Mark McGurl, *The Program Era: Postwar Fiction and the Rise of Creative Writing* (Cambridge: Harvard University Press, 2009). In regards to Morrison, see McGurl 56–57; in regards to Pynchon, see McGurl 62–63.

12. Pynchon's shorter novel *The Crying of Lot 49* (1966), and his previous expansive novel *V.* (1963) were somewhat less controversial and are therefore more often taught at the undergraduate level, though they are less prominent in culture at large.

13. *Miller* was argued in January and November 1972 and decided on June 21, 1973; *Gravity's Rainbow* was published in February 1973.

14. Peter Kihss, "Pulitzer Jurors Dismayed on Pynchon," *New York Times*, May 8, 1974: 38

15. Louis Menand, "Entropology," Review of *Mason and Dixon*, *New York Review of Books*, June 12, 1997.

16. For example, though the novel was denied the Pulitzer, it shared the National Book Award that year with Isaac Bashevis Singer's *A Crown of Feathers and Other Stories* (1973).

17. Toon Staes, "When You Come to a Fork in the Road—Marcuse, Intellectual Subversion and Negative Thought in *Gravity's Rainbow* and *Against the Day*," in *Against the Grain: Reading Pynchon's Counternarratives*, ed. Sascha Pöhlmann (Amsterdam: Rodopi, 2010), 100.

18. See Molly Hite, Toon Staes, and Joseph W. Slade. Scholarly consensus is that Pynchon was familiar with Marcuse and *Eros and Civilization* when he wrote *Gravity's Rainbow*. Slade charts connections to Max Weber and Thorstein Veblen.

19. Michael Harris, "To Historicize Is to Colonize: Colonialism in *V.* and *Gravity's Rainbow*," in *Approaches to Teaching Pynchon's "The Crying of Lot 49 and Other Works*," ed. Thomas Schaub (New York: Modern Language Association, 2008), 104.

20. Joseph W. Slade, "Religion, Psychology, Sex, and Love in *Gravity's Rainbow*," in *Approaches to "Gravity's Rainbow*," ed. Charles Clerc (Columbus: Ohio State University Press, 1983), 160.

21. There is further evidence that Pynchon was thinking about the long narratives of American national identity at the time. Menand notes that in 1973 the author signed a contract to write *Mason and Dixon*, which was not released until 1997, but which is explicitly about colonial politics and imperialism in the American imagination.

22. Thomas Pynchon, *Gravity's Rainbow* (New York: Penguin, 1973), 26.

23. Hannah Arendt's essay on the banality of evil suggests that such tolerance of extreme acts was often valorized by those who were complicit in the Nazi enterprise as necessary parts of achieving a greater vision.

24. Herbert Marcuse, *Eros and Civilization: A Philosophical Inquiry into Freud* (Boston: Beacon, 1966), 107–8.

25. Cf. Hite, "Reading," where the author contends that the post-war Zone is a chance to explore the utopic movement of society that Marcuse advocates (41–42). Slade would disagree, as he states that "the uncertainty of the Zone offers hope that is soon defeated: an old world may or may not be dying, but a new one clearly is powerless to be born" (178). Staes notes, similarly, that ultimately the Zone is defined as a space of death and not utopia (Staes 100).

26. This notion is something I discuss extensively in the introduction.

27. Susan Sontag highlights the discourse that makes this possible. "War-making is one of the few activities that people are not supposed to view 'realistically'; that is, with an eye to expense and practical outcome. In all-out war, expenditure is all-out, unprudent—war being defined as an emergency in which no sacrifice is excessive" (*AIDS and Its Metaphors* [New York: Farrar, 1989], 11).

28. See Slade's argument that multi-national corporations are an extension of the logic of the nation-state and that national status was merely a name given to a fundamentally economic entity continuous with the corporation (158).

29. For example, one of the Pulitzer board members who denied the novel the fiction award apparently confessed to only getting a third of the way through the book (see Peter Kihss, "Pulitzer Jurors Dismayed on Pynchon").

30. James R. Lindroth, review of *Gravity's Rainbow*, by Thomas Pynchon, *America* (May 12, 1973): 446; W. T. Lhamon, "The Most Irresponsible Bastard," review of *Gravity's Rainbow*, by Thomas Pynchon, *New Republic* (April 14, 1973): 24.

31. Scott Simmon, "Gravity's Rainbow Described," *Critique* 16, no. 2 (1974): 54.

32. Robert K. Morris, "Jumping off the Golden Gate Bridge," Rev. of *Gravity's Rainbow* by Thomas Pynchon, *The Nation* (July 16, 1973): 53.

33. For more, see Clive Jordan.

34. Toni Morrison, *The Bluest Eye* (New York: Vintage, 2007), 135.

35. Jennifer Gillan, "Focusing on the Wrong Front: Historical Displacement, the Maginot Line, and *The Bluest Eye*," *African American Review* 36, no. 2 (2002): 284.

36. Jerome Bump provides examples of interpretations of the novel that foreground the psychological impacts of racism, building the archive around the doll test and its epistemology.

37. Gwen Bergner, "Black Children, White Preference: *Brown v. Board*, the Doll Tests, and the Politics of Self-Esteem," *American Quarterly* 61, no. 2 (2009): 310.

38. For example, Thaggert describes the flexibility of the Moynihan Report's logic: "Depending on one's ideological inclinations, the report could be used either to advocate for more government programs to assist African Americans or to excoriate African Americans for failing to take advantage of the programs that already existed" (Miriam Thaggert, "Marriage, Moynihan, Mahogany: Success and the Post-Civil Rights Black Female Professional in Film," *American Quarterly* 64, no. 4 [2012]: 727).

39. George Lipsitz, "The Possessive Investment in Whiteness: Racialized Social Democracy and the 'White' Problem in American Studies," *American Quarterly* 47, no. 3 (1995): 379.

40. Cholly is described as "dangerously free" (Morrison, *Bluest Eye*, 159). In this way, his complete alienation from moderating social norms makes him similar to Bigger Thomas.

41. Cheryl A. Wall, "On Dolls, Presidents, and Little Black Girls," *Signs* 35, no. 4 (Summer 2010): 797. See also, Hortense J. Spillers, Afterword in *Conjuring: Black Women, Fiction, and Literary Tradition*, ed. Marjorie Pryse and Spillers, 249–61 (Bloomington: Indiana University Press, 1985).

42. Malin Walther Pereira, "Periodizing Toni Morrison's Work from *The Bluest Eye* to *Jazz*: The Importance of *Tar Baby*," *MELUS* 22, no. 3 (1997): 73–74.

43. See, for example, Werrlein, Rosenberg, Klotman, Wall, and Roye.

44. See, for example, Werrlein and Middleton.

45. See Davis, NCAC, Milhoan, Stephens, ACLU, Williams, Hui, Alexander, and Rekhi.

46. The ALA also ranks *The Bluest Eye* fifteenth on its list of one hundred most challenged books of 2000–2009, and thirty-fourth on the same list for 1990–1999.

47. See Stephens, for example.

48. Kimberly Millhoan, "The Bluest Eye Blues: Standing Up for Toni Morrison," *ACLUOhio.org*, ACLU of Ohio, September 17, 2013, quoted in Sara Gates, "Ohio Schools Leader Calls for Ban of 'The Bluest Eye,' Labels Toni Morrison Book 'Pornographic,'" *Huffington Post*, September 13, 2013.

49. Carolyn P. Henly, "Reader-Response Theory as Antidote to Controversy: Teaching *The Bluest Eye*," *The English Journal* 82, no. 3 (March 1993): 14.

50. Mary Ella Randall et al., "Antidote to Controversy? Responses to Carolyn Henly," *The English Journal* 82, no. 3 (March 1993): 21.

51. Allen Alexander calls Soaphead Church "easily Morrison's most detestable character in a novel that is replete with them." Allen Alexander, "The Fourth Face: The Image of God in Toni Morrison's *The Bluest Eye*," *African American Review* 32, no. 2 (Summer 1998): n.p.

52. Daniel Patrick Moynihan, *The Negro Family: The Case for National Action* (Washington, D.C.: Office of Policy Planning and Research, United States Department of Labor, 1965), 48.

53. Eden Osucha points out that Moynihan's subjection of the African American family to state intervention also results in the racialization of the private.

54. I draw this notion from Ferguson, who himself credits Audre Lorde with articulating it. Ferguson writes: "Lorde was referring to the discursive and material formations that came to characterize the 1960s, the 1970s, and the 1980s—the pathologization of difference, the displacement of those pathologies onto surplus populations, and the political and cultural challenges to such conservative formations" (Roderick A. Ferguson, *Aberrations in Black: Toward a Queer of Color Critique* [Minneapolis: University of Minnesota Press, 2004], 110).

55. He writes, for example, that "In the context of the United States, the women's movement became hegemonic as it engaged in racial and class exclusions, thereby normalizing white citizenship; the civil rights movement complied with liberal exclusions through its sexist ideologies and practices, thereby normalizing heteropatriarchal citizenship" (*Aberrations*, 115).

56. Angela Davis's account of the Moynihan Report takes issue with the report's hypothesis about black matriarchy, arguing that the Moynihan Report founds a negative ideology on inaccurate information.

57. Notably, the report celebrates higher levels of male educational achievement and employment among the white population—gender inequality—as a sign of the health of the white family, while denigrating gender parity in the African American community (31, 32).

58. The report celebrates the benefits of military service, asserting, "Given the strains of the disorganized and matrifocal family life in which so many Negro youth come of age, the Armed Forces are a dramatic and desperately needed change: a world away from women, a world run by strong men of unquestioned authority, where discipline, if harsh, is nonetheless orderly and predictable, and where rewards, if limited, are granted on the basis of performance" (Moynihan, *Negro Family*, 42).

59. See the section on "Alienation" (Moynihan, *Negro Family*, 43–45).

60. See James Berger, "Ghosts of Liberalism: Morrison's *Beloved* and the Moynihan Report," *PMLA* 111, no. 3 (May 1996): 412.

61. As Jennifer Gillan notes, it does so by shifting attention *to* perceived variations in African American sexual practices and *away from* the documented sexual practices in slavery including concubinage and rape (287).

62. See Patricia Hill Collins, *Black Feminist Thought: Knowledge, Consciousness, and the Politics of Empowerment*, revised 10th anniversary ed. (New York: Routledge, 2002), 18 et passim.

63. Rose M. Brewer, "Black Women in Poverty: Some Comments on Female-Headed Families," *Signs* 13, no. 2 (1988): 331.

64. Hortense J. Spillers, "Mama's Baby, Papa's Maybe: An American Grammar Book," *Diacritics* 17, no. 2 (1987): 66.

65. Eden Osucha, "Race and the Regulation of Intimacy in the Moynihan Report, the Griswold Decision, and Morrison's Paradise," *American Literary History* 27, no. 2 (2015): 262–63.

66. Morrison *does* suggest the African American community is also to blame for rushing to judgment and victim blaming, however. Late in the novel, Claudia and Frieda overhear their neighbors discussing Pecola's situation, and note that they did not find "eyes creased with concern" and that "our sorrow was the more intense because nobody else seemed to share it" (190). That the town feels personally guilty or shamed is indicated by their habit of looking away from Pecola in the novel's closing sections (see Morrison, *Bluest Eye*, 195).

67. Toni Morrison, *Unspeakable Things Unspoken: The Afro-American Presence in American Literature*, Tanner Lecture on Human Values (Ann Arbor: University of Michigan, 1988), 148.

68. Cf. Osucha, who contends that Berger fails to identify the ways that Morrison is shifting or altering the logic of the Moynihan Report.

69. Mark McGurl, *The Program Era: Postwar Fiction and the Rise of Creative Writing* (Cambridge: Harvard University Press, 2009), 57.

70. Werrlein points out that the novel also signifies on the *Dick and Jane* primers that were part of a national literacy campaign that excluded African Americans (62).

3. Porn Wars and Pornotroping: Counter-Narratives of Obscenity amid Transitions in Feminist Activism

1. Hélène Cixous suggests that requiring women authors to be sexless is a result of patriarchal derogation of the contributions of women authors. Hélène Cixous, "Castration or Decapitation?," trans. Annette Kuhn, *Signs* 7, no. 1 (1981): 52.

2. Kathy Acker's exploration of the language and politics of the body through an interest in bodybuilding is well-documented and something she wrote about herself. See her essay "Against Ordinary Language: The Language of the Body," in *Bodies of Work* (London: Serpent's Tail, 1997), 143–51.

3. Acker was diagnosed with breast cancer in 1996 and had a double mastectomy that year. Del LaGrace Volcano took two portraits of Acker in 1997 that speak to Acker's determination to make visible her post-surgery body, provoking discussions about gender and the non-normative body; see Volcano ("Kathy Acker," e-mail to the author, March 12, 2012). In *Sublime Mutations*, Volcano calls Acker "one of the most radical sex writers of the century" (Tübingen: Konkursbuchverlag, 2000), 107.

4. Acker's novel is stylistically innovative and culturally important because of its impact on the New York punk scene of the time. It is not widely read but has an avid cult following.

5. Such a similarity suggests connections as well to novels like Toni Morrison's *The Bluest Eye* (1970) and Sapphire's *Push* (1996). See Martha J. Cutter and Missy Dehn Kubitschek.

6. Kathy Acker, *Empire of the Senseless* (New York: Grove Press, 1988).

7. C[ynthia] Carr, "Theoretical Grrrl: The Legacy of Kathy Acker," *The Village Voice*, November 5, 2002, n.p.

8. Emphasizing the centrality of the body in her work, she wrote, "I am looking for the body, my body, which exists outside its patriarchal definitions. Of course, that is not possible. But who is any longer interested in the possible?" "Seeing Gender," in *Bodies of Work* (London: Serpent's Tail, 1997), 158–68.

9. Nicola Pitchford, *Tactical Readings: Feminist Postmodernism in the Novels of Kathy Acker and Angela Carter* (Lewisburg: Bucknell University Press, 2002).

10. Acker also engages Lacan directly; see Christopher Kocela.

11. Nicola Pitchford describes Roy Hoffman's critique and others in her exploration of Acker's changing fortunes in the literary world (66).

12. Ellen G. Friedman, "'Now Eat Your Mind': An Introduction to the Works of Kathy Acker," *The Review of Contemporary Fiction* 9, no. 3 (1989): 40.

13. Andrea Dworkin, *Pornography: Men Possessing Women* (Perigee, 1981), 24.

14. As the 1986 Meese Commission Report notes, the statutes they succeeded in passing cannot sustain Constitutional challenges because their definition of pornography is too broad to withstand the *Miller* test. See Attorney General's Commission on Pornography, *Attorney General's Commission on Pornography: Final Report* (Washington, D.C.: United States Department of Justice, 1986). That this continues to be an active front in feminist discussions and public policy debates is attested to by the recent consideration by the European Union of a measure that would ban all forms of pornography as part of an effort to reduce gender bias. See, for example, Amanda Hess, Zack Whittaker, and European Parliament.

15. Judith Butler, "Force of Fantasy: Feminism, Mapplethorpe, and Discursive Excess," *Differences* 2, no. 2 (1990): 105–25.

16. For more on the potential for affirmation and empowerment through non-mainstream pornography, see Tina Vasquez.

17. Nina Hartley, "Reflections of a Feminist Porn Star" (1992), Red Garter Club Blog [July 2012], emphasis in the original.

18. Though perhaps recognizing the complexity of decisions about sexual freedom, Acker was ambivalent about her own experiences as a sex worker. See "Devoured by Myths: An Interview with Sylvere Lotringer," in *Hannibal Lecter, My Father* (New York: Semiotext(e), 1991).

19. From the novel: "Evil enchanters such as Ronald Regan and certain feminists, like Andrea Dworkin, who control the nexuses of government and culture,'re [sic] persecuting and will continue to persecute us until they have buried and downed, drowned us in our own human forgetfulness" (Acker, *Don Quixote, Which Was a Dream* [New York: Grove Press, 1986], 102). As Alex Houen notes, this attack on Dworkin is ambiguous, steeped in an irony that complicates the simplistic discourse that Dworkin's logic seems to produce (Alex Houen, "Novel Biopolitics: Kathy Acker and Michel Foucault," in *Powers of Possibility: Experimental American Writing since the 1960s* [Oxford: Oxford University Press, 2012], 177).

20. Ellen G. Friedman, "A Conversation with Kathy Acker," *The Review of Contemporary Fiction* 9, no. 3 (1989): 13.

21. Butler notes, for example, the ironic similarities between Dworkin's and Jessie Helms's conceptions of art, reminding us that the latter's bill restricting state funding for certain sexual representations in media "virtually cites the MacKinnon/Dworkin

bill." She calls this overlap a "sorry discursive alliance" based on "a common theory of fantasy and the phantasmatic that informs both views" (108). Similarly, Gayle Rubin notes, "Feminist rhetoric has a distressing tendency to reappear in reactionary contexts" (Gayle Rubin, "Thinking Sex: Notes for a Radical Theory of the Politics of Sexuality," in *Deviations: A Gayle Rubin Reader* [Durham: Duke University Press, 2011], 169). Rubin is noting how anti-porn conservatives and those who wish to see a more limited experience of sexual variation use the language of objectification to argue that sex is fundamentally debasing. Neither critic argues that these moves are feminist. Rather, Butler is condemning Dworkin's ideology and Rubin decrying the ease with which dominant voices co-opt the language of resistance.

22. Audre Lorde, "The Master's Tools Will Never Dismantle the Master's House," in *This Bridge Called My Back*, ed. Cherríe Moraga and Gloria Anzaldúa (New York: Kitchen Table, 1981), 99.

23. Cherríe Moraga, "A Long Line of Vendidas," in *Loving in the War Years* (Boston: South End Press, 1983), 128.

24. Qtd. in Michael Hardin, "Kathy Acker: An Introduction," in *Devouring Institutions*, ed. Michael Hardin (San Diego: San Diego State University Press, 2004), xii.

25. Acker's works are not, however, strictly autobiographical. For more on the relationship between Acker and her characters, as well as her use of diary material in her writing, see Friedman ("Conversation," 12) and Acker's "Devoured by Myths" (607); Houen characterizes Acker's work as *allobiography*, that is, "the writing of one's life *as other*" (152).

26. See Cynthia Carr, Terry Engebretsen, Houen, Kocela, and Barrett Watten; see also Acker's "Reading the Lack" (73); "Against Ordinary Language"; "Seeing Gender" (160–61); and "Colette," (154) in *Bodies of Work* (London: Serpent's Tail, 1997), and "A Few Notes on Two of My Books" (1989), *Review of Contemporary Fiction* 19, no. 3 (1999): 118–19, 120 for examples of such engagement.

27. This experience influenced Acker immensely. She says of her time as a sex worker, "It changed my politics. . . . The 42nd Street experience made me learn about street politics. You see people from the bottom up, and sexual behavior, especially sex minus relationship—which is what happens in 42nd Street—is definitely bottom" ("Devoured by Myths," 4–5).

28. Gloria Anzaldúa, "Speaking in Tongues: A Letter to 3rd World Women Writers," in *This Bridge Called My Back*, ed. Cherríe Moraga and Gloria Anzaldúa (New York: Kitchen Table, 1981), 167.

29. One can read Anaïs Nin's preface to the 1961 edition of *Tropic of Cancer* in parallel to this. Nin refers to *Tropic* this way: "And it is blood and flesh which are here given us. Drink, food, laughter, desire, passion, curiosity, the simple realities which nourish the roots of our highest and vaguest creations. The superstructure is lopped away. This book brings with it a wind that blows down the dead and hollow trees whose roots are withered and lost in the barren soil of our times" (Anaïs Nin, Preface to *Tropic of Cancer* by Henry Miller [New York: Grove Press, 1961], xxxiii). Nin's terms suggest that Miller's celebration of the body can be a source of freedom in ways that echo Moraga's. However, it is crucial to recognize the different social possibilities for women of color and that Miller's freedom to undertake this work is underwritten by his whiteness.

30. Kathy Acker, *Hannibal Lecter, My Father* (New York: Semiotext(e), 1991), 145.

31. The German declaration finds, for example, that the novel "mostly deals with male power and potency," though it then confoundingly concludes that this means the novel is not feminist (Acker, *Hannibal*, 147).

32. It is at this point that drawings of genitalia appear in the text. The novel's first sentence, which concludes with "Janey depended on her father for everything and regarded her father as boyfriend, brother, sister, money, amusement, and father" (Kathy Acker, *Blood and Guts in High School* [New York: Grove Press, 1984], 7), is followed on the next page by a drawing of two views of a man's body with the penis in full view but with the head out frame. The caption for this image is "boyfriend, brother, sister, money, amusement, and father" (8).

33. In the text, this is represented as a vertical list, emphasizing that Janey is symbolically *beneath* these other subjects (or non-subjects).

34. This critique becomes somewhat explicit when President Carter gets a particularly filthy treatment (Acker, *Blood and Guts*, 119–21). Carter had been inaugurated the year before the book's completion.

35. Ellen G. Friedman contends that Acker does not fundamentally believe that such a utopia can come to pass: "Acker's questers' searches for identity and a new healing myth lead to silence, death, nothingness, or reentry into the sadomasochism of patriarchal culture. . . . The attempts to subvert male texts and thus male culture result in revelation rather than revolution; the path to an alternate site of enunciation blocked by the very forces this path is meant to escape" ("Now Eat," 44).

36. The recurrence of the word "prison" evokes Friedman's description of Acker's notion of the interpellation of women into a misogynistic culture, which she calls "patriarchal cultural incarceration" ("Now Eat," 41). Jon Stratton links this passage to Fredric Jameson's 1972 *The Prison-House of Language* (93), indicating a close connection between Structuralist conceptions of language and the cultural models (including capitalism) that Acker is resisting. Further metaphors of imprisonment in relation to the heterosexual order are found in Acker's "Reading the Lack of the Body" (69) and "Colette" (154). That all of this is related directly to Acker's interventions in contemporary material conditions is demonstrated by Houen, who notes that "*Empire*'s passages on incarceration were topical considering the increase in the prison population under Reagan" (185).

37. See also Lisa Lowe, *Immigrant Acts* (Durham: Duke University Press, 1996), 25.

38. Audre Lorde, "The Master's Tools Will Never Dismantle the Master's House," in *This Bridge Called My Back*, ed. Cherríe Moraga and Gloria Anzaldúa (New York: Kitchen Table, 1981), 98.

39. For other elaborations of the concept of pornotroping, see Jennifer C. Nash and Alexander G. Weheliye.

40. In this vein, we might interpret Lauren Berlant's comment in regards to *The Color Purple* that "For Celie and Nettie's biological father, race functions much as gender functions for the sisters: not as a site of positive identification for the victim, but as an excuse for the oppressor's intricate style of cultural persecution. Lynching, in his narrative, has a structural equivalence to Celie's rape, in its violent reduction of the victim to a 'biological' sign, an exemplum of subhumanity" (Lauren Berlant, "Race, Gender, and Nation in *The Color Purple*," *Critical Inquiry* 14, no. 4 [1988]: 840).

41. Mel Watkins, "Some Letters Went to God," review of *The Color Purple* by Alice Walker, *New York Times Review of Books*, July 25, 1982: NewYorkTimes.com.

42. In this way, the novel might be said to be even more similar to Acker's since it, too, faced the criticism that its political project was ineffective against the danger that it reinforced the stereotypes it attempted to challenge.

43. Trudier Harris, "On *The Color Purple*, Stereotypes, and Silence," *Black American Literature Forum* 18, no. 4 (1984): 155.

44. For more, see Chapter 2.

45. See Hazel V. Carby, *Reconstructing Womanhood: The Emergence of the Afro-American Woman Novelist* (Oxford: Oxford University Press, 1987), 6.

46. Jacqueline Bobo, "Sifting through the Controversy: Reading *The Color Purple*," *Callaloo* 39 (1989): 335.

47. Patricia Holt, Introduction to *Alice Walker Banned* by Alice Walker (San Francisco: Aunt Lute, 1996), 1–2.

48. "Banned & Challenged Classics," American Library Association, February 1, 2016, https://www.ala.org/advocacy/bbooks/frequentlychallengedbooks/classics.

49. Martha J. Cutter, "Philomela Speaks: Alice Walker's Revisioning of Rape Archetypes in *The Color Purple*," *MELUS* 25, no. 3–4 (2000): 163.

50. Linda Abbandonato, "A View from 'Elsewhere': Subversive Sexuality and the Rewriting of the Heroine's Story in *The Color Purple*," *PMLA* 106, no. 5 (1991): 1109–10.

51. See Whitney Strub, "Lavender, Menaced: Lesbianism, Obscenity Law, and the Feminist Antipornography Movement," *Journal of Women's History* 22, no. 2 (2010): 83–107.

52. Michel Foucault, *The History of Sexuality: An Introduction*, Vol. I, trans. Robert Hurley (New York: Vintage Books, 1990), 6.

4. AIDS Politics Is Local: Narratives of Plague and Place in the Culture Wars

1. From the heading: Roy Cohn, qtd. in Albin Krebs, "Roy Cohn, Aide to McCarthy and Fiery Lawyer, Dies at 59," *New York Times*, August 3, 1986.

2. William F. Buckley, "Roy Cohn, RIP," *National Review*, August 29, 1986, 18.

3. When referring to the real-life figure of Roy M. Cohn, I will use his last name in keeping with academic convention. However, when referring to the character by the same name in Tony Kushner's play, I will call him "Roy," as the play does. Tony Kushner, *Angels in America: A Gay Fantasia on National Themes* (New York: Theater Communications Group, 2003).

4. Roderick A. Ferguson, *Aberrations in Black: Toward a Queer of Color Critique* (Minneapolis: University of Minnesota Press, 2004), 3.

5. David L. Eng, *Racial Castration: Managing Masculinity in Asian America* (Durham: Duke University Press, 2001), 17.

6. Judy Tzu-Chun Wu, "Asian American History and Racialized Compulsory Deviance," *Journal of Women's History* 15, no. 3 (Autumn 2003): 60.

7. Didi Herman, *The Antigay Agenda: Orthodox Vision and the Christian Right* (Chicago: University of Chicago Press, 1998), 50.

8. Whitney Strub, *Perversion for Profit: The Politics of Pornography and the Rise of the New Right* (New York: Columbia University Press, 2010), 179–80.

9. See Whitney Strub (116–45 and 179–212) and Didi Herman (1–59). Herman notes the complex relationship between anti-communist activism and antigay activism: "CR [Christian Right] antigay discourse has some antecedents in CR anticommunist

and anti-Semitic discourses, but the differences between these understandings are also important" (28).

10. See the chapter conclusion for more, including protestations by certain justices that this phrasing does not imply local standards.

11. From the heading: Quoted from Cindy Patton, *Inventing AIDS* (New York: Routledge, 1990), 45.

12. AVERT, "History of HIV & AIDS in the U.S.," May 30, 2014.

13. At the time, two separate labs had isolated what they believed to be the same virus, using different names. The International Committee on Taxonomy of Viruses would not officially name the virus *Human Immunodeficiency Virus*, or HIV, until 1986 ("History").

14. See An Act Making Appropriations for the Department of the Interior and Related Agencies for the Fiscal Year Ending September 30, 1990, and for Other Purposes, Pub. L. 101–121, 103 Stat. 701–56 (October 23, 1989).

15. Jesse Helms, letter to the editor, "Only Morality Will Effectively Prevent AIDS from Spreading," *New York Times*, November 23, 1987, A22.

16. See United States, AIDS Control Act of 1987, 100th Cong. (Washington: GPO, 1988).

17. Senate Amendment to House Resolution 3058, S. Amdt.963 to H.R. 3058, 100th Cong. (1988), subsection 2536a.

18. Rose M. Brewer confirms this process, writing, "There is an intense American cultural bias that assumes that the male-headed household, with woman as homemaker, is the norm—despite the fact that only about 14 percent of American households now have such an arrangement. The nuclear family imperative is rooted in upper-class, white, patriarchal prerogatives that are unevenly shared across race and class lines" ("Black Women in Poverty: Some Comments on Female-Headed Families," *Signs* 13, no. 2 [1988]: 332). Gayle Rubin theorizes the cultural mechanism by which this proceeds: "All these hierarchies of sexual value . . . function in much the same ways as do ideological systems of racism, ethnocentrism, and religious chauvinism. They rationalize the well-being of the sexually privileged and the adversity of the sexual rabble" ("Thinking Sex: Notes for a Radical Theory of the Politics of Sexuality," in *Deviations: A Gayle Rubin Reader* [Durham: Duke University Press, 2011], 150–51).

19. Susan Sontag, *AIDS and Its Metaphors* (New York: Farrar, 1989), 27.

20. Susan Sontag notes the serviceability of disease metaphors for nativist sentiment: "Authoritarian political ideologies have a vested interest in promoting fear, a sense of the imminence of takeover by aliens—and real diseases are useful material. Epidemic diseases usually elicit a call to ban the entry of foreigners, immigrants. And xenophobic propaganda has always depicted immigrants as bearers of disease" (61–62). War metaphors were also used by AIDS activists to evoke the scale of loss associated with the epidemic and to suggest the nature of a unifying national tragedy or struggle; see Marita Sturken, "Conversations with the Dead: Bearing Witness in the AIDS Memorial Quilt," *Socialist Review* 22, no. 2 (1992): 69–70.

21. See Herman, 29–30.

22. The LGBTQ+ community resisted this stigmatization by deliberately publicizing the experience of living with AIDS and humanizing sufferers. The most monumental of these was the NAMES Project AIDS Memorial Quilt. In particular, the AIDS Quilt resists the invisibility of those who lived with and died of the disease and the characterization of LGBTQ+ individuals as outside the domestic, family, and affective

mainstream. This strategy was not without controversy, as some questioned its efficacy and appropriateness; see Douglas Crimp, Elaine Showalter, and Sturken (86–89).

23. Richard Berkowitz and Michael Callen, *How to Have Sex in an Epidemic: One Approach* (New York: News from the Front, 1983), 39.

24. This was true in mainstream national campaigns and after AIDS became a national issue. However, the kinds of sex-positive or gay-positive campaigns that characterized early efforts at control were quite different. *How to Have Sex in an Epidemic* is a good example of material that did not construe domestic monogamy and other middle-class virtues as the obvious solution. As the authors of the booklet cannily lament, "Gay men have always been criticized for having 'too much sex' with 'too many' different partners. . . . Wherever we turn we are reminded of the joys of romance and dating by those who claim they are only concerned with our health" (35).

25. See Patrick J. Buchanan, Speech to the Republican National Convention, Houston, Texas, August 17, 1992.

26. Qtd. in Isaac Butler and Dan Kois, *The World Only Spins Forward* (New York: Bloomsbury, 2018), 275.

27. David Joselit, "Robert Mapplethorpe's Poses," in *Robert Mapplethorpe: The Perfect Moment*, ed. Janet Kardon (Philadelphia: Institute of Contemporary Art, 1988).

28. Janet Kardon, "The Perfect Moment," in *Robert Mapplethorpe: The Perfect Moment*, ed. Kardon (Philadelphia: Institute of Contemporary Art, 1988), 9.

29. Barbara Gamarekian, "Corcoran, to Foil Dispute, Drops Mapplethorpe Show," *New York Times*, June 14, 1989. It is hard to ignore pecuniary considerations because the Corcoran was campaigning to increase its endowment and federal funding at the time (Gamarekian, "Corcoran"); being embroiled in a public scandal might have hurt its bottom line. The Corcoran's attempt to avoid controversy was, nonetheless, controversial, as the choice not to champion freedom of expression was unpopular in the art world and at the Gallery, and the director of the Corcoran was asked to resign later that year (Barbara Gamarekian, "Arts Nominee Speaks Out against Helms Amendment," *New York Times*, September 23, 1989: 9).

30. See Cathleen McGuigan and Shawn D. Lewis. Also see Isabel Wilkerson.

31. Though they were acquitted, Dennis Barrie and the museum faced a number of hurdles, including a hostile judge. See Cathleen McGuigan and Shawn D. Lewis. Barrie remarked that Judge Albanese even declared the CAC not to be a museum. Barrie goes on to address the issue of the severability of offensive content, describing how Albanese "declared that the seven Mapplethorpe photographs in question could be presented at trial out of the context of the exhibition, even out of the context of their portfolios. And he agreed with the prosecution that exhibitions have no intellectual rhyme or thought behind them" (Dennis Barrie, "The Scene of the Crime," *Art Journal* [Fall 1991]: 30). Barrie's account accurately reflects the judge's rulings; see *City of Cincinnati v. Contemporary Arts Center*. Despite fairly clear federal jurisprudence on the issue, Albanese ruled in ways apparently intended to narrowly construe the artwork and highlight its prurience to privilege the outcome at trial.

32. Barrie, "The Scene of the Crime," 29.

33. Patti Smith, *Just Kids* (New York: Harper Collins, 2010), 215.

34. However, it is also important to note that while the suturing of male nudes to sculpture and flower photography lends cultural capital to the erotic work, the shuttling of signification cannot be easily contained, and the eroticization of other subjects can be troubling.

35. Lyon's inclusion here recalls Kathy Acker's interest in bodybuilding and my earlier discussion of her conscious transgression of gender norms as an expression of feminist ideology. Mapplethorpe also photographed Acker for his portraits series.

36. This echoes something Sontag wrote of sitting for Mapplethorpe: "It is obvious [that] many of Mapplethorpe's photographs record objects of his desire. . . . But the look trained upon the subject when photographed is sightless, generic: the look that discerns form" ("Certain Mapplethorpes").

37. Roland Barthes, *Camera Lucida: Reflections on Photography*, trans. Richard Howard (New York: Hill, 1981), 41.

38. Despite presenting a contextualizing discussion of various genres of Mapplethorpe's photos (nudes, portraits, etc.), Janet Kardon only briefly mentions "Mapplethorpe's S&M photographs" in passing, describing how viewing them in the "conventional gallery or museum environment can be startling" (10) before moving on.

39. Early drafts not only prohibited certain sexual content but also themes that disparaged protected groups. This language is part of an effort among conservatives to ally with anti-pornography feminists including Andrea Dworkin. In "The Force of Fantasy," Judith Butler points out the aporia in Jesse Helms's logic, which conflates depictions of sexual acts and discrimination. Helms's use of this pretext seems patently disingenuous and was ultimately stripped from the bill.

40. The bill stops just short of naming *The Perfect Moment* directly when they note "recently works have been funded which are without artistic value but which are criticized as pornographic and shocking by any standards" (An Act, sec. 304b2, p. 41). Moreover, Kardon's home institution, the Institute for Contemporary Art, was subjected to specific clearance guidelines. A similar provision was included to oversee the Southeastern Center for Contemporary Art, which had awarded the NEA grant to Serrano.

41. The rarity of specific lists of prohibited content is attested to by the FCC's reluctance to stipulate which words you can't say on television. Even such a public-facing and far-reaching standard has never been clarified, despite multiple broadcast-industry requests.

42. From Kushner, *Angels in America*, 142. Cindy Patton, *Inventing AIDS* (New York: Routledge, 1990), 131.

43. The New York–based AIDS Coalition to Unleash Power (or ACT UP), took this notion literally by encouraging direct action and through its famous slogan "Silence = Death."

44. Michael Cadden, "Strange Angel: The Pinklisting of Roy Cohn," in *Approaching the Millennium: Essays on Angels in America*, ed. Deborah R. Geis and Steven F. Kruger (Ann Arbor: University of Michigan Press, 1997), 84. See also David Román, "November 1, 1992: AIDS / *Angels in America*," in *Approaching the Millennium: Essays on Angels in America*, ed. Deborah R. Geis and Steven F. Kruger (Ann Arbor: University of Michigan Press, 1997), 42.

45. In keeping with the *Miller* ruling and previous cases, North Carolina obscenity statutes shielded work that could be shown to have artistic merit; see Offenses against Public Morality and Decency, North Carolina Gen Stat Subchapter VII, Article 26, subsection 14-190.1.

46. The Blumenthal Performing Arts Center, where the play was to be staged, was criticized by free speech advocates for requiring legal pre-clearance and for requesting the nude scenes be removed. The criticism was similar to that directed at the Corcoran

for insufficient fortitude in the face of government restriction of the arts; see V. Cullum Rogers.

47. Reporter Perry Tannenbaum puts the number of anti-*Angels* protestors at about fifteen and the number in support at more than ten times that number (Butler and Kois 287).

48. See Butler and Kois, 289–90.

49. See also Stephen Nunns, 23.

50. The author of the measure, Hoyle Martin, also used plague rhetoric, suggesting that the imputed moral failing of homosexuality is the reason for AIDS (Nunns 26).

51. Jonathan Freedman, *Klezmer America: Jewishness, Ethnicity, Modernity* (New York: Columbia University Press, 2008), 42.

52. For more on the exact timeline of this staging, see Román, 51–52. Both parts of the play were staged together for private audiences and reviewers beginning November 1, 1992—two days prior to the election—while public performances began on November 8—five days after it (42–53).

53. Tony Kushner, *Angels in America: A Gay Fantasia on National Themes* (New York: Theater Communications Group, 2003), 180.

54. Additionally, talks to ratify the Strategic Arms Reduction Treaty were underway at the time of the 1990 workshop of *Millennium Approaches*, and the 1991 premiere of a complete *Millennium Approaches* preceded the dissolution of the Soviet Union by a matter of months.

55. See also Román, 53.

56. See Herman (19–24) on the role of Christian millennialism and apocalyptic themes in American national mythologies.

57. Qtd. in Stephen Nunns, "Is Charlotte Burning?" *American Theater* (February 1999): 23.

58. See *Federal Communications Commission v. Pacifica*.

Epilogue

1. See Gary Trust, "Cardi B. and Megan Thee Stallion's 'WAP' Debuts at No. 1 on Billboard Hot 100 with Record First-Week Streams," *Billboard*, August 17, 2020.

2. Lakin Starling, "Cardi B. 'WAP' [ft. Megan Thee Stallion] Review," *Pitchfork*, August 7, 2020.

3. "The Results Are In: WAP Is a Bop," *WSJ Noted*, August 18, 2020.

4. Charles Holmes, "The Conservative Crusade against 'Wet-Ass Pussy,'" *Rolling Stone*, August 2020.

5. Raisa Bruner and Andrew R. Chow, "The 10 Best Songs of 2020," *Time*, November 23, 2020 (updated November 30, 2020).

6. Ben Sisario, "Cardi B's 'WAP' Proves Music's Dirty Secret: Censorship Is Good Business," *New York Times*, October 27, 2020.

7. See Nicholas Kristof, Samantha Cole, and Kate Cox.

8. See National Center on Sexual Exploitation (NCOSE), "Porn Harms," Endsexualexploitation.org, accessed February 20, 2020.

9. International Center on Sexual Exploitation (ICOSE), "RE: International Concern Over Your Company's Involvement in Sexual Exploitation," Endsexualexploitation.org, National Center on Sexual Exploitation, May 5, 2020.

10. See National Center on Sexual Exploitation (NCOSE), "NCOSE History," Endsexualexploitation.org, accessed February 20, 2020.

11. Group members arranged the purchase of *Fanny Hill* that led to *Memoirs* and the complainant in *Pacifica* was a member of the group's national planning board. See Stephen Bates and Steve Weinstein, respectively. Stephen Bates, "Father Hill and *Fanny Hill*: An Activist Group's Crusade to Remake Obscenity Law," *First Amendment Law Review* 8, no. 2 (March 1, 2010). Steve Weinstein, "How 'Jerker' Helped Ignite Obscenity Debate: Comedian Carlin Has a Few Choice Words for Media Watchdogs," *Los Angeles Times*, August 18, 1987.

12. See Dana Kennedy, "Controversial Photo Exhibit Opens in City Where Artist Died of AIDS," *Associated Press*, July 31, 1990.

Works Cited

Aarons, Debra, and Marc Mierowsky. "Obscenity, Dirtiness, and License in Jewish Comedy." *Comedy Studies* 5, no. 2 (2014): 165–77.

Abbandonato, Linda. "A View from 'Elsewhere': Subversive Sexuality and the Rewriting of the Heroine's Story in *The Color Purple*." *PMLA* 106, no. 5 (1991): 1106–15.

Acker, Kathy. "Against Ordinary Language: The Language of the Body." In *Bodies of Work*, 143–51.

———. *Blood and Guts in High School*. New York: Grove Press, 1984.

———. *Bodies of Work: Essays*. London: Serpent's Tail, 1997.

———. "Colette." In *Bodies of Work*, 152–57.

———. "Devoured by Myths: An Interview with Sylvère Lotringer." In Acker, *Hannibal Lecter, My Father*, 1–24.

———. *Don Quixote, Which Was a Dream*. New York: Grove Press, 1986.

———. *Empire of the Senseless*. New York: Grove Press, 1988.

———. "A Few Notes on Two of My Books." *Review of Contemporary Fiction* 19, no. 3 (1999): 117–22.

———. *Hannibal Lecter, My Father*. New York: Semiotext(e), 1991.

———. "An Interview with Kathy Acker." Interview by Larry McCaffery. *Mississippi Review* 20, no. 1–2 (1991): 83–97.

———. "Reading the Lack of the Body: The Writing of the Marquis de Sade." In *Bodies of Work*, 66–80.

———. "Seeing Gender." In *Bodies of Work*, 158–68.

ACLU of Ohio. "Defending Toni Morrison," October 1, 2013. https://www.acluohio.org/archives/issue-information/defending-toni-morrison. Accessed August 24, 2018.

An Act Making Appropriations for the Department of the Interior and Related Agencies for the Fiscal Year Ending September 30, 1990, and for Other Purposes. Pub. L. No. 101–121. 103 Stat. 701–56 (1989).

Adler, J., and C. McGuigan. "The Killing of a Gory Novel." *Newsweek*, November 26, 1990, 85.

Afflerbach, Ian. "Liberalism's Blind Judgment: Richard Wright's *Native Son* and the Politics of Reception." *Modern Fiction Studies* 61, no. 1 (2015): 90–113.

AIDS Control Act of 1987. S. 1352, 100th Cong. (1988).

Alexander, Allen. "The Fourth Face: The Image of God in Toni Morrison's *The Bluest Eye*." *African American Review* 32, no. 2 (Summer 1998): 293–303.

Alexander, Michelle. *The New Jim Crow: Mass Incarceration in the Age of Colorblindness*. New York: New Press, 2010.

American Library Association. "Banned & Challenged Classics." https://www.ala.org/advocacy/bbooks/frequentlychallengedbooks/classics.

Anzaldúa, Gloria. "Speaking in Tongues: A Letter to Third World Women Writers." In *This Bridge Called My Back*, edited by Cherríe Moraga and Gloria Anzaldúa, 165–73.

Attorney General's Commission on Pornography. *Attorney General's Commission on Pornography: Final Report*. Washington, D.C.: United States Department of Justice, 1986.

AVERT. "History of HIV & AIDS in the U.S." May 30, 2014.

Baldwin, James. "Everybody's Protest Novel." In *Notes of a Native Son*, 13–23. Boston: Beacon, 1955.

Barrie, Dennis. "The Scene of the Crime." *Art Journal* 50, no. 3 (Fall 1991): 29–32.

Barthes, Roland. *Camera Lucida: Reflections on Photography*. Trans. Richard Howard. New York: Hill, 1981.

Bates, Stephen. "Father Hill and *Fanny Hill*: An Activist Group's Crusade to Remake Obscenity Law." *First Amendment Law Review* 8, no. 2 (March 1, 2010).

Berger, James. "Ghosts of Liberalism: Morrison's Beloved and the Moynihan Report." *PMLA* 111, no. 3 (May 1996): 408–20.

Bergner, Gwen. "Black Children, White Preference: *Brown v. Board*, the Doll Tests, and the Politics of Self-Esteem." *American Quarterly* 61, no. 2 (2009): 299–332.

Berkowitz, Richard, and Michael Callen. *How to Have Sex in an Epidemic: One Approach*. New York: News from the Front, 1983.

Berlant, Lauren. "Race, Gender, and Nation in *The Color Purple*." *Critical Inquiry* 14, no. 4 (1988): 831–59.

Blake, Emily, et al. "Year in Review: The Best Pop Collaborations of 2020." *Rolling Stone*, December 15, 2020.

Bobo, Jacqueline. "Sifting through the Controversy: Reading *The Color Purple*." *Callaloo* 39 (1989): 332–42.

Bomberger, Ann. "The Efficacy of Shock for Feminist Politics: Kathy Acker's *Blood and Guts in High School* and Donald Barthelme's *Snow White*." In

Gender Reconstructions: Pornography and Perversions in Literature and Culture, edited by Cindy L. Carlson, Robert Mazzola, and Susan M. Bernardo, 189–204. Aldershot: Ashgate, 2002.

Brew, Kathy. Photograph of Kathy Acker. 1991.

Brewer, Rose M. "Black Women in Poverty: Some Comments on Female-Headed Families." *Signs* 13, no. 2 (1988): 331–39.

Bruce, Lenny. *Lenny Bruce: Let the Buyer Beware*, produced by Marvin Worth and Hal Wilner, Shout! Factory, 2004.

Bruner, Raisa, and Andrew R. Chow. "The 10 Best Songs of 2020." *Time*, November 23, 2020 (updated November 30, 2020).

Buchanan, Patrick J. Speech to the Republican National Convention. Houston, Texas. August 17, 1992.

Buckley, William F. "Roy Cohn, RIP." *National Review*, August 29, 1986, 18–19.

Butler, Isaac, and Dan Kois. *The World Only Spins Forward*. New York: Bloomsbury, 2018.

Butler, Judith. "Force of Fantasy: Feminism, Mapplethorpe, and Discursive Excess." *Differences* 2, no. 2 (1990): 105–25.

Cable-Porn and Dial-a-Porn Control Act (S. 1090), *Hearing before the Subcommittee on Criminal Law of the Committee on the Judiciary*, first session, 99th Cong. (1985).

Cadden, Michael. "Strange Angel: The Pinklisting of Roy Cohn." In *Approaching the Millennium: Essays on Angels in America*, edited by Deborah R. Geis and Steven F. Kruger, 78–89. Ann Arbor: University of Michigan Press, 1997.

Carby, Hazel V. *Reconstructing Womanhood: The Emergence of the Afro-American Woman Novelist*. Oxford: Oxford University Press, 1987.

Carr, C[ynthia]. "Theoretical Grrrl: The Legacy of Kathy Acker." *The Village Voice*. November 5, 2002: n.p.

Chong, Sylvia Shin Huey. *The Oriental Obscene: Violence and Racial Fantasies in the Vietnam Era*. Durham: Duke University Press, 2011.

City of Cincinnati v. Contemporary Arts Center (and City of Cincinnati v. Barrie). 57 Ohio Misc. 2d 9. Hamilton County Municipal Court, Ohio. 1990.

Cixous, Hélène. "Castration or Decapitation?" Trans. Annette Kuhn. *Signs* 7, no. 1 (1981): 41–55.

Clarke, Cheryl. "Lesbianism: An Act of Resistance." In *This Bridge Called My Back*, edited by Cherríe Moraga and Gloria Anzaldúa, 128–37.

Clinton, William Jefferson. Inaugural Address. Washington, D.C. January 20, 1993.

Cole, Samantha. "How a Petition to Shut Down Pornhub Got Two Million Signatures." *Vice*, Vice Media Group, September 1, 2020.

Collins, Patricia Hill. *Black Feminist Thought: Knowledge, Consciousness, and the Politics of Empowerment*. Revised 10th anniversary ed. New York: Routledge, 2002.

Cox, Kate. "Millions of Videos Purged from Pornhub amid Crackdown on User Content." *Vice*, Vice Media Group, December 14, 2020.

Crimp, Douglas. "Mourning and Militancy." *October* (Winter 1989): 3–18.
Cutter, Martha J. "Philomela Speaks: Alice Walker's Revisioning of Rape Archetypes in *The Color Purple*." *MELUS* 25, no. 3–4 (2000): 161–80.
Davis, Angela Y. *Women, Race & Class*. New York: Vintage, 1983.
Davis, Stacy. "Brookfield Residents Ask the Board to Drop Book from Curriculum." Newstimes.com. Hearst Media Services Connecticut, October 6, 2011.
de Grazia, Edward. *Girls Lean Back Everywhere: The Law of Obscenity and the Assault on Genius*. New York: Vintage, 1993.
Dore, Florence. *The Novel and the Obscene: Sexual Subjects in American Modernism*. Stanford: Stanford University Press, 2005.
Durrell, Lawrence. "From Lawrence Durrell to Alfred Perlès." In *Art and Outrage: A Correspondence about Henry Miller*, by Durrell, Alfred Perlès, and Henry Miller, 7–10. New York: E. P. Dutton, 1961.
———. "From Lawrence Durrell to Alfred Perlès." In *Art and Outrage: A Correspondence about Henry Miller*, by Durrell, Alfred Perlès, and Henry Miller, 14–17. New York: E. P. Dutton, 1961.
Dworkin, Andrea. *Pornography: Men Possessing Women*. New York: Perigee, 1981.
Dworkin, Andrea, and Catharine A. MacKinnon. *Pornography and Civil Rights: A New Day for Women's Equality*. Minneapolis: Organizing Against Pornography, 1988.
Edelman, Lee. *No Future: Queer Theory and the Death Drive*. Durham: Duke University Press, 2004.
"Editorial Judgment or Censorship?" *Writer*, May 1991: 20–23.
Ellison, Ralph. "Richard Wright's Blues." *The Antioch Review* 50, no. 1–2 (1992): 61–74.
Eng, David L. *Racial Castration: Managing Masculinity in Asian America*. Durham: Duke University Press, 2001.
Engebretsen, Terry. "Re-Educating the Body: Kathy Acker, Georges Bataille, and the Postmodern Body in My Mother: Demonology." In *Devouring Institutions*, edited by Michael Hardin, 69–84.
European Parliament. "Report on Eliminating Gender Stereotypes in the EU." *European Parliament*. December 6, 2012.
Federal Communications Commission [FCC]. "Obscene, Indecent, and Profane Broadcasts." Consumer Fact Sheet. Washington: FCC [May 17, 2011].
Federal Communications Commission v. Fox Television Stations. 129 S. Ct. 1800. Supreme Court of the US. 2009. Google Scholar.
Federal Communications Commission v. Fox Television Stations. 567 US n.p. Supreme Court of the US. 2012. Supremecourt.gov.
Federal Communications Commission v. Pacifica. 438 US 726–80. Supreme Court of the US. 1978.
Ferguson, Roderick A. *Aberrations in Black: Toward a Queer of Color Critique*. Minneapolis: University of Minnesota Press, 2004.

Foster, Steven. "A Critical Appraisal of Henry Miller's *Tropic of Cancer*." *Twentieth Century Literature* 9, no. 4 (1964): 196–208.
Foucault, Michel. *Discipline and Punish: The Birth of the Prison*. Trans. Alan Sheridan. New York, Vintage, 1995.
———. *The History of Sexuality: An Introduction*. Volume I. Trans. Robert Hurley. New York: Vintage, 1990.
Fredericksen, Barbara L. "Fascinating Lives of a Risque Trio." *St. Petersburg Times*. January 24, 2003.
Freedman, Jonathan. *Klezmer America: Jewishness, Ethnicity, Modernity*. New York: Columbia University Press, 2008.
Friedman, Ellen G. "A Conversation with Kathy Acker." *The Review of Contemporary Fiction* 9, no. 3 (1989): 12–22.
———. "'Now Eat Your Mind': An Introduction to the Works of Kathy Acker." *The Review of Contemporary Fiction* 9, no. 3 (1989): 37–49.
Gamarekian, Barbara. "Arts Nominee Speaks Out against Helms Amendment." *New York Times*. September 23, 1989: 9.
———. "Corcoran, to Foil Dispute, Drops Mapplethorpe Show." *New York Times*. June 14, 1989: n.p.
Gates, Sara. "Ohio Schools Leader Calls for Ban of 'The Bluest Eye,' Labels Toni Morrison Book 'Pornographic.'" *Huffington Post*. September 13, 2013.
Gillan, Jennifer. "Focusing on the Wrong Front: Historical Displacement, the Maginot Line, and *The Bluest Eye*." *African American Review* 36, no. 2 (2002): 283–98.
Glass, Loren. *Counterculture Colophon: Grove Press, the Evergreen Review, and the Incorporation of the Avant-Garde*. Stanford: Stanford University Press, 2013.
Grice, Helena. "'The Voice in the Picture': Reversing the Angle in Vietnamese American War Memoirs." *Journal of American Studies* 46, no. 4 (2012): 941–58.
Grove Press, Inc. v. Christenberry. 175 F.Supp. 488–503. 1959.
Grove Press, Inc. v. Christenberry. 276 F.2d 433–43. 1960.
Hagler-Geard, Tiffany. "The Historic 'Napalm Girl' Pulitzer Image Marks Its 40th Anniversary." *ABC News*. Yahoo-ABC News Network, June 8, 2012.
Halberstam, Jack. *The Queer Art of Failure*. Durham: Duke University Press, 2011.
Hardin, Michael, ed. *Devouring Institutions*. San Diego: San Diego State University Press, 2004.
———. "Fighting Desires: Henry Miller's Queer *Tropic*." *Journal of Homosexuality* 42, no. 3 (2002): 129–50.
———. "Kathy Acker: An Introduction." Introduction. In *Devouring Institutions*, edited by Michael Hardin, x–xvi.
Harris, Michael. "To Historicize Is to Colonize: Colonialism in *V.* and *Gravity's Rainbow*." In *Approaches to Teaching Pynchon's "The Crying of Lot 49*

and Other Works," edited by Thomas Schaub, 99–105. New York: Modern Language Association, 2008.

Harris, Trudier. "On *The Color Purple*, Stereotypes, and Silence." *Black American Literature Forum* 18, no. 4 (1984): 155–61.

Hartley, Nina. "Reflections of a Feminist Porn Star." 1992. Red Garter Club Blog.

Hassan, Ihab. *The Literature of Silence: Henry Miller and Samuel Beckett*. New York: Knopf, 1967.

Helms, Jesse. "Only Morality Will Effectively Prevent AIDS from Spreading." Letter to the editor. *New York Times*. November 23, 1987: A22.

Henly, Carolyn P. "Reader-Response Theory as Antidote to Controversy: Teaching *The Bluest Eye*." *The English Journal* 82, no. 3 (March 1993): 14–19.

Herman, Didi. *The Antigay Agenda: Orthodox Vision and the Christian Right*. Chicago: University of Chicago Press, 1998.

Hess, Amanda. "Think the Porn Industry Discriminates against Women? Lean In." *The XX Factor*. Slate.com. March 8, 2013.

Higgonet, Anne. *Pictures of Innocence: The History and Crisis of Ideal Childhood*. London: Thames, 1998.

Hogue, W. Lawrence. "Can the Subaltern Speak? A Postcolonial, Existential Reading of Richard Wright's *Native Son*." *Southern Quarterly* 26, no. 2 (2009): 9–39.

Holmes, Charles. "The Conservative Crusade against 'Wet-Ass Pussy.'" *Rolling Stone*, August 2020.

Holt, Patricia. Introduction to *Alice Walker Banned* by Alice Walker, 1–18. San Francisco: Aunt Lute, 1996.

hooks, bell. Introduction to *Body and Soul* by Andres Serrano. New York: Takarajima, 1995.

Horning, Kathleen T. "The Naked Truth." *School Library Journal* (August 2012): 32–35.

Houchin, John. *Censorship of the American Theatre in the Twentieth Century*. Cambridge: Cambridge University Press, 2003.

Houen, Alex. "Novel Biopolitics: Kathy Acker and Michel Foucault." In *Powers of Possibility: Experimental American Writing since the 1960s*, 145–92. Oxford: Oxford University Press, 2012.

Hui, T. Keung. "Common Core Critics Attack Use of 'The Bluest Eye' in Schools." News & Observer Publishing Co., September 2, 2014.

Hutchison, E. R. *"Tropic of Cancer" on Trial: A Case History of Censorship*. New York: Grove Press, 1968.

International Center on Sexual Exploitation (ICOSE). "RE: International Concern Over Your Company's Involvement in Sexual Exploitation." National Center on Sexual Exploitation, May 5, 2020.

Jackson, Paul R. "Henry Miller, Emerson, and the Divided Self." *American Literature* 43, no. 2 (1971): 231–41.

Jacobellis v. Ohio. 378 U.S. 184–204. Supreme Court of the U.S. (1964).

JanMohamed, Abdul R. "Sexuality on/of the Racial Border: Foucault, Wright, and the Articulation of 'Racialized Sexuality.'" In *Discourses of Sexuality: From Aristotle to AIDS*, edited by Domna Stanton, 94–116. Ann Arbor: University of Michigan Press, 1992.

Jordan, Clive. "World Enough, and Time." *Encounter* 42 (February 1974): 61–65.

Joselit, David. "Robert Mapplethorpe's Poses." In *Robert Mapplethorpe: The Perfect Moment*, edited by Janet Kardon, 19–21. Philadelphia: Institute of Contemporary Art, 1988.

Kalk, Bruce H. "The Carswell Affair: The Politics of a Supreme Court Nomination in the Nixon Administration." *American Journal of Legal History* 42, no. 3 (1998): 261–87.

Kardon, Janet. "The Perfect Moment." In *Robert Mapplethorpe: The Perfect Moment*, edited by Kardon, 9–13. Philadelphia: Institute of Contemporary Art, 1988.

———, ed. *Robert Mapplethorpe: The Perfect Moment*. Philadelphia: Institute of Contemporary Art, 1988.

Kennedy, Dana. "Controversial Photo Exhibit Opens In City Where Artist Died of AIDS." *Associated Press*, July 31, 1990.

Kihss, Peter. "Pulitzer Jurors Dismayed on Pynchon." *New York Times*, May 8, 1974: 38.

Kincaid, Larry, and Grove Koger. "Tropic of Cancer and the Censors: A Case Study and Bibliographic Guide to the Literature." *Reference Services Review* 25, no. 1 (1997): 31–38.

Klein, Alvin. "Three Funny Women, Joking through the Pain." *New York Times*, April 28, 1996.

Kocela, Christopher. "A Myth beyond the Phallus." *Genders* 34 (2001).

Krebs, Albin. "Roy Cohn, Aide to McCarthy and Fiery Lawyer, Dies at 59." *New York Times*. August 3, 1986: 1, 33.

Kristof, Nicholas. "The Children of Pornhub." *New York Times*, Late ed. December 6, 2020.

Kubitschek, Missy Dehn. "Subjugated Knowledge: Toward a Feminist Exploration of Rape in Afro-American Fiction." In *Black Feminist Criticism and Critical Theory*, edited by Joe Weixlmann and Houston A. Baker, Jr., 43–56. Greenwood: Penkeville, 1988.

Kushner, Tony. *Angels in America: A Gay Fantasia on National Themes*. New York: Theater Communications Group, 2003.

Lambert, Josh. *Unclean Lips: Obscenity, Jews, and American Culture*. New York: New York University Press, 2013.

Lee, James Kyung-Jin. *Urban Triage: Race and the Fictions of Multiculturalism*. Minneapolis: University of Minnesota Press, 2004.

Lhamon, W. T. "The Most Irresponsible Bastard," review of *Gravity's Rainbow*, by Thomas Pynchon. *New Republic* (April 14, 1973): 24–28.

Lindroth, James R. Review of *Gravity's Rainbow*, by Thomas Pynchon. *America* (May 12, 1973): 446.

Lipsitz, George. "The Possessive Investment in Whiteness: Racialized Social Democracy and the 'White' Problem in American Studies." *American Quarterly* 47, no. 3 (1995): 369–87.

Lorde, Audre. "The Master's Tools Will Never Dismantle the Master's House." In *This Bridge Called My Back*, edited by Cherríe Moraga and Gloria Anzaldúa, 98–101.

———. "An Open Letter to Mary Daly." In *This Bridge Called My Back*, edited by Cherríe Moraga and Gloria Anzaldúa, 94–97.

Love, Matthew. "50 Best Stand-Up Comics of All Time." RollingStone.com. February 14, 2017.

Lowe, Lisa. *Immigrant Acts*. Durham: Duke University Press, 1996.

Mapplethorpe, Robert. *Certain People: A Book of Portraits*, introduction by Susan Sontag. Santa Fe: Twelvetrees Press, 1985.

Marcuse, Herbert. *Eros and Civilization: A Philosophical Inquiry into Freud*. 1955. Boston: Beacon, 1966.

McCarthy, Harold T. "Henry Miller's Democratic Vistas." *American Quarterly* 23, no. 2 (1971): 221–35.

McGuigan, Cathleen, and Shawn D. Lewis. "Showdown in Cincinnati." *Newsweek* 116, no. 15 (1990): 73.

McGurl, Mark. *The Program Era: Postwar Fiction and the Rise of Creative Writing*. Cambridge: Harvard University Press, 2009.

McNally, Joe, and Janet Mason. "Caught in Time." *Life*, May 1995, 38–44.

McNeill, David. Introduction. *Language and Gesture*. Cambridge: Cambridge University Press, 2000, 1–10.

———. "Why Gestures?" In *Gesture and Thought*. Chicago: University of Chicago Press, 2005, 3–21.

Memoirs v. Massachusetts. 383 U.S. 413. Supreme Court of the U.S. 1966.

Menand, Louis. "Entropology." Rev. of *Mason and Dixon*. *The New York Review of Books*. NYREV. June 12, 1997.

Miller, Henry. "From Henry Miller; To Lawrence Durrell." In *Art and Outrage: A Correspondence about Henry Miller*, by Lawrence Durrell, Alfred Perlès, and Henry Miller, 27–37. New York: E. P. Dutton, 1961.

———. *Tropic of Cancer*. New York: Grove Press, 1961.

Miller v. California. 413 U.S. 15–48. Supreme Court of the U.S. 1973.

Millet, Kate. *Sexual Politics*. Champaign: University of Illinois Press, 2000.

Millhoan, Kimberly. "The Bluest Eye Blues: Standing up for Toni Morrison." ACLU of Ohio. September 17, 2013.

Moraga, Cherríe. "Entering the Lives of Others: Theory in the Flesh." In *This Bridge Called My Back*, edited by Cherríe Moraga and Gloria Anzaldúa, 23.

———. "A Long Line of Vendidas." In *Loving in the War Years*, 90–142. Boston: South End Press, 1983.

Moraga, Cherríe, and Gloria Anzaldúa, eds. *This Bridge Called My Back*. New York: Kitchen Table, 1981.
Morris, Robert K. "Jumping off the Golden Gate Bridge." Rev. of *Gravity's Rainbow* by Thomas Pynchon. *The Nation*, July 16, 1973.
Morrison, Toni. *The Bluest Eye*. New York: Vintage, 2007.
———. *Playing in the Dark: Whiteness and the Literary Imagination*. Cambridge: Harvard University Press, 1992.
———. *Unspeakable Things Unspoken: The Afro-American Presence in American Literature*. Tanner Lecture on Human Values. Ann Arbor: University of Michigan Press, 1988.
Moynihan, Daniel Patrick. *The Negro Family: The Case for National Action*. Washington, D.C.: Office of Policy Planning and Research, United States Department of Labor, 1965.
Muñoz, José Esteban. *Disidentifications: Queers of Color and the Performance of Politics*. Minneapolis: University of Minnesota Press, 1999.
Nash, Jennifer C. "Black Anality." *GLQ: A Journal of Lesbian and Gay Studies* 20, no. 4 (2014): 439–60.
National Center on Sexual Exploitation (NCOSE). "NCOSE History." https://endsexualexploitation.org/about/history/. Accessed February 20, 2020.
———. "Pornography and Public Health Research Summary." Endsexualexploitation.org. https://endsexualexploitation.org/wp-content/uploads/NCOSE_Pornography-PublicHealth_ResearchSummary_1-14-19_FINAL.pdf. Accessed November 2, 2021.
National Council Against Censorship (NCAC). "In Broomfield, CO *The Bluest Eye* Is Removed without Being Banned." August 23, 2013.
———. Letter to Members of the Northville Public Schools Board of Education. April 12, 2016. https://ncac.org/wp-content/uploads/2016/04/NCAC-letter-to-NPS-re-The-Bluest-Eye.pdf.
Nietzsche, Friedrich. *Thus Spoke Zarathustra: A Book for Everyone and Nobody*. Translated and with an introduction and notes by Graham Parkes. Oxford: Oxford University Press, 2005.
Nin, Anaïs. Preface. In Henry Miller, *Tropic of Cancer*, xxxi–xxxiii.
Nodelman, Perry. "On Nakedness and Children's Books." *Children's Literature Association Quarterly* 9, no. 1 (1984): 25–30.
"No Gays, Please, We're Carolinian." *The Economist*, April 26, 1997, 26–27.
Nunns, Stephen. "Is Charlotte Burning?" *American Theater* (February 1999): 22–27, 74–77.
Offenses against Public Morality and Decency. North Carolina Gen Stat Subchapter VII, Article 26. Subsection 14-190.1.
Osucha, Eden. "Race and the Regulation of Intimacy in the Moynihan Report, the Griswold Decision, and Morrison's Paradise." *American Literary History* 27, no. 2 (2015): 256–84.

Overbeke, Grace. "Subversively Sexy: The Jewish 'Red Hot Mamas' Sophie Tucker, Belle Barth, and Pearl Williams." *Studies in American Humor* 3, no. 25 (2012): 33–58.
Patton, Cindy. *Inventing AIDS*. New York: Routledge, 1990.
Pereira, Malin Walther. "Periodizing Toni Morrison's Work from *The Bluest Eye* to *Jazz*: The Importance of *Tar Baby*." *MELUS* 22, no. 3 (1997): 71–82.
Pitchford, Nicola. *Tactical Readings: Feminist Postmodernism in the Novels of Kathy Acker and Angela Carter*. Lewisburg: Bucknell University Press, 2002.
Plagens, Peter. "Confessions of a Serial Killer." *Newsweek* (March 4, 1991): 58–59.
Pynchon, Thomas. *Gravity's Rainbow*. New York: Penguin, 1973.
Rampersad, Arnold. "Note on the Text." *Native Son* (restored text), by Richard Wright, introduction by Rampersad, 485–88.
Randall, Mary Ella, Sandra Stotsky, Linda M. Christensen, and Bill Lyons. "Antidote to Controversy? Responses to Carolyn Henly." *The English Journal* 82, no. 3 (March 1993): 20–23.
Rekhi, Tanja. "Some Buncombe County Parents Upset about School Reading Assignment." WLOS.com. Sinclair Broadcast Group. September 21, 2017.
Rembar, Charles. *The End of Obscenity: The Trials of "Lady Chatterley," "Tropic of Cancer," & "Fanny Hill" by the Lawyer Who Defended Them*. New York: Harper and Row, 1986.
Ressner, Jeffrey. "Biafra Trial Ends in Hung Jury." *Rolling Stone*, October 1987, 22.
"The Results Are In: 'WAP' Is a Bop." *Wall Street Journal*, August 18, 2020.
Rogers, V. Cullum. "Tempest in a Dixie Cup: 'Angels in America' vs. Charlotte." *Back Stage* (March 29, 1996).
Román, David. "November 1, 1992: AIDS / *Angels in America*." In *Approaching the Millennium: Essays on Angels in America*, edited by Deborah R. Geis and Steven F. Kruger, 40–55. Ann Arbor: University of Michigan Press, 1997.
Rowley, Hazel. "The Shadow of the White Woman: Richard Wright and the Book-of-the-Month Club." *Partisan Review* 66, no. 4 (1999): 625–34.
Rubin, Gayle. "Thinking Sex: Notes for a Radical Theory of the Politics of Sexuality." In *Deviations: A Gayle Rubin Reader*. Durham: Duke University Press, 2011.
Ryan, Patrick. "The 10 Best Songs of 2020, Including Billie Eilish, The Weeknd and Cardi B." *USA Today*, December 16, 2020.
School District of Abington Township, Pennsylvania et al. v. Schempp et al. 374 US 203. Supreme Court of the U.S. 1963.
Senate Amendment to House Resolution 3058. S. Amdt.963 to H.R. 3058, 100th Cong. (1988).
Shapiro, Karl. "The Greatest Living Author." In *Tropic of Cancer*, by Henry Miller, preface by Anais Nin, v–xxx. New York: Grove Press, 1980.
Sheppard, R. Z. "A Revolting Development." *Time*, October 1990, 100.
Showalter, Elaine. *Sister's Choice: Tradition and Change in American Women's Writing*. Oxford: Oxford University Press, 1991.

Simmon, Scott. "Gravity's Rainbow Described." *Critique* 16, no. 2 (1974): 54–67.
Sisario, Ben. "Cardi B's 'WAP' Proves Music's Dirty Secret: Censorship Is Good Business." *New York Times*, October 27, 2020.
Slade, Joseph W. "Religion, Psychology, Sex, and Love in *Gravity's Rainbow*." In *Approaches to "Gravity's Rainbow,"* edited by Charles Clerc. Columbus: Ohio State University Press, 1983.
Smith, Patti. *Just Kids*. New York: Harper Collins, 2010.
Sontag, Susan. *AIDS and Its Metaphors*. New York: Farrar, 1989.
———. "Certain Mapplethorpes." In *Certain People: A Book of Portraits*, by Robert Mapplethorpe. Santa Fe: Twelvetree Press, 1985.
Speaker, Dixon. "'Holy the Lone Juggernaut!' Miller, Ginsberg, and the Autobiography of the Individual." *Nexus: The International Henry Miller Journal* 11 (2016): 25–36.
Spillers, Hortense J. Afterword in *Conjuring: Black Women, Fiction, and Literary Tradition*, edited by Marjorie Pryse and Spillers, 249–61. Bloomington: Indiana University Press, 1985.
———. "Mama's Baby, Papa's Maybe: An American Grammar Book." *Diacritics* 17, no. 2 (1987): 64–81.
Staes, Toon. "When You Come to a Fork in the Road—Marcuse, Intellectual Subversion and Negative Thought in *Gravity's Rainbow* and *Against the Day*." In *Against the Grain: Reading Pynchon's Counternarratives*, edited by Sascha Pöhlmann, 97–111. Amsterdam: Rodopi, 2010.
Starling, Lakin. "Cardi B. 'WAP' [ft. Megan Thee Stallion] Review." *Pitchfork*, August 7, 2020.
Stephens, Challen. "Alabama Senator Calls for Removal of Toni Morrison Novel Aligned with Common Core." *Alabama Media Group*, August 28, 2013.
Stratton, Jon. "The Banality of Representation: Generation, Holocaust, Signification and Empire of the Senseless." *New Formations: A Journal of Culture/Theory/Politics* 51 (2003): 80–98.
Strub, Whitney. "Lavender, Menaced: Lesbianism, Obscenity Law, and the Feminist Antipornography Movement." *Journal of Women's History* 22, no. 2 (2010): 83–107.
———. *Perversion for Profit: The Politics of Pornography and the Rise of the New Right*. New York: Columbia University Press, 2010.
Sturken, Marita. "Conversations with the Dead: Bearing Witness in the AIDS Memorial Quilt." *Socialist Review* 22, no. 2 (1992): 65–95.
Sumner, Charles. "For Profit's Sake! Don't Look at That White Lady!" *Southern Quarterly* 26, no. 2 (2009): 134–40.
Thaggert, Miriam. "Marriage, Moynihan, Mahogany: Success and the Post–Civil Rights Black Female Professional in Film." *American Quarterly* 64, no. 4 (2012): 715–40.
Trust, Gary. "Cardi B. and Megan Thee Stallion's 'WAP' Debuts at No. 1 on Billboard Hot 100 with Record First-Week Streams." *Billboard*, August 17, 2020.

Turner, Frederick. *Renegade: Henry Miller and the Making of "Tropic of Cancer."* New Haven: Yale University Press, 2011.
Ut, Huynh Cong "Nick." *The Terror of War [Napalm Girl].* June 8, 1972. Photograph.
Vasquez, Tina. "Ethical Pornography." *Herizons* 25, no. 4 (2012): 32.
Volcano, Del LaGrace. "Kathy Acker." E-mail to the author. March 12, 2012.
———. *Sublime Mutations.* Tübingen: Konkursbuchverlag, 2000.
Walker, Alice. *The Color Purple.* San Diego: Harcourt, 1982.
Wall, Cheryl A. "On Dolls, Presidents, and Little Black Girls." *Signs* 35, no. 4 (Summer 2010): 769–801.
Wallen, Joellyn. "Barth, Belle (1911–1971)." In *Jewish Women in America: An Historical Encyclopedia*, edited by Paula E. Hyman and Deborah Dash Moore, 24–25. New York: Routledge, 1998.
Watkins, Mel. "Some Letters Went to God." Rev. of *The Color Purple* by Alice Walker. *New York Times Review of Books*, July 25, 1982. https://www.nytimes.com/books/98/10/04/specials/walkercolor.html.
Watten, Barrett. "Foucault Reads Acker and Rewrites the History of the Novel." In *Lust for Life: On the Writings of Kathy Acker*, edited by Amy Scholder, Carla Harryman, and Avital Ronell, 58–77. London: Verso, 2006.
Weheliye, Alexander G. "Pornotropes." *Journal of Visual Culture* 7, no. 1 (2008): 65–81.
Weinstein, Steve. "How 'Jerker' Helped Ignite Obscenity Debate: Comedian Carlin Has a Few Choice Words for Media Watchdogs." *Los Angeles Times*, August 18, 1987.
Werrlein, Debra T. "Not So Fast, Dick and Jane: Reimagining Childhood and Nation in *The Bluest Eye*." *MELUS* 30, no. 4 (2005): 53–72.
Westwell, Guy. "Accidental Napalm Attack and Hegemonic Visions of America's War in Vietnam." *Critical Studies in Media Communication* 28, no. 5 (2011): 407–23.
Whittaker, Zack. "EU to Vote on Porn Ban, Calls for Internet Enforcement." CNET News. March 6, 2013.
Wilkerson, Isabel. "Cincinnati Jury Acquits Museum in Mapplethorpe Obscenity Case." *New York Times*, October 6, 1990: 1.
Williams, Maren. "Bluest Eye Banned from Classrooms in North Carolina High School." Comic Book Legal Defense Fund, September 12, 2014.
———. "VICTORY in Michigan: The Bluest Eye Remains in Northville AP Class." Comic Book Legal Defense Fund, April 13, 2016.
Winslow, Donald R. "Napalm Girl 40 Years Later." *New Photographer* (July–August 2012): 18–20.
Wright, Richard. "How Bigger Was Born." *Native Son* (restored text), by Wright, introduction by Arnold Rampersad, 431–62.
———. *Native Son* (restored text), introduction by Arnold Rampersad. New York: Harper Perennial Modern Classics, 2005.

Wu, Judy Tzu-Chun. "Asian American History and Racialized Compulsory Deviance." *Journal of Women's History* 15, no. 3 (Autumn 2003): 58–62.
Yamada, Mitsuye. "Invisibility Is an Unnatural Disaster: Reflections of an Asian American Woman." In *This Bridge Called My Back*, edited by Cherríe Moraga and Gloria Anzaldúa, 35–40.
Young, John K. *Black Writers, White Publishers: Marketplace Politics in Twentieth-Century African American Literature*. Jackson: University Press of Mississippi, 2006.

INDEX

2 Live Crew, 15, 25

Abington v. Schempp. See *School District of Abington Township, Pennsylvania et al. v. Schempp et al.*
Acker, Kathy, 25–26, 102–21, 123–25, 133–34, 139, 155, 185n46, 190nn2–4, 191nn10,18, 192nn25,27, 193nn32,34–36, 194n42, 197n35. See also *Blood and Guts in High School*
AIDS 26, 28, 137–39, 141–49, 156–57, 160–61, 163, 165–67, 195nn20,22, 196n24, 197n43, 198n50
Albert, 123, 129, 131
American Library Association (ALA), 84, 127, 188n46
Angels in America, 24, 26, 28, 40, 138, 141–42, 148, 156–68, 194n3, 198n47; *Millennium Approaches* 160, 165, 198n54; *Perestroika*, 160–61, 164
Anzaldúa, Gloria, 35, 103, 112–13, 119, 133–34. See also *This Bridge Called My Back*

Baldwin, James, 43–45
Barrie, Dennis, 150–51, 168, 196n31
Barth, Belle, 3, 5, 27–28, 179n3
Barthes, Roland, 152–53
Biafra, Jello, 2–4. See also Dead Kennedys
Bigger Thomas, 24, 30, 41–44, 47–61, 182nn1–2, 184nn25,35, 185nn38,43–44, 188n40

Black Boy, 42, 46, 184nn27,30
Blood and Guts in High School, 25, 104–6, 108, 113–18, 123, 130, 134, 193nn32,34
The Bluest Eye, 5, 15, 24–26, 28, 68, 70, 81–90, 92–98, 100–1, 127, 186n10, 188n46, 189n51, 190nn66,5
Book-of-the-Month Club, 24, 30, 41–42, 47–48, 51–52, 55–58, 62, 184n30, 185n43
Brown v. Board of Education of Topeka, 12, 81–82, 100
Bruce, Lenny, 1–5, 27–28, 118, 179n1
Brew, Kathy, 102–3
Buchanan, Patrick J., 148, 166
Burroughs, William S., 6, 24, 29, 80, 115
Butler, Judith, 109, 134–35, 191–92n21, 197n39

canon, 4–9, 11, 15, 18, 20, 22–23, 25, 29–31, 37–38, 40, 56, 61–62, 70, 78, 81, 83, 99, 111, 125, 127, 133, 183n20
Carby, Hazel V., 23, 125
Cardi B., 171–73. See also "WAP"
Carlin, George, 2–4, 168–69, 180–81n22
Celie, 123–32, 193n40
Charlotte Repertory Theater, 158–59, 168
Chicago School of Sociology, 41, 50
Cholly Breedlove, 81–82, 87–90, 93–97, 188n40
Chong, Sylvia Shin Huey, 68, 72, 186n1
Cincinnati Contemporary Arts Center, 26, 141–42, 150–51, 168, 196n31
Cixous, Hélène, 106–7, 116, 121, 123, 190n1

216 / INDEX

Clark, Kenneth B. and Mamie Phipps, 82–83, 97–98
Claudia MacTeer, 94–95, 190n65
Clinton, William Jefferson, 160, 166
Cohn, Roy (historical figure), 136–38, 140, 194n3. *See also* Roy Cohn
The Color Purple, 25–26, 40, 104, 123–32, 193n40
Comics Code Authority, 16, 56
Comstock Laws, 11–12, 18–19, 21, 171
Corcoran Gallery, 141, 150, 157, 168, 196n29, 197–98n46
counterculture, 2, 24–25, 29–30, 35–36, 100, 147
culture wars, 2, 26 136, 138, 140–41, 143, 146–49, 151, 155, 157, 160, 162, 165–69, 171
Cutter, Martha J., 128

Dead Kennedys, 2, 15, 25, 168
Denton, Jeremiah, 65–66
doll test, 82–83, 97–98, 188n36
Dore, Florence, 46–47, 53–54, 184n33
Dostoevsky, Fyodor, 33, 182n6
Dworkin, Andrea, 105, 108–110, 174, 191n19, 191–92n21, 197n39

Ellison, Ralph, 46, 63, 64
Emerson, Ralph Waldo, 31–32, 182n6
Eng, David L., 139

Federal Communications Commission v. Pacifica, 174, 180–81n22, 199n11
Ferguson, Roderick A., 21–22, 35, 41, 46, 48–50, 90, 92–93, 138–40, 189n54
feminism, 2, 8, 25, 93, 103–113, 118–21, 123–24, 128–29, 140, 183n19, 191nn14,19, 193n31, 197nn35,39
Fields, Totie, 3
Fisher, Dorothy Canfield, 42, 182n2
Foucault, Michel, 6–7, 15–17, 35, 51, 133, 180n12, 183n21, 185n39
Freedman, Jonathan, 159, 161, 164–65
Frieda MacTeer, 94–95, 190n66

genius, 8, 11, 28, 31, 34, 101; identity and, 5–8, 11, 64, 99–101, 142, 169; Tony Kushner as, 165–66; Henry Miller as, 6, 24, 32, 36–39, 61–62, 183nn11,13,20; obscenity and, 4–6, 8, 11, 21, 26, 29–30, 36–39, 61, 70, 78–80, 95, 98, 100, 119, 133, 138, 142, 166, 169; Thomas Pynchon as, 6, 78–81

Glass, Loren, 18–19, 37, 40, 61–62
Gravity's Rainbow, 5, 24–25, 28, 66, 68–80, 98, 101, 187n18
Grove Press, 18–19, 29, 31, 36–38, 40, 81, 180n17
Grove Press, Inc. v. Christenberry (1959 & 1960), 180n17
Grove Press, Inc. v. Gerstein, 31, 69, 180n17

Harris, Trudier, 124–26, 128
Hartley, Nina, 109–10
Hassan, Ihab, 31–31, 35–36, 62–63, 185n47
Hays Code, 16, 56
Helms, Jesse, 143, 148–50, 155–59, 167, 181n22, 191n21, 197n39
Herman, Didi, 139, 140, 194–95n9
high cultural pluralism, 9, 69, 98–99
Hogue, W. Lawrence, 42, 56, 182n2
hooks, bell, 141, 149
"How Bigger Was Born," 43–44, 57–58, 60, 182n1, 185n41
How to Have Sex in an Epidemic, 144, 147–48, 196n24

Jacobellis v. Ohio, 13, 169, 180nn18–19, 182n34
Janey, 113–17, 123, 130, 134, 193nn32–33
JanMohamed, Abdul R., 51–52, 55, 180n12, 183n21
Joe, N.Y.C., 154
Joe Pitt, 160–64
Joyce, James, 12, 31, 37–39, 78, 79

Kardon, Janet, 150–53, 197nn38,40
Kim Phúc, Phan Thị, 66–68, 96. See also *Terror of War*
Kushner, Tony, 24, 26, 40, 137–38, 141, 146, 148, 157, 160–63, 165–67, 194n3. See also *Angels in America*

Lambert, Josh, 17, 19–21, 27, 181n22
Lawrence, David Herbert, 12, 18, 31–32, 38–39
Lipsitz, George, 82
Lorde, Audre, 111, 120–21, 189n54
Louis Ironson, 157, 160–64
Lowe, Lisa, 22
Lyon, Lisa, 152, 197n35

MacKinnon, Catharine A., 105, 108–9, 191–92n21
Manfred, 151

Man in Polyester Suit, 153
Mapplethorpe, Robert, 24, 26, 133, 136–38, 141–42, 146, 148–56, 167, 174, 196n31, 197nn35–36,38. *See also The Perfect Moment*
Marcuse, Herbert, 71, 76, 112, 187nn18,25
Mary Dalton, 47–48, 50–56, 58–61, 184n, 185n
McGurl, Mark, 8–9, 69, 98–99, 186n11
Megan Thee Stallion, 171, 173. *See also* "WAP"
Memoirs v. Massachusetts, 13–14, 174, 181n23, 199n11
Miller, Henry, 5–6, 8, 24–25, 29–40, 47, 61–64, 69, 71, 78, 80, 98, 117–18, 180n19, 182nn1,6, 183nn9,11,13,20, 184n34, 192n29. *See also Tropic of Cancer*
Miller v. California, 14–15, 20, 25, 66, 70, 86, 114, 132, 152, 154, 169, 180–81n22, 181n23, 187n13, 191n14, 197n45; Miller test, 14–15, 132, 154, 169, 191n14
modernism, 32, 37, 99
Moraga, Cherríe, 24, 26, 33, 35, 103, 111, 113, 119–21, 133–34, 183n19, 192n29. *See also This Bridge Called My Back*
Morrison, Toni, 5, 7–9, 22, 24–25, 68–69, 81–84, 86–89, 92–93, 95–101, 125, 127–28, 181–82n32, 186n10, 189n51, 190n66. *See also The Bluest Eye*
Moynihan Report, 81, 83, 90–98, 124–25, 140, 188n38, 189n56, 190n68
Mr. _____. *See* Albert
Muñoz, José Esteban, 46

National Book Award, 124, 187n16
National Center on Sexual Exploitation (NCOSE), 174
National Endowment for the Arts (NEA), 141, 148–49, 155–56, 167, 197n40
Napalm Girl. *See Terror of War*
Native Son, 24, 29–30, 40–63, 68, 87, 92, 97, 182n2, 184nn30,34, 185n44, 186n10
naturalism, 60, 184n25
The Negro Family: The Case for National Action. *See* Moynihan Report
Nettie, 123, 129, 131, 193n40
Nietzsche, Friedrich, 31, 33
Nin, Anaïs, 39, 183n, 192n29

obscenity, definition 10–14; First Amendment and 29, 39, 169
Orwell, George, 38

Parents Music Resource Center, 15, 70, 127, 173
pathology, 11, 21, 24, 42, 50, 57, 60–61, 90, 93, 96, 101, 148, 159, 165–66, 189n54; AIDS and, 141–42, 144–47, 149, 163, 166–67; Bigger Thomas and, 58; canon and, 56, 83; Cholly Breedlove and, 89, 96; crime and, 7, 50, 55, 170; family and, 83, 87, 90, 125, 140, 170; identity and, 6–8, 11, 22–23, 25–26, 30, 40, 44, 55, 57, 61, 64, 82, 83, 87, 90–91, 96–97, 125–27, 130, 133, 138–40, 144, 155, 160, 166–67, 169–70, 172; obscenity and, 4, 6–8, 11, 21, 23, 29, 30, 40, 42, 46, 50, 56, 58, 61, 70, 83, 95, 96–98, 100, 125–27, 130, 133, 138–42, 155, 166–67, 169–70; sexuality and, 3, 16, 21, 87, 114, 116, 138, 140, 144, 146, 155, 170, 172
Patton, Cindy, 144–45, 156–57, 165
Pecola Breedlove, 82, 86–89, 93–97, 190n66
The Perfect Moment, 24, 26, 138, 141–42, 148–55, 157, 166–68, 174, 197n40
Piss Christ, 141, 148–49
pornography, 12–14, 17, 20, 65, 84, 103, 105–11, 119, 121, 134, 140, 151, 152–53, 174, 180n18, 186n7, 191n14, 197n39
pornotroping, 26, 33, 121–23, 126, 130–31, 133, 193n39
postmodernism, 99; Kathy Acker and, 104, 106, 119; Thomas Pynchon and, 9, 71
post-structuralism, 106, 118–20
Prior Walter, 160–61, 163–66
Pulitzer Prize: *Angels in America*, 26, 141; *The Color Purple*, 124; *Gravity's Rainbow*, 25, 69–71, 78, 80, 187n16, 188n29; *Terror of War*, 66
Pynchon, Thomas, 5, 6, 9, 24, 25, 66, 68–73, 76, 78–81, 83, 98–100, 186nn11–12, 187nn18,21, 188n29. *See also Gravity's Rainbow*

Rampersad, Arnold, 41, 52
Rembar, Charles, 180n17
Rosset, Barney, 18–20, 37
Roth, Philip, 6, 24
Roth v. United States, 12–14, 180n17
Roy Cohn (dramatic character), 160, 162, 164–65, 194n. *See also* Cohn, Roy

School District of Abington Township, Pennsylvania et al. v. Schempp et al., 65, 100
Serrano, Andres, 141, 148–49, 197n40. *See also Piss Christ*

sexual revolution, 17, 25, 30, 116, 139
sex work, 109–12, 145, 173–74, 191n18, 192n27
Shug Avery, 124, 129, 131–32
Smith, Patti, 151, 155
Sontag, Susan, 145–47, 165, 187n27, 195n20, 197n36
Spillers, Hortense J., 26, 33, 91–92, 121–24, 126
Strub, Whitney, 20, 27–28, 33, 129, 139–41
Sumner, Charles, 41–42, 48, 53
Supreme Court of the United States, 10, 12–18, 26–27, 29, 35–37, 141–42, 180nn17,19,22, 181n23; Burger Court, 12–15, 65–66, 77–78, 181n23; Warren Court, 12–14, 17, 31, 77–78, 82, 100, 169, 181n23, 182n34

technomodernism, 9, 69, 98–99
Terror of War (Napalm Girl), 66–68, 78, 149
This Bridge Called My Back, 103, 120
Tropic of Cancer, 5, 16, 19, 24, 29, 31–39, 61–62, 68–69, 71, 80, 180n19, 184n34, 186n49, 192n29

Tucker, Sophie, 3, 179n9
Tyrone Slothrop, 73–75, 89

Ut, Huynh Cong "Nick," 66–68, 78, 96–97, 186n7. See also *Terror of War*
utopia, 75–77, 115, 117, 128, 133–35, 161, 165–66, 185n46, 187n25, 193n35

Vietnam War, 65–66, 69–72

Wagner, Richard, 71, 79
Walker, Alice, 25–26, 40, 104, 111, 119, 123–28, 130–34, 139. See also *The Color Purple*
"WAP," 171–73, 175
Whitman, Walt, 31–32, 38, 182n6, 183n20
Williams, Pearl, 3, 5
Williams, William Carlos, 38
World War II, 69, 71–73, 75–76
Wright, Richard, 24, 25, 29, 40–44, 46–64, 69, 87, 92, 98, 182nn1,2, 184nn22,27–28,33–34, 185n36, 186n10. See also *Native Son*

X Portfolio, 148, 150, 153–55, 196n31

Patrick S. Lawrence is Associate Professor of English at the University of South Carolina, Lancaster.

www.ingramcontent.com/pod-product-compliance
Lightning Source LLC
Chambersburg PA
CBHW020407080526
44584CB00014B/1208